OCR

Critical Thinking

OCR and Heinemann are working together to provide better support for you

Jo Lally
Colin Hart
Tony McCabe

www.pearsonschoolsandfe.co.uk

✓ Free online support
✓ Useful weblinks
✓ 24 hour online ordering

0845 630 33 33

LiveText
CD-ROM INSIDE

OCR
RECOGNISING ACHIEVEMENT

Heinemann

Official Publisher Partnership

Heinemann is an imprint of Pearson Education Limited, a company incorporated in England and Wales, having its registered office at Edinburgh Gate, Harlow, Essex, CM20 2JE. Registered company number: 872828

www.heinemann.co.uk

Heinemann is a registered trademark of Pearson Education Limited

Text © Pearson Education Ltd, 2010

First published 2010

12 11 10

10 9 8 7 6 5 4 3 2 1

British Library Cataloguing in Publication Data
A catalogue record for this book is available from the British Library.

ISBN 978 0 435 23590 1

Produced by Pearson Education Ltd

Typeset by Geoff Ward, Tower Designs UK Ltd

Original illustrations © Pearson Education Ltd, 2010
Illustrated by Sam Thompson, Calow Craddock Ltd

Picture research by Lindsay Lewis

Cover photo: M.C. Escher's 'Symmetry Drawing E72'© 2007 The M.C. Escher Company-Holland. All rights reserved. www.mcescher.com

Printed in Spain by Graficas Estella

Acknowledgements
The authors and publisher would like to thank the following individuals and organisations for permission to reproduce photographs:

(Key: b-bottom; c-centre; l-left; r-right; t-top)

Alamy Images: Colin Underhill 136, CountryCollection - Homer Sykes 63, david pearson 231, ImageState 213, PHOTOTAKE Inc. 177, Ray Roberts 128; **Bridgeman Art Library Ltd:** 82; **Clark Wiseman/Studio 8:** / Pearson Education Ltd. 24tc; **Corbis:** Alessandra Benedetti 75, Peter Andrews 162; **Digital Railroad:** Bill Bachmann / Danita Delimont 35; **Fotolia:** Wendy Kaveney 184; **Image Source Ltd:** Nigel Riches. 24c, 24cl; **iStockphoto:** 188, Bryce Kroll 6, kreicher 160, René Mansi 210, Snezana Negovanovic 108; **Jupiterimages:** / Photos.com 58; **MindStudio:** Pearson Education Ltd. MindStudio 24; **National Geographic:** 126; **Pearson Education Ltd:** Brand X Pictures 44, Jack Star 144, Jules Selmes 43, Steve Cole 52; **PhotoDisc:** / Kevin Peterson 24tl; **Photolibrary.com:** Craig Cozart 174, Dennis Hallinan / Nonstock 236, Gavin Blue / Stock Photos 138, SGM SGM 77; **Press Association Images:** Stefan Rousseau 186; **Rex Features:** 20, Brian Rasic 202, Simon Roberts 39, Sipa Press 47, Ted Blackbrow 120; **Shutterstock:** Alan Freed 170, Luciano Mortula 112, Monkey Business photos 30; **TopFoto:** Haydn West 72

All other images © Pearson Education

Every effort has been made to contact copyright holders of material reproduced in this book. Any omissions will be rectified in subsequent printings if notice is given to the publishers.

Websites
The websites used in this book were correct and up-to-date at the time of publication. It is essential for tutors to preview each website before using it in class so as to ensure that the URL is still accurate, relevant and appropriate. We suggest that tutors bookmark useful websites and consider enabling students to access them through the school/college intranet.

OCR A2 Critical Thinking

Contents

Introduction to the Student Book and CD-ROM   2

Introduction to Unit 3   4

Introduction to Unit 4   6

Unit 3   Ethical reasoning and decision-making

Chapter 1   Dealing with evidence   8

Chapter 2   Choices and criteria   30

Chapter 3   Making difficult decisions   44

Chapter 4   Applying principles to make
difficult decisions   52

Chapter 5   Applying ethical theories to make
difficult decisions   72

Exam Café Unit 3

Relax, refresh, result!   98

Practice Unit 3 exam paper   104

Unit 4   Critical reasoning

Chapter 6   Analysing different forms of real-life
reasoning   108

Chapter 7   Analysing framework reasoning in real texts   126

Chapter 8   Analysing reasoning in detail   144

Chapter 9   Evaluating reasoning: structural strength
and weakness in real-life reasoning   160

Chapter 10   Evaluating reasoning: other strength
and weakness in real-life reasoning   184

Chapter 11   Developing your own arguments   210

Exam Café Unit 4

Relax, refresh, result!   244

Practice Unit 4 exam paper   247

Glossary   250

Introduction to the Student Book and CD-ROM

Student Book

Units 3 and 4

Your A2 Critical Thinking course is divided into two units. This Student Book provides an exact match to the OCR specification and as well as teaching material, it includes activities, examiner tips and 'stretch and challenge' opportunities.

Exam Café

In our unique Exam Café you'll find lots of ideas to help you prepare for your Unit 3 and Unit 4 exams. You'll see the Exam Café at the end of Unit 3 and again at the end of Unit 4. You can **Relax and prepare** because there's handy advice on getting started on your A2 Critical Thinking course, **Refresh your memory** with summaries and checklists of the key ideas you need to revise and **Get the result!** through practising exam-style questions, accompanied by hints and tips from the examiners.

Student CD-ROM

LiveText

On the CD-ROM you will find an electronic version of the Student Book, powered by LiveText. As well as the Student Book and the LiveText tools, there is:

■ guidance to the activities – indicated by this icon.

Within the electronic version of the Student Book, you will also find the interactive Exam Café.

Exam Café

Immerse yourself in our contemporary interactive Exam Café environment! With a click of your mouse you can visit three separate areas in the café to **Relax and prepare**, **Refresh your memory** or **Get the result!** You'll find a wealth of material including:

■ Revision tips from students, Key concepts, Common mistakes and Examiner tips (all of which you can read and hear!)

■ Language of the exam (an interactive activity)

■ Revision flashcards, Revision checklists and the Basics

■ Sample exam questions (which you can try) with student answers and examiner comments.

OCR A2 Critical Thinking

Critical Thinking at A2 is both the same as at AS Level and different from it. There is an obvious and necessary sense of continuity: you will still be using the skills and language acquired in your AS modules. You will still be assessed on your ability to:

■ analyse critically the use of different kinds of reasoning in a wide range of contexts (AO1)

■ evaluate critically the use of different kinds of reasoning in a wide range of contexts (AO2)

■ develop and communicate relevant and coherent arguments clearly and accurately in a concise and logical manner (AO3).

However, you will find that both of the A2 modules will be more challenging because:

■ the arguments and evidence will be more complex

■ you will explore more deeply the concepts, issues and problems involved

■ some of the reasoning will be more complex and is likely to require a more focused approach from you and greater powers of concentration

■ you will need to use and understand a greater range of specialist language at this higher level of Critical Thinking.

You will also develop some new skills, particularly:

■ applying principles and ethical theories to resolve dilemmas

■ assessing the impact of reasoning upon claims.

Assessment at A2 Critical Thinking

Assessment will consist of two examinations:

■ **Unit 3: Ethical reasoning and decision-making**
This is a written paper of 1 hour and 30 minutes and will account for 50 per cent of the marks at A2. The structured questions are based on an issue or topic, for which evidence will be provided in the form of a Resource Booklet. You are also required to produce a piece of extended writing. You should attempt **all** questions. Nearly half of the marks for this unit will be allocated on the basis of how well you develop and communicate your arguments.

■ **Unit 4: Critical reasoning**
This paper will consist of structured questions set on an extended stimulus passage. You will also have to produce a piece of extended writing in response to the passage. Again, you need to attempt **all** the questions. The paper lasts 1 hour and 30 minutes and will account for 50 per cent of the marks at A2.

You can find full details in the OCR specification, available at www.ocr.org.uk.

Another Heinemann textbook covers Units 1 and 2 (the AS units).

The Cambridge Assessment definition of Critical Thinking

■ Critical Thinking is the analytical thinking which underlies all rational discourse and enquiry.

■ It is characterised by a meticulous and rigorous approach.

■ As an academic discipline, it is unique in that it explicitly focuses on the processes involved in being rational.

■ These processes include:

  ● analysing arguments

  ● judging the relevance and significance of information

  ● evaluating claims, inferences, arguments and explanations

- constructing clear and coherent arguments
- forming well-reasoned judgements and decisions.

■ Being rational also requires an open-minded yet critical approach to one's own thinking as well as that of others.

'Stretch and challenge' questions

In response to allegations that A Level exams were becoming easier, the government instructed exam boards in 2005 that the new A Level exams must include questions which would 'stretch and challenge' students and thereby give the ablest students an opportunity to show what they could do. This is being achieved by means of:

■ a particular style of questions; a greater variety of introductions to questions; for example, analyse, evaluate, discuss

■ structuring questions in a more coherent way which shows more connections between sections of the specification; for example, a) to b) to c)

■ including extended writing in all subjects except where it is clearly inappropriate

■ using a wider range of question types; for example, case studies, open-ended questions, rather than just short-answer questions

■ developing improved synoptic assessments, not just superficial links between areas relating to question types, etc.

In Unit 3 of the Critical Thinking qualification, question 4 is regarded as a 'stretch and challenge' question. In Unit 4 the 'stretch and challenge' questions are 3 and 4. They are marked by levels of response, of which level 4 describes the work of the ablest students.

In this textbook, the green 'stretch and challenge' boxes, found on some pages, are intended particularly for students aiming for the highest grades.

Introduction to Unit 3

Unit 3 – Ethical reasoning and decision-making

You should see Unit 3 as a decision-making unit. It takes you through a process; from identifying a problem all the way to arriving at a solution. Unit 3 gives you the opportunity to develop and use your advanced skills in the context of issues that are topical, interesting and involving.

There will be fewer questions in the Unit 3 exam than in the AS Critical Thinking exams. The questions will require you to:

■ **analyse** and **evaluate** evidence provided in a Resource Booklet

■ use relevant **criteria** to evaluate **choices**

■ write an argument which attempts to resolve an issue arising from the evidence supplied in the Resource Booklet. This issue may be expressed in the form of a dilemma. In this argument you will be required to identify and apply **principles** to help you resolve the issue.

How will this book help me to cover Unit 3?

The five chapters follow the pattern of the Unit 3 exam, as follows:

Chapter 1: Dealing with evidence

This chapter will explain how to:

- evaluate resource documents of various kinds
- draw conclusions and make inferences from evidence of various kinds
- demonstrate critical awareness of problems of definition and implementation
- use evidence provided to identify and explain relevant factors that might affect the way people view the issue under discussion.

Chapter 2: Choices and criteria

This chapter will help you to:

- examine evidence critically and identify appropriate choices in response to issues of concern
- develop and assess the relevance of criteria to decide upon a course of action
- evaluate the choices made in the context of the evidence provided and criteria identified.

Chapter 3: Making difficult decisions

This chapter will:

- examine in more detail what we mean when we talk in terms of a dilemma
- identify dilemmas arising from various situations
- set out and explain a dilemma.

Chapter 4: Applying principles to make difficult decisions

This chapter will:

- define and explain what we mean by 'principles'
- explore how to best apply some principles in attempting to resolve an issue or dilemma.

Chapter 5: Applying ethical theories to make difficult decisions

This chapter will:

- examine some ethical theories
- explore how to best apply ethical theories in attempting to resolve an issue or dilemma.

Exam Café

This section will explain the exam paper and the thinking behind it, what it will be asking you to do and what the examiner will be looking for in your answers. This will be very useful to you in terms of helping to improve your exam performance.

Introduction to Unit 4

Unit 4 – Critical reasoning

Unit 4 is the synoptic unit of your Critical Thinking exam and should bring together all the skills that you have developed during the Critical Thinking course. You will be asked to analyse and evaluate one or more longer passages of reasoning and to develop your own reasoning on a related theme. At AS you needed to demonstrate that you had some very specific skills, one at a time. At A2 the emphasis is on selecting the right skills to use and applying them to a wider task.

At AS you are likely to have answered specific questions: for example, in AO2, Evaluation of Reasoning, about the weakness of the use of evidence in paragraph 4; or you may have identified a flaw in paragraph 6 and explained why this flaw meant that the reasoning did not work. In Unit 4 you will answer fewer questions, in more depth. You will be asked to evaluate the support given to a particular claim. You will be expected to notice flaws and weak use of evidence for yourself and evaluate the extent to which these flaws weaken the argument in one sustained answer.

Chapter 6: Analysing different forms of real-life reasoning

This chapter will:

■ revise how to identify arguments

■ identify and analyse a wide range of forms of reasoning.

Chapter 7: Analysing framework reasoning in real texts

This chapter will help you to:

■ revise and extend AS understandings of (some) AS analysis skills

■ analyse the framework reasoning in a longer passage, identifying elements of reasoning

■ analyse strands of reasoning.

Chapter 8: Analysing reasoning in detail

This chapter will help you to:

■ analyse arguments into elements

■ analyse the structure of reasoning, identifying joint and independent reasons

■ use argument diagrams to show argument structure.

Chapter 9: Evaluating reasoning: structural strength and weakness in real-life reasoning

This chapter will evaluate structural strength and weakness in reasoning by considering:

■ how effectively reasons support conclusions

■ how effectively evidence supports reasoning

■ the effect of structural/logical flaws.

Chapter 10: Evaluating reasoning: other strength and weakness in real-life reasoning

This chapter will evaluate the effect of other reasoning devices on the strength of an argument including:

■ appeals

■ rhetorical persuasion

■ counter argument

■ hypothetical reasoning

■ analogy.

Chapter 11: Developing your own arguments

In this chapter you will learn to write your own arguments with:

■ a clear structure of reasoning with reasons which support intermediate and main conclusions as well as strands of reasoning

■ identifying possible counter-arguments and responding to them

■ clarification of key terms.

Exam Café

This section will explain the exam paper and the thinking behind it, what it will be asking you to do and what the examiner will be looking for in your answers. This will be very useful to you in terms of helping to improve your exam performance.

Unit 3 Ethical reasoning and decision-making

Dealing with evidence

Learning objectives

- Evaluate resource documents of various kinds.
- Draw conclusions and make inferences from evidence of various kinds.
- Demonstrate critical awareness of problems of definition and implementation.
- Use evidence provided to identify and explain relevant factors that might affect the way people view the issue under discussion.

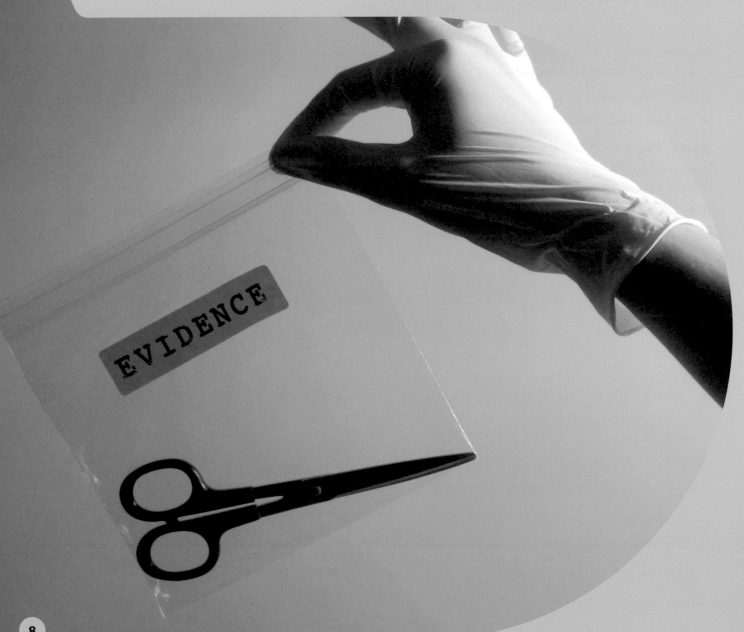

Unit 3 is about using Critical Thinking skills in the context of decision-making. We are going to take an evidence-based approach to help us through this process.

In the Unit 3 exam you will be required to:

■ examine evidence provided on a particular issue in a critical and focused manner

■ use **criteria** to evaluate choices related to this issue

■ use principles to *resolve* the issue.

These tasks will require you to refer closely to the evidence provided.

Using evidence in Unit 3

Throughout Unit 3 you are required to use evidence in a critical and constructive manner. You need to be able to analyse and evaluate various types of evidence with some considerable skill, avoiding comments which are vague and over-generalised.

It is important that you see the close links between Unit 3 and the three other units that make up the A Level in Critical Thinking. You will be aware from Units 1 and 2 of the importance that Critical Thinking places upon the use and evaluation of evidence. In this unit, we are following on from Units 1 and 2, particularly in relation to evaluating evidence.

In the exam you will be provided with a separate Resource Booklet containing between three and five documents. It is very likely that these documents will contain a variety of different types of evidence: for example, statistical/numerical evidence in the form of graphs, tables, charts; statements of policy; opinions; and explanations. Sources may include government departments or ministers, religious leaders, commentators and pressure groups.

When using evidence, for whatever purpose, we need to consider how useful it is for that purpose. Our aim throughout this unit is to use evidence to help us in the decision-making process. Establishing how useful evidence might be involves us in asking the right sort of questions of it. In other words, we need to interrogate our evidence.

The exam you take will almost certainly begin with some short questions testing your ability to interpret the resource documents. They are most likely to cover some of the following:

■ Problems of using documents. In answer to this type of question, the reasons you give may refer to the reliability of the evidence, or the inferences, which can be drawn from it.

■ Problems of definition.

■ Problems of implementation.

■ Factors affecting views. These questions may ask you to identify *either* factors influencing views contained in a document *or* items contained in a document which could influence the views of people who read it.

> **REMEMBER**
>
> Critical Thinking is concerned mainly with skills rather than knowledge. Because it is not primarily a content-based subject, you will not be required to have any in-depth knowledge of the topic covered by the evidence that will be provided. It is what you do with the evidence that is important.

KEY TERM

Criteria

The plural of *criterion*, which is a standard by which something may be judged or decided.

You should avoid the common mistake of using *criteria* as singular.

EXAM TIPS

If you are asked to provide a specific number of points (e.g. two), it is a good idea to number them, so that the examiner can see clearly that you have given the correct number of separate points.

It is essential that you take time to study the Resource Booklet carefully before attempting the questions and that you refer to the evidence contained in the resource documents when answering the questions.

Problems in using evidence: (1) Reliability

The skills you learned in the AS course are likely to be relevant to your use of the resource documents provided for the Unit 3 exam. If question 1 or 2 asks you to identify problems in using a document, issues of credibility or plausibility may well be acceptable answers. You should remember from the AS course that credibility refers to the source of a claim, while plausibility refers to its content.

The main problems of credibility which could occur are that:

■ the source may have a poor *reputation* for accuracy

■ they may have limited access to **reliable** information (*ability to observe*)

■ they may have a *vested interest* to select, exaggerate or even falsify the evidence in favour of their own point of view

■ they may lack *expertise* (training and experience)

■ and their presentation of the facts or the arguments may be one-sided (lacking *neutrality*).

When a resource document includes a survey, you should question its findings by asking about:

■ the size of the sample

■ the **representativeness** of the sample

■ the nature of the questions asked

■ whether the survey was conducted individually

■ whether the survey was anonymous.

> **WORKED EXAMPLE 1**
>
> According to pharmaceutical giant, DrugsUR, animal testing is a vital part of developing new medicine and protecting the general public from side effects. Moreover, a study it commissioned indicates that 89% of the population is in favour of animal testing.

Comment

DrugsUR would have a strong vested interest in encouraging people to accept animal testing. It should be authoritative on the need for some testing, but its vested interest probably outweighs this. The study was commissioned by the company, but we do not know who the sample group was – employees, perhaps? We cannot be sure that these results can really be extended to the general population. So this evidence does not give strong support to a conclusion about animal testing being either necessary or popular.

ACTIVITY

Read Documents A and B and then use credibility criteria to answer the following question.

With reference to Documents A and B, identify and briefly explain *two* of the problems that might arise in using Documents A and B in assessing the extent to which animal testing can be considered necessary.

Document A: Chemical testing on animals – the views of the British Union for the Abolition of Vivisection (BUAV)

(Note: The BUAV is an organisation which campaigns to end animal experimentation.)

Chemical toxicity (the testing of poisons) on animals basically involves subjecting animals to different levels of potentially toxic substances to assess how and in which way they are affected.

This approach to chemical testing, which uses animals and is mainly observational and descriptive, is extremely crude. Animal tests tell us little about why a substance is toxic, as the results tend to demonstrate effects rather than causes of toxicity. The test results are difficult to extrapolate from sterile laboratory conditions to real-life exposure of humans or even wildlife. Scientists simply cannot rely on animal test results accurately reflecting chemical effects on humans.

The underlying problems are the inevitable and significant differences between species in biochemistry, pharmacology, physiology and even anatomy. Here are just two of many examples:

Skin irritation:

Rabbits and guinea pigs are usually used for skin irritation testing but lack the varied range of human responses, partly due to a difference in the distribution of fine blood vessels. Their skin reacts to a limited degree and does not distinguish between very mild and moderate irritants.

Carcinogenicity (testing to see if chemicals might cause cancer):

Rodents are used in large numbers in cancer tests which attempt to replicate life-long exposure. However, while humans live an average of 75 years, rodents only live for two or three years.

Document B: The use of animals in medical research – the views of the Research Defence Society (RDS)

(Note: The RDS is an organisation which aims to promote an understanding of animal research in medicine.)

Those who would seek to abolish animal research often claim that the use of animals in medical research is unnecessary because information can be obtained by alternative methods, such as test tubes and computers.

What is often not realised is that scientists have strong ethical, economic and legal obligations to use animals in research only when absolutely necessary. A lot of effort goes into trying to reduce the number of animals used, and trying to develop new methods to replace animals. As a result, the number of laboratory animals used annually in the UK has almost halved in the last 20 years.

Non-animal methods – such as computer-modelling and studies of patients and populations – are very widely used. In fact, only about ten pence in every pound spent on medical research goes on animal studies. The word 'alternatives', often used to describe these non-animal methods, can lead to confusion because these methods are generally used alongside animal studies, not instead of them. All these techniques have their place, and it is rarely possible to substitute one for the other.

It is unethical and illegal to expose patients to new medicines without being confident that they are likely to benefit them and not be seriously harmed. Treatments must, therefore, be tested on animals to establish their probable effectiveness and safety. They are then tested on human volunteers. The process is not perfect, but testing on animals is by far the best way to protect people. Animal tests ensure that obviously toxic substances are not given to human beings and that doctors in charge of human volunteers are made aware of serious side effects.

Problems in using evidence: (2) Inferences

'Infer' and 'draw a conclusion' are different ways of saying the same thing. If we look at reasons or evidence and decide which conclusions can be supported by these reasons or this evidence, we are making an inference or drawing a conclusion.

There is a very strict sense of inference, where we claim that if **x** is the case, **y** must also be the case. For example, what can be inferred from the following information?

> Sparrows are birds. Birds have wings.

From this information we can infer that sparrows have wings. It is not very interesting, but it must be the case. It is difficult to think of many examples in everyday life, which allow us to draw certain conclusions that we don't already know. There is almost always a gap in our knowledge or an element of uncertainty which means that we can look only at what is probable.

Let's look at another example.

> The tide is coming in fast. You are having a picnic well below the tide line.

What can we infer here? Well, we can be sure that if you stay where you are, you will get wet. You may be swept up by the incoming tide. We cannot be sure of this, but it is possible. It depends on the tidal range, the strength of the tide and how quickly you react when you notice what is happening. If you cannot swim (or cannot swim well fully dressed in tidal waters), you may need to be rescued or you may drown. None of this is as certain as our inference in the previous example that sparrows must have wings. On the other hand, it is probable that you are in danger and that this less certain reasoning will have consequences for your life and health, which matter far more than the certainty that sparrows have wings.

If we can infer something, we can say it follows from the evidence. Let's take another piece of evidence. Making an inference from this evidence is harder and is more like the kind of task which you may encounter in the exam.

> 50% of faulty gadgets returned to shops turned out to be too complex for their users to operate.
>
> Source: *New Scientist*, 15 March 2006

What follows from this? Let's take four options, as follows:

- 50 per cent of people are stupid.
- Gadgets should be simpler.
- We do not need such complex gadgets.
- Clearer instructions are needed.

- 50 per cent of people are stupid. We definitely cannot conclude this. We cannot use a statistic about 50 per cent of 'faulty' gadgets to draw a conclusion about 50 per cent of people. We do not know what percentage of people who have bought gadgets have returned them: it may be a very small proportion. The evidence that 50 per cent of 'faulty' gadgets are too complex for their users does not even mean that these users are stupid: some of them may be highly intelligent but baffled by gadgetry.

- Gadgets should be simpler. This seems to be a safer inference. If people cannot use their gadgets, then perhaps these gadgets should be simpler so that people can use them. However, there are two problems with this. Again, we do not know what percentage of people who have bought gadgets have returned them. If 99 per cent of people who buy gadgets are able to use them, 1 per cent return them and half of those find them too complex, then perhaps there is not a strong case for gadgets to be simpler. We also need to question what is meant by simpler. Do we mean that they should have simpler functions? There may be a good case for retaining the complexity of function because it is useful to those who can cope with it. Or do we mean that gadgets should retain the same functions but be simpler to use? This would be a safer conclusion. Perhaps, then, we could conclude that it would be a good idea if gadgets were simpler to use.

- We do not need such complex gadgets. This claim is far too strong to be concluded from the evidence that 50 per cent of 'faulty' gadgets are too complex for their users. We may well need things that are complex.

- Clearer instructions are needed. This seems to be quite reasonable. However, we would need to know how clear the instructions for these gadgets are before making a claim that they should be clearer.

So it seems that the best conclusion we can come to is that it would be a good idea if gadgets were simpler to use – or perhaps more user friendly.

WORKED EXAMPLE 2

The gender pay gap

Despite all the efforts of successive governments to ensure that career prospects for men and women are equal to one another, the average pay of men is still higher than that of women. One possible cause for this problem may be that education and career guidance encourage girls to aim lower than boys.

Study the following evidence provided by the Women's Equality Unit of the Office for National Statistics.

Suggest some problems you think might arise in using this evidence to support a decision to invest more in career guidance and education for girls, in order to help close the gender pay gap.

The job gap – occupational segregation in Britain, percentages

Occupations	% women	% men
Receptionists	95	5
Nurses	88	12
Primary and nursery teachers	87	13
Cleaners and domestics	80	20
Retail cashiers and check-out operators	77	23
Office managers	67	33
Retail and wholesale managers	35	65
Marketing and sales managers	26	74
Software professionals	17	83

Source: The Women's Equality Unit of the Office for National Statistics

Comment

While this evidence is relevant to the issue of unequal pay and could be of some use in suggesting there is a link between education and lower pay, we must be careful not to base reasoning upon a simplistic, and therefore flawed, view of cause and effect. Some of the problems with using the evidence to support the choice might therefore include:

■ The evidence only gives us information about the types of job which are more or less likely to be occupied by women. We might assume from this that most of the occupations the majority of women are employed in are lower paid, and in turn infer that this could be a major factor in women earning less (the gender pay gap), but it is important to recognise that this particular piece of evidence does not, in itself, prove this to be the case.

■ Also the figures in themselves do not explain why women are more represented in some occupations than in others. To support the choice to invest more in career guidance and education for girls we would need to establish a link between deficiencies in education or poor career guidance and women occupying the majority of lower paid professions, but the evidence does not provide this link.

■ There are also other important factors, which could explain why women might occupy the majority of lower paid occupations, rather than deficiencies in education or poor career guidance. For example, some of these lower paid occupations might allow women to work more 'child friendly' hours. (However, you could still argue that the problem is education in its broadest sense, i.e. society's expectations of who should bear the primary responsibility for looking after children.)

■ Trying to establish a link between deficiencies in education and women occupying the majority of lower paid occupations is also likely to be problematic because some of the occupations in which women dominate, such as primary school teaching, require higher level educational qualifications. Neither can nursing be viewed as unskilled in any way.

ACTIVITY 2

What problems might arise in using the evidence provided below when assessing whether or not Anti-Social Behaviour Orders (ASBOs) should continue to play a significant role in combating anti-social behaviour?

ASBOs issued between 1999 and 2005

Area	Total number of ASBOs issued
Avon and Somerset	150
Cheshire	140
Devon and Cornwall	135
Greater London	670
Greater Manchester	938
Humberside	169
Merseyside	172
Nottinghamshire	173
West Midlands	485
Surrey	62
Total for England	6227
Wales – total	270

Source: www.crimereduction.gov.uk

EXAM TIP

Look at the date of the evidence given in the Resource Booklet. If the data is several years old, you can point that out as a problem of weakness (because the situation may have changed subsequently). However, it is inevitable that data presented in the exam will be at least a year or so out of date, but such a short delay is not normally significant.

Information is often presented visually, as a graph, table or diagram. You may be expected to show that you can understand data presented in these ways. So here is an example of that kind of data, with some questions of the kind which could occur in the exam.

ACTIVITY 3

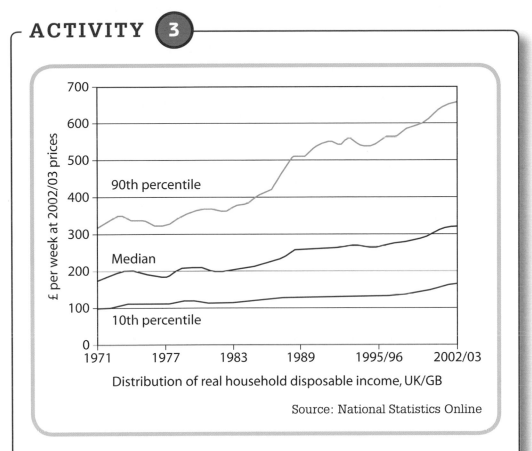

Distribution of real household disposable income, UK/GB

Source: National Statistics Online

a) **Suggest and briefly explain one difficulty in using the data in this graph to support the claim that standards of living have risen generally while the income gap between rich people and poor people has widened.**

b) **Suggest and briefly explain one difficulty in using the data in this graph to support the claim that for rich people to become richer indirectly benefits poorer people.**

c) **Suggest and briefly explain two difficulties in using the data in this graph to support the claim that family poverty in the UK is decreasing.**

Problems of definition and implementation

We are going to examine some sources of information on different topics in order to:

■ identify possible problems when defining and using certain words/phrases in a particular context.

■ explain how and why these problems might arise

■ assess the extent to which such problems might present difficulties when deciding on how best to respond to an issue.

WORKED EXAMPLE 3

Bullying in schools

Read this short passage and then look at the questions and comments that follow.

> When surveyed, most schools stated that they took incidents of bullying very seriously. A high proportion of schools either are currently reviewing their policies or review them annually.
>
> One school made the comment that, owing to the rapidly changing forms in which bullying is happening, for example the use of modern technology like the Internet, they review their policy every six months to keep pace with the changing environment.
>
> In view of these rapidly changing forms of bullying, this practice of regular reviews of policy is worth sharing with other professionals.

1 Working on your own, attempt to write a brief definition of what constitutes bullying.

2 Compare your definition with others in your group. As a group try to agree on a common definition of bullying.

Comment

We could try to define bullying in two ways:

■ By means of a short and inclusive statement, such as: *The inappropriate use of power.*

■ By producing a list of what constitutes acts of bullying, such as:

Bullying is any activity that involves the following: deliberate aggression; inflicting pain and distress; the use of unequal power relationships; the persistent use of such activity/behaviour.

Both of these attempts at definition can often be found in school handbooks. And both illustrate some problems we face when trying to define a very commonly used word 'bullying'.

WORKED EXAMPLE 3 (CONT.)

3 Identify and briefly explain what some of the problems with these definitions might be.

Comment

■ The first definition – the inappropriate use of power – contains within itself problems of definition, such as:

● It lacks clarity or precision as to what is meant by 'inappropriate'. (Is there some scale or measurement of behaviour that will enable us to judge what is and is not inappropriate?)

- An action which might be viewed as an inappropriate use of power by a child in a school environment may be viewed as appropriate if carried out by a teacher – for example, as making somebody sit next to someone they do not want to sit next to.

- A similar kind of problem can occur when dealing with the sensitive issue of how far we should allow parents to go in dealing with their child's misbehaviour: where does discipline end and abuse begin?

■ The second attempt at defining bullying could be said to be a description and not a definition as such. A particular problem with a list like this is that it fails to define its terms (What, for example, does 'persistent' mean?).

■ Both definitions could be viewed as over-influenced by factors such as 'political correctness', 'liberalism' or the 'nanny state'. (Each of these terms, of course, in itself poses an issue of definition.)

WORKED EXAMPLE 3 (CONT.)

4 **One school refers to the use of modern technology like the Internet as representing a new form of bullying.**

How might this affect any policy we might draw up to deal with bullying?

Comment

This question is the kind of thing which is referred to as 'problems of implementation' in the exam. What we can see at work here is how change – cultural, economic, political or technological – can affect the way we define behaviour. Such changes can, in turn, affect how we might respond to a problem. In the case of bullying, we might well decide that to be fully effective any anti-bullying policy has to go beyond just looking at what can be done during school hours. For example, we might want to ask parents to regulate their children's access to the Internet. It becomes in this sense part of the debate about policing the World Wide Web.

Problems of definition

Depending upon the issue you will be discussing in the exam and upon the context in which the words/phrases occur, relevant problems could include:

■ ambiguity in language and usage

■ context – words and phrases can convey different meanings/messages depending on social/political/cultural contexts

■ different types of sources might define/use certain key words in different ways, each of which could well be acceptable in its own setting; for example, scientific/non-scientific, legal/non-legal usage.

■ established/majority/common definitions/usage might not allow for minority views/ interpretations, based perhaps on ethnic/religious/political perspectives.

■ certain key words may be used in such a way as to influence policy or public opinion unfairly, thus shaping the terms of the debate.

EXAM TIP

Questions about implementation may ask   :

• what problems might be encountered implementing a policy
• what problems might occur   the policy is implemented?

These questions do not mean the same and the answer to one would not be an answer to the other.

Problems of implementation

Another kind of question about problems refers to implementation. A resource document might propose a particular policy or course of action and you might be asked to suggest one or two ways in which that policy or course of action might be difficult to implement. The precise kind of answer you can make will vary according to the kind of concept being discussed, but appropriate answers might include:

■ lack of public support

■ lack of clear guidance (to citizens, police and judges)

■ inconsistent enforcement.

Questions of this kind are sometimes linked to problems of definition. As in worked example 4 below, a question on problems of definition is followed by a question asking how the problems you have identified might cause problems of implementation. In such cases, make the link to the problems of definition explicit and clear.

WORKED EXAMPLE 4

Animal rights protesters

Read the following extract from a BBC news story.

Animal rights extremists were blamed when a building contractor pulled out of work on a controversial animal research centre for Oxford University after shareholders received threatening letters leading to a temporary drop in the company's share prices.

But Oxford University officials say they remain committed to building the £18-million project, which will see mice, amphibians and monkeys being used in the search for cures for conditions like leukaemia, Alzheimer's and asthma.

Research scientists reacted angrily to what they said was 'blatant terrorism' and the government promised to clamp down on 'internal terrorists' and give better protection to such companies.

Source: www.news.bbc.co.uk

a) **Identify two words which might present problems of definition and briefly explain why they might present such problems.**

b) **Explain how these problems of definition might in turn lead to problems for the government in dealing with animal rights protesters.**

Comment

a) Two words which might present problems of definition are 'extremists' and 'terrorists'/'terrorism'. The use of the words 'extremists' and 'terrorists' to describe any direct action group could give rise to a number of problems. A sample answer might make some of the following points below.

Extremist

- The use of the word 'extremist' can be used to influence public opinion unduly against the views represented by animal rights protesters.

- There is perhaps an implication here that the views of the protesters are somehow dangerous and marginal, whereas animal rights protesters might claim that it is the practice of animal experimentation that is extremist, and what they are doing is therefore quite reasonable.

- As there is no objective definition of the word 'extremist', actions must be viewed and judged in context. There are no defined boundaries of what is normal.

Terrorist

- 'Internal terrorist' implies that society as a whole is at serious risk of attack and injury.

- 'Terrorist' here is being used in a fairly imprecise way: we would need to know more about what sort of threats are being made and if there is strong evidence of them being carried out or of any intention to carry them out.

- There could be a legal definition of what constitutes 'terrorism' that may be different from the one intended by the research scientists referred to in the news report.

- It might be that 'terrorists' are so defined because they represent unpopular/minority views or because they are threatening established/privileged groups such as shareholders, in which case 'terrorists' might not be an appropriate word to use.

- We could argue that, in the case of both words under discussion, it is in the interests of the building contractors and the shareholders to use words like these in order to present animal rights protesters in the worst possible light.

b) It is the duty of the state/government to protect its citizens when they are exposed to the actions/threats of others that may cause them harm. Therefore, threats made by animal rights protesters call for a *response*.

The problem, though, comes in deciding upon what is an appropriate level of response. This is a problem of *implementation*.

- In modern society anyone described as 'extreme' or as a 'terrorist' is very likely to be viewed as a serious threat that needs to be acted against quickly and with some severity. However, should the threat posed by some animal rights protesters – 'internal terrorists' – be taken as seriously as that presented by international terrorism?

EXAM TIP

We have commented at some length here in order to show you that much can be said about problems of definition and implementation. You would not be expected to make this number of points in the exam. Two relevant problems that are well developed should be enough to gain a very good mark.

■ This might well be a matter of opinion, but there certainly appears to be an implication here in the use of these words that the same kind of measures should be taken against animal rights 'extremists' as are being taken against other forms of terrorism. The shareholders threatened or attacked may well demand of the government that it be consistent.

■ It might, therefore, be difficult for the government – or security forces – to respond in a more low-key, and perhaps more appropriate, manner to any threat posed by animal rights protesters.

■ An unduly severe reaction on the part of the security forces might run the risk of encouraging protesters to be more 'extreme' and to be more likely to commit acts of 'terrorism'.

■ Labelling protesters as extremist/terrorists might make it more difficult for the government/the scientific establishment to respond rationally and fairly to what might be legitimate views held by opponents of animal experimentation.

ACTIVITY 4

Read the following report from the BBC news website and then answer the questions.

Tony Blair's so-called 'respect agenda' emerged as a broad idea during the 2005 general election campaign. He said that it was about putting the law-abiding majority back in charge of their local communities:

'Whether it is in the classroom, or on the streets in town centres on a Friday or Saturday night, I want to focus on this issue. We have done a lot so far with anti-social behaviour orders and additional numbers of police. I want to make this a particular priority for this government, how we bring back a proper sense of respect in our schools, in our communities, in our towns and villages.'

ASBOs [anti-social behaviour orders] and extra numbers of police have been used to try to tackle bad behaviour and encourage people – particularly younger people – to be more respectful.

Source: www.news.bbc.co.uk

a) **Explain in what ways the use of the word 'respect' here could present us with problems of definition.**

b) **Suggest some ways in which these problems of definition might lead to difficulties when it comes to implementing polices aimed at reducing anti-social behaviour in our communities.**

EXAM TIP

If you are asked a general question about problems in using a document for a particular purpose, you are likely to be able to answer in terms of any of the following:

• credibility
• plausibility
• inference
• flaws
• assumptions
• definition

Problems in reasoning

Documents may also fail to justify conclusions drawn from them because the reasoning in them is flawed. For example, if a document offers only a single example in support of a claim, it may be accused of rash generalisation. Similarly, the use of evidence may be weakened by a causal fallacy, conflation, confusion between necessary and sufficient conditions, etc. These would be acceptable answers to a general question asking about problems in using a document, so it is useful to revise the flaws you learned in the AS course.

Another problem with the reasoning can be reliance on dubious assumptions. To draw attention to such reliance is another way of answering questions asking you to identify problems in the reasoning.

Factors influencing evidence/opinions

The evidence you will be dealing with in the exam will help you to identify the factors that might affect people's views on the issue you are exploring.

Two different kinds of question can be asked about factors influencing opinions, and you should make sure you do not confuse them. Both kinds of question refer specifically to one or more resource documents, and you should mention the documents in your answers. The two kinds of questions refer to authors and readers.

■ The first kind of question asks what may have motivated the author of a document or someone referred to in the document to take the approach they have.

■ The second kind of question asks you to identify information in the document which might influence a reader's response to the issue. You must state what opinion could be derived from the information.

The most significant factors, which might influence the views expressed in a document, are already familiar to you as credibility criteria: vested interest/bias and expertise/ability to observe. It is often possible to explain why someone takes a particular view in terms of their motivation or their specialist knowledge and experience.

In turn, vested interest and expertise can often be explained by reference to other factors, especially the background of the person or their underlying values. In other cases, these factors can influence opinions more directly.

Aspects of personal background which may influence someone's opinion include:

- age and gender (older people sometimes see things from a different perspective from younger, or men from women)

- marriage and family (single, married or co-habiting, with or without children)

- education (people who have been to university, for example, may have a broader and more intellectual perspective than someone who has read little and never left home)

- culture and religion (religious and cultural communities tend to share certain perceptions)

- geography (where people live may influence their response to issues, such as conservation or house building)

- economic factors (wealth, employment, etc.)

Underlying values may include matters of:

- ethics (convictions that certain things are morally right or wrong)

- politics (supporting a political party, concern about intrusion by government into private life, etc.)

- aesthetics (judgments about what is beautiful and beliefs about how important it is to protect beautiful things).

WORKED EXAMPLE 5

Read Documents A and B, then answer the questions which follow.

Document A: Free contraception for under-age school children

Free morning-after pills will be handed out to pupils under the age of consent at every school in England, it emerged last night. School nurses are to be told to dish out contraception and could even arrange secret abortions for teenagers without their parents' knowledge under a controversial push by the government to tackle teenage pregnancy.

The teenage pregnancy plan outraged family campaigners who warned it would only fuel soaring rates of conception among teenagers.

Ministers have claimed that 'conception rates are now at their lowest levels since the mid-1980s'. But the latest available figures, which cover 2004, show the number of girls who became pregnant before the age of 18 was 39,545. The total is 4,174 higher than the number of under-18 conceptions in England in 1995, which was 35,371.

Thousands of 13-year-old girls have been handed the morning-after pill by health service staff without their parents' permission. Last year it emerged that as many as one in three children has easy access to condoms and emergency contraception at secondary school. Among 302 primary care trusts across the country, around 2,400 girls aged 13 or younger received the morning-after pill on the NHS last year. They are able to get hold of the morning-after pill and other contraception without their parents' knowledge.

Source: Edited from *The Daily Mail*

Document B

These are based on contributions to an online discussion responding to the report in Document A, but they have been re-named and lightly edited for copyright reasons.

Andrew: As a parent of three children I am appalled at this. While I worry that one day a child of mine may find themselves in this situation, I am more concerned that they would be able to hide it from me. I mean what is the government thinking? Encouraging our children to go behind our backs? This will just create more problems in the long run. A lot of parents have enough trouble trying to get their children to come to them with problems as it is.

Brenda: I doubt they will just be handed out willy-nilly, I expect there'll be very strict controls. As for not informing parents, not every child has the type of parent who'll support them emotionally or physically, so they are entitled to put their trust in a professional, safe in the knowledge of confidentiality. No, I wouldn't be happy if my kids were given this kind of service without my knowledge, but at the end of the day whose fault would it be if they felt they couldn't trust me?

Caroline: Yes, school nurses can issue condoms and the emergency contraceptive pill in school AFTER there have been comprehensive talks with parents and school governors – it isn't done automatically. As school nurses we encourage young people to talk to their parents about relationships, sexual health and contraception, but unfortunately many young people are unable to do so, and we must be able to signpost these young people to services and give them support and information whenever we can. The report clearly highlights a lack of school nurses across the country; more school nurses would be able to support and teach young people about self-esteem, relationships and lifestyle choices allowing, hopefully, for a better outcome for all.

Debbie: I agree with the plan, maybe because I'm in my early 20s and not so naive about the actions of young people. Promoting abstinence and preaching that sex is wrong will not work. The fact is that many young people can't talk to their parents, for varying reasons, so having a non-judgemental professional on hand to help them out is a good idea. I know that it would have been a good thing to have had when I was at school!

Ernie: Weren't we lucky in 1939? Taken from home, no parents, no counselling, no sex education, no sex and so no HIV or AIDS, no nanny government, etc., and later, still on rationing, a working week of 55 hours plus evening classes. I rejoice that I am old-ish, have enjoyed 57 years with a wonderful wife and look forward to having a few more years to laugh at and despair of all the nonsense that is turned out by all these so-called do-gooders and their social experts, whom no doubt we pay for in national or local taxes.

a) **With reference to Document A, identify and briefly explain _two_ factors that might affect how people react to the provision of contraception to girls below the age of 16.**

b) **With reference to Document B, identify and briefly explain _two_ factors that may have influenced the views stated concerning the provision of contraception to girls below the age of 16.**

Comment

a) You could reasonably choose any two of the following factors:

■ People who feel that 13 is too young for a girl to be sexually active may be influenced against the proposal by the newspaper's claim that 'thousands of 13-year-old girls have been handed the morning-after pill by health service staff without their parents' permission'.

■ Many parents are likely to oppose the proposal because they resent the claim that contraception and abortions can be arranged 'without their parents' knowledge'.

■ People who are concerned about the rising number of teenagers becoming pregnant are likely to approve of the proposal to make contraception and abortion even more readily available to children, but the newspaper claims that some pressure groups believe it will have the opposite effect.

b) It is not difficult to identify factors which might have affected each of the contributions to this discussion. You could make any two of the following points:

■ Being a parent has influenced Andrew's contribution to the discussion. He opposes the proposal because he feels that the government is undermining his parental rights and responsibilities.

■ However, being a parent has influenced Brenda in the opposite direction. She appears to be confident enough in her relationship with her children to conclude that parents whose children do not consult them are probably failures, whose children need to be able to access help outside the family. So she approves of the proposal.

■ Caroline is evidently a school nurse (she refers to them as 'we'), and this professional role seems to affect her attitude considerably. She is in favour of trusting school nurses to take responsibility in the area of child sexuality and takes a balanced view of parental rights.

■ Debbie states that her opinion is affected by her age, and this appears likely to be the case. She identifies with the teenagers rather than their parents and strongly approves of the proposal.

■ Age is also the main factor acknowledged by Ernie, but in this case his remoteness from the age of the people concerned leads him to an unfocused opposition to the proposal, based mainly on his conviction that things were better in his day.

ACTIVITY 5

Documents A and B are about the differences between what men and women are paid. This is referred to as the 'gender pay gap'. Read the documents carefully and then use them to answer the following questions:

a) **Refer to Document A. Identify and briefly explain one factor from Document A which might lead someone to conclude that action must be taken to close the gender pay gap.**

b) **Refer to Document A. Identify and briefly explain one factor from Document A which might lead someone to conclude that it is not necessary to take any action to close the gender pay gap.**

c) **Refer to Document B. Identify and briefly explain two factors which might have influenced the opinions expressed in Document B.**

Document A: Extracts from the Women and Work Commission Report, February 2006

■ Female workers suffer one of the biggest pay gaps in Europe – 17 per cent for full-time staff and 38 per cent for part-time staff – because they are more likely to be in low paid jobs and then slip down the career ladder after having children.

■ Lady Prosser, the Chairwoman of the Commission, said: 'Many women are working, day in day out, far below their abilities. This waste of talent is an outrage.'

■ Recommendations of the Report were that the government should:
  • take action to tackle gender stereotypes
  • encourage skilled part-time jobs
  • support women returning to work
  • extend flexible working rights to parents of older children
  • provide £5 million to train trade union equality representatives to monitor pay.

Document B: Some reactions to the Women and Work Commission Report

■ **Dr Katherine Rake**, Director of the Fawcett Society (an organisation that campaigns for equal opportunities for women)
'This report has short-changed a generation of women. If this government wants to go down in history as having closed the pay gap, it is going to have to try a lot harder. The time is long overdue for rigorous measures that will actually work.'

■ **John Cridland**, Deputy Director of the CBI (Confederation of British Industry – an organisation representing employers)
'I was staggered at how poor career guidance and education has become; we are failing a whole generation of young people – especially young girls.'

■ **George Osborne**, the Shadow Chancellor of the Exchequer (speaks for the opposition party in the House of Commons; a leading member of the Conservative Party)
'In the past, Conservatives have given the impression that young mothers should stay at home. Today, the Labour Party gives the impression that all young mothers should work. Both are wrong … We should support the choice that young mothers make for themselves.'

Using evidence in questions 3 and 4

Although the issues we have been looking at so far are raised explicitly in questions 1 and 2 on the exam paper, you must not forget them in question 4. In order to gain a high mark for 'Use of Resources' you need to show that you have questioned the reliability of the documents you refer to in your answer. You could do this in any of the following ways:

■ by use of credibility criteria

■ by questioning the plausibility of the claims

■ by asking whether the evidence really does support the conclusion which the author has drawn from it

■ by identifying flaws, weaknesses or strengths in the reasoning of the document.

You do not necessarily have to refer to the resource documents to support your answer to question 3, and if you do, you do not need to discuss their credibility. However, you should ensure that you use only documents which are credible for the purpose for which you are using them. Especially, if you have already explained in answer to question 1 or 2 that a particular document lacks credibility, you should not use that document in question 3 as if it was credible.

Summary

You should now be able to:

■ explain difficulties in understanding and using evidence

■ use evidence to demonstrate your awareness that how we might define certain key words and phrases can be problematic

■ explain how such problems of definition can, in turn, make it more difficult to devise and implement policies

■ use evidence in identifying factors that might affect how people view a range of issues.

2 Choices and criteria

Learning objectives

- Examine how we use evidence critically to help us identify what might be appropriate choices in response to issues of concern.

- Examine how we need to develop and assess the relevance of criteria to enable us to decide upon a course of action.

- Use criteria we have identified, in the context of the evidence provided, to evaluate the choices made.

In Chapter 1 we examined evidence for three particular purposes:

- to interpret and evaluate data

- to explore problems of definition and implementation

- to help us to identify and explain factors that influence how people react to certain issues or problems.

These are the skills which are likely to be tested in one or both of the short questions at the beginning of the exam.

Question 3 in the exam will ask you to identify one or two choices and to evaluate it or them by a number of appropriate criteria.

In Chapter 2 you will:

- examine how we use evidence critically to help us identify what might be appropriate choices in response to issues of concern

- examine how we need to develop and assess the relevance of criteria to enable us to decide upon a course of action

- use criteria we have identified, in the context of the evidence provided, to evaluate the choices made.

Identifying possible choices

Here we could talk in terms of framing **choices** or policy alternatives. Whether we are deciding upon which university to apply to or what to do about nuclear energy, the process is more or less the same.

It is likely that we will start off with at least some sort of a view about the problem or issue. We might even think that we know straightaway what should or should not be done. However, this is where we might need to be very careful not to base our decisions on emotion or prejudice.

Think in terms of some of the issues looked at in Chapter 1:

- anti-social behaviour

- teenage pregnancy

- the gender pay gap.

Each of these issues is the subject of much analysis and debate. All three are of concern to us, on both individual and **collective** levels. It follows, then, that responses to each of these issues – and to any number of other problems – are likely to involve us acting collectively. This may well mean government intervention, for example, via the police and the courts. Decisions have to be made: what to do; what not to do; what policies to put in place; how effective such policies are likely to be. Before reaching decisions we need to examine relevant evidence.

The issues raised in the exam may involve collective and/or individual choices. From session to session, there will probably be an approximate balance between issues which focus on:

- public policy (at global, national or local levels)

- public institutions (such as schools or hospitals)

- commercial institutions (such as manufacturers or shops)

- individuals (such as consumers, parents, employers etc.)

KEY TERMS

Choices
The different options that might be available to us when we are responding to situations where decisions need to be made.

Collective
Refers to situations where groups of people are affected as a whole rather than just on an individual level.

Collective decisions
Are those made by, or on behalf of, society or institutions as a whole, as in the state or any organisation we might belong to, such as school, business, family and so on.

Different types of choice

In the exam you will be required to identify one or more possible choices in response to the issue and the documents supplied. One of the short questions at the beginning of the question paper might ask you to identify two or three choices. The issue may present you with different types of choice. Some of the different types of choice you might identify may include the following:

- a range of options
- alternatives
- a continuum of choice.

A range of options

This is where we are presented with a number of different options and might select one or more, or even all of them, depending largely on what our resources will permit us to do. For example, a school or college or a workplace might decide to improve the health of its personnel with a health promotion. A number of suggestions spring to mind – posters, education, healthy eating options on the menu, subsidies to encourage the use of the gym, sports halls and the like; even organised work-outs for all every morning. The option or options chosen might be determined as much by resources as anything else.

Alternatives

Here we are presented with options where we do have to choose between one or the other; for example, choosing which university you would like to attend: here you have to choose one university (once you have decided to go to university of course). You cannot go to more than one university at a time.

A continuum of choice

A continuum of choice involves us considering options of increasing intervention or severity. Take the case of responding to the gender pay gap. Here we might decide that the key thing is to encourage employers to employ more women in higher paid posts. In this case the following continuum represents a series of choices which could be made:

- introduce a voluntary code of practice whereby employers agree to try to move towards employing a quota of women in higher paid posts
- introduce a compulsory scheme of quotas for women in higher paid positions, under which firms will be liable to fines if they do not comply
- introduce such a scheme where the penalty for non-compliance is imprisonment.

You may find the continuum of choice approach a useful way of identifying possible choices, but you will not be tested on your ability to put them into the 'right' order.

Question 3 may state the extreme positions and require you to choose and discuss a different choice.

If the topic is the use of animals for research, the extreme choices might be to 'allow animal testing to continue as it is at present' and to 'ban all animal testing'. The most fruitful choices for evaluation would be 'significantly strengthen the regulation of animal testing' or 'restrict animal testing to cases where scientists are developing new treatments for serious illnesses'.

WORKED EXAMPLE 6

According to Document A in worked example 5, page 25–26, the government has introduced a policy allowing school nurses to issue emergency contraception (the morning-after pill) to schoolgirls, including those under the age of consent, without informing their parents. Suggest *three* other choices which the government could make about the provision of emergency contraception to teenagers.

EXAM TIP

• The best approach to identifying choices is probably to begin by listing all the variables which need to be taken into account. It should then be quite easy to generate at least three choices (and probably many more) by mixing and matching these variables.

• Make sure that you define a choice fully, including all aspects.

Comment

There are four variables in this situation, and the choices we identify should consist of permutations of these variables:

■ the age of the girl

■ who can prescribe the pill

■ the role of parents

■ any other safeguards.

It is important to give full answers. For example, the answer 'allow school nurses to prescribe emergency contraception to girls over 16 without informing their parents' would be incomplete, because it does not say what happens about girls under 16. So although that may look like a good answer, it would probably receive only 1 mark out of 2, or 2 out of 3.

Here are examples of answers which would receive full marks, but many variations would be equally valid and acceptable. For example, you might reasonably argue that 18 (the age of majority) is the crucial age for not informing parents, rather than 16 (the age of consent).

■ Allow school nurses to prescribe emergency contraception to girls over the age of 16 without informing their parents, and to girls under 16 whose parents consent.

■ Allow school nurses to prescribe emergency contraception to girls over the age of 16 without informing their parents, and allow doctors to prescribe it to girls under 16 without informing their parents.

■ Allow school nurses to prescribe emergency contraception to girls over the age of 16 without informing their parents, and to girls under the age of 16 with the consent of either their parents or a senior social worker.

■ Allow school nurses to prescribe emergency contraception to girls over the age of 16 without informing their parents, and to girls under the age of 16 subject to a formal psychological assessment.

■ Allow school nurses to prescribe emergency contraception to girls over the age of 16 without informing their parents, and to girls under the age of 16 subject to an informal psychological assessment.

Other choices could include allowing emergency contraception to be prescribed only by a woman or girl's own GP, or only by a Family Planning Clinic or – in the case of teenagers or girls under the age of consent – only by staff at a Young Person's Sexual Health clinic. The permutations are many.

ACTIVITY 6

a) It has been suggested that learning to play a musical instrument should become part of the National Curriculum for schools. This would mean that all children would have to learn an instrument and the tuition would be provided by schools free of charge. Suggest *three* other choices which the government could make about providing instrumental tuition.

b) Many people believe that eating meat is morally wrong, either for economic reasons or because of concerns for animal welfare. They may decide that neither they nor their families should eat any meat or products derived from animals. Suggest *three* other choices which individuals may make about eating meat.

c) Some hospitals have chosen not to make scarce medical resources available to patients whose medical problems could be regarded as being their own fault (e.g. smokers or obese people). Suggest *three* other choices which hospitals could make about the provision of scarce medical resources.

Criteria

Before we decide on which course of action to take, we need to identify and explore relevant criteria. Criteria are the means by which we decide on a reasoned course of action.

The role and importance of criteria in making choices

Even in the most everyday situations where decisions are required, we need to have some means of judging what might be our best course of action. For instance, when deciding where to go on holiday, a family might apply a criterion based upon what facilities are available for the children. There will almost certainly be the criterion of cost to consider too.

We also need some way of assessing whether or not we have done the right thing. Decisions we make often require us to make further decisions in the future: 'should we continue doing what we originally decided to do?' is a fairly obvious one.

It is very important in all this that we select the criteria that are the most appropriate to the type of decision we are considering.

Identifying and developing relevant criteria

We need to be aware that there are different types of criteria. This is important to us in Unit 3 because there are likely to be different ways of testing whether or not criteria have been met.

Although distinctions between types of criteria cannot always be precise, one useful way of broadly categorising criteria is as follows:

■ moral/ethical

■ pragmatic

■ political

■ economic.

- We apply certain criteria when we are making choices.

Moral/ethical

Moral (or ethical) criteria are concerned with right and wrong behaviour and the goodness or badness of the actions of individuals or groups. Under this heading we would include criteria concerned with considerations such as: *fairness*; *equality*; *harm*.

Pragmatic

A pragmatic approach to decision-making involves trying to deal with a problem and making choices in a way that is based on practical rather than theoretical considerations. If you are being pragmatic, you will try to be realistic rather than idealistic. The sort of criteria here would include such considerations as: *ease of implementation*; *effectiveness*; *efficiency*; *sustainability*.

Political

This is a word that can be used in a number of different ways, not all of them complimentary! Strictly speaking, it refers to the state, the government or the public affairs of the country. It is also used to refer to the ideas and activities of the various political parties. In a more derogatory sense, a decision might be described as political because it has an eye to what might prove popular and to what advantage there could be in it for an individual or a party. Political criteria are often also pragmatic and can include considerations such as: *public acceptability* (will such a measure be popular?); *does it fit in with party policy?*; *will our international allies approve?*

Economic

Economic factors are concerned with the use and distribution of resources. We will be using a fairly broad definition of economic criteria, which will include things such as *employment, costs, the creation of wealth and its distribution, overseas trade, the local economy, government spending and taxation.* We will consider, too, issues concerning *the effective use of resources* and *value for money.*

When we come to use criteria to help us to make choices, we may aim for a range of different types of criteria.

REMEMBER

In order to succeed in the Unit 3 exam, it is essential that you have a good understanding of the importance of using criteria in the decision-making process.

ACTIVITY 7

Here is a list of some criteria which you might choose to use in the exam, depending on what issue is set for consideration:

legality, public safety, sustainability, impact on the environment, value for money, personal freedom, effects on wildlife, equality of opportunity, impact on community relations, adherence to international norms and conventions.

Look at the following three issues, each of which throws up options for us to consider:

■ nuclear energy
■ smoking
■ public demonstrations, such as protest marches.

a) From the list above, identify two criteria that are likely to play an important or necessary role in assessing policies in relation to each of the three issues.

b) Explain why you have chosen each criterion.

Using criteria: identifying relevance and problems

You can expect to get a question requiring you to identify a choice (or possibly more than one) and evaluate it by appropriate criteria. About a quarter of the marks for the whole exam will be allocated to this question, so you should aim to spend about 20 minutes on it. The question will probably help you by identifying one suitable criterion, but you should use more than the one given.

For criteria to be applied effectively they should be:

■ *readily understood* – your criteria ought to be clearly phrased

■ *relevant* to the possible choices you have identified – there should be a good fit between the criterion and the situation under discussion. Some criteria are likely to be more appropriate in the evaluation of certain courses of action than others. Making a decision about whether we allow some form of euthanasia, for instance, is hopefully much more likely to involve ethical rather than economic considerations

■ *measurable* where possible/appropriate. Some of the criteria you choose may be precisely measurable – for example, one of the resource documents may provide data which you can use – whereas in other cases you may need to make an educated guess, but for a criterion to be of any use at all you must be able to make some kind of judgement as to how well it is satisfied by the choice you are evaluating.

You will need to bear these points closely in mind throughout the rest of this chapter.

When considering a course of action we might ask some, or all, of the following questions (bearing in mind the classifications of moral, pragmatic, political and economic factors we have discussed earlier).

■ Should we do this because it is the *right* thing to do? For instance, will it involve people being treated equally?

■ Will it work?

■ Will it be popular?

■ Will it represent an effective use of resources?

These questions will, in effect, form the basis of our criteria (however we might choose to phrase them). These criteria could be stated as equality, practicality, popular opinion and cost-effectiveness.

However, it is more than likely that any criterion we identify as being relevant and useful will also bring with it some problems of which we need to be aware.

EXAM TIP ●

When answering questions which require you to use criteria, be precise in your explanations and applications of relevant criteria. Remember to test the criteria you identify against a particular choice.

WORKED EXAMPLE 7 ✓

Handling anti-social behaviour

Consider using *public opinion* as a criterion in choosing how to respond to young people who display disruptive and disorderly behaviour.

Consider first these options.

■ Increase the number of ASBOs handed out to young people.

■ Impose more Dispersal Orders, which give the police powers to break up groups of people congregating in public places and to move them on.

■ Impose a curfew on young people being out between certain hours.

We might choose one of these options, or we might adopt two of them, or even all three: the criteria we decide to use might very well determine which option we take. We might, of course, decide to do none of these things, though this seems unlikely when we consider the growing strength of public opinion on this topic. The first two require no additional powers. Imposing a curfew, however, would probably be seen as a more drastic action and would probably lead to considerable debate.

Whatever we choose to do, it is very likely that public opinion will play a part in our decision.

1 **What importance do you think should be attached to public opinion as a criterion in formulating a policy to deal with disruptive and disorderly behaviour amongst young people?**

Comment

Remember that we have already said that for a criterion to be of real use to us it should be:

- *readily understood* – a criterion should be relatively easy to understand and concisely phrased. Phrases such as 'public opinion' or 'public acceptability' are easily recognisable.

- *relevant* – does such a criterion fit? In other words, are the views and demands of the public likely to be a significant factor in influencing what is being decided here? We could argue that public support for a measure such as a curfew is vital because, without widespread support, it would be very difficult to enforce. Evidence we looked at earlier confirms that disorderly or anti-social behaviour amongst young people is an issue of public concern. (Over 6000 ASBOs were issued between 1999 and 2005.) The success or otherwise of any policies is very likely to have to be tested in terms of public acceptability.

- *measurable* – we do have ways of trying to assess what the public is thinking and what it might or might not be in favour of, via surveys, opinion polls, meetings, consultations and so on.

It would appear, then, that using public opinion/acceptability as a criterion to help us to make choices in this context would be clear, appropriate and measurable and that we should therefore, attach a great deal of importance to it.

However, we have to go on to ask the question below.

WORKED EXAMPLE 7 (CONT.)

2 **What *problems* are likely to arise in using public opinion/ acceptability as a criterion in deciding how to respond to anti-social behaviour in young people?**

Comment

What we have to think about here is whether or not anything could be said against using public opinion as a criterion in helping us to make decisions about what to do about our unruly 15- and 16-year-olds. Is there an argument for being careful here?

There certainly is and it could include points such as:

- To use public acceptability as a criterion we need to be confident that we have indicators of public opinion that are accurate, credible and representative:

  - *Accurate*: because we need to be sure that the standards of statistical analysis and handling have clearly been applied (this is vital for any form of measurement to be of use). Raw data which show what the public is thinking (gleaned from opinion polls or other forms of survey) must be handled with great care.

- Should the use of ASBOs be increased?

  - **Credible**: if we are using indicators to help us to make decisions, we need to be reasonably confident that what they tell us is actually the case. For instance, we might look at a breakdown of the results of a survey that has been undertaken amongst the residents of an estate. The survey seeks to find out what the residents think should be done about gangs of teenagers who are causing a nuisance. This breakdown might be presented in the form of graphs, pie charts, bar charts, percentages, etc. and reflect the highest standards of statistical analysis. But we would still need to consider various points of credibility in relation to those who conducted the research, those who responded to the survey and those who have reported the results.

    - Did those who conducted the survey have a vested interest which affected how they worded the questions? Do they work for a polling organisation which has a reputation for reliability?

    - Did those who responded do so on the basis of knowledge (expertise and ability to observe)? Did they have a vested interest which might have affected their answers?

    - Do those who have reported the results have a vested interest to use them to draw particular conclusions?

  - **Significance**: what if the results of such a survey might be different depending on the time of year at which opinions are canvassed? For example, the summer holiday period can provoke a lot more complaints from older people about the behaviour of young people.

  - *Representative*: we want to be sure that the result of any survey shows us what a range of people are thinking. For example, even if you only want to know what the over-sixties feel about the idea of a curfew, you will still need to be sure that you have not just polled a particularly grumpy set of older people.

KEY TERM

Credible/Credibility
Whether the evidence is believable.

Significance
The weight of support or importance of evidence.

You would want, of course, to ask a representative sample, based perhaps upon gender, family type, race or ethnic group, social class and so on. But, as a local authority or as a chief of police, you would not just want to look at the results of a survey that shows you only what the over-sixties think should be done with young people. You would want an indicator that at least represents a spread of age groups amongst other things.

■ There is another serious problem that could arise from using public opinion as a criterion for action. This revolves around what happens if the public's view on what should be done might be considered in itself to be unacceptable – perhaps on the basis of being extreme or discriminatory or impracticable.

Using criteria to evaluate choices

In this final section of Chapter 2 we are going to bring together what we have been looking at in terms of *framing choices* and *identifying relevant criteria*.

We will do this by using criteria and referring to evidence to evaluate possible choices that we have identified.

Examining a decision to impose a curfew on young people

How might we have reached a decision such as to impose a curfew on young people being on the streets between certain hours? We could have started by asking these two questions:

1 Will this work?
2 Will it cost much?

If, after considering relevant evidence, we decided that the answer was 'yes' to the first question and 'no' to the second, then our decision would seem to be a good one. It would certainly meet the pragmatic criterion of being an effective course of action. It would also appear to be an effective use of resources, thereby giving value for money and fulfilling our economic criterion.

But what if the answer is 'yes' to both questions? Then we have a more complicated situation on our hands. Some kind of balance has to be struck, just as one might need to strike a balance between the moral and the political. This, then, becomes a question of judgement: how far does one criterion outweigh the other?

Finally, what if the answer is 'no' to the first question? In other words, we don't think the curfew will work. Does it then matter what the answer to the second question is?

To attempt to answer this we need to bring in a consideration of moral and political types of criteria. Consider the following scenario:

> A suggested course of action is, after consideration, thought unlikely to have much effect. It might even prove to be quite costly. (Though why bother if it is not going to work, even if it is relatively cheap to implement?) Yet the government decides to go ahead with it anyway.

On the face of it, this is something of a riddle. How might we solve it and explain the government's actions? We can do this by applying additional criteria to help us to evaluate the choice that has been made.

Look again at the suggestion that we place a curfew on young people between, for example, the hours of 9 pm and 6 am. What happens if further research strongly suggests that such a policy just will not work because it will be unenforceable? What if, in addition, we are not too sure how much the curfew scheme is going to cost but, nonetheless, we decide to go ahead with the scheme anyway?

How could we defend such a choice? Because we are stupid?

No, because we are smart, if somewhat unscrupulous, politicians. We have equally convincing evidence that such a curfew will be very popular with voters. As the voting age is 18, young people under that age will not be able to register their opinion in the polling booths anyway.

But also, on a less unworthy note, we might be convinced that, ineffective as it might be, a curfew is the right and moral thing to do. It is wrong for young people to be out after nine o'clock at night.

Therefore, if we consider it necessary to fulfil both political and moral criteria, choosing to impose a curfew might appear to be quite a reasonable step to take even if we are not sure that it will be effective.

ACTIVITY 8

Evaluate the three possible responses to anti-social behaviour listed in worked example 7 (on pages 37–38) by reference to the following criteria:

- **ease of implementation**
- **public safety**
- **fairness.**

Supporting your evaluation

Unless the question specifically asks you to refer to the resource documents, you do not need to do so. However, your evaluation will be better (and achieve a higher mark) if you support your judgement by reasoning and/or by reference to evidence. This evidence could come from your personal knowledge or from the resource documents.

If you do refer to the resource documents, make sure that the use you make of them is credible. For example, if you have already shown in question 1 or 2 that a source lacks expertise, or has a vested interest to misrepresent the truth, do not then quote it in support of your evaluation as if it were reliable.

ACTIVITY 9

Supermarket expansion

Examine the evidence about supermarkets in Documents A, B and C. Then complete the task which follows.

> **Document A: MPs declare war on power of the supermarket giants**
>
> MPs will demand a series of draconian curbs on the power of the supermarkets in a hard-hitting report into the future of the high street.

The report by the All-Party Parliamentary Small Shops Group will call for the Office of Fair Trading to trigger a full-blown investigation into the supermarket sector. Recommendations include:

■ an end to what MPs will say is the unfair advantage supermarkets derive from offering free car parking while shoppers wishing to use local stores have to pay to park on the high street

■ the wiping out of advantageous business rates for supermarkets

■ measures to allow local authorities to find resources to fight planning applications by supermarkets

■ stiff sanctions if supermarkets exceed the floorspace they are given planning permission for. Earlier this month, a Friends of the Earth report concluded that there is a growing trend for supermarket groups to flout restrictions.

Supermarket chiefs insisted that they will fight off any plans to increase their business rates or tax their free car parks. And they urged regulatory authorities to resist calls for a time-consuming investigation.

Source: Nick Mathiason, *The Observer*, 29 January 2006

Document B: Simon Hoggart's Week

It is heartening to see the wave of opposition billowing out towards Tesco. And it is producing results too. Near where my parents live in Norwich, a persistent local campaign has stopped Tesco getting permission for a store that would wipe out a street of local shops, including two terrific butchers, a greengrocer, a fishmonger, an old-fashioned pharmacist who delivers, and two fine bakeries. Money spent with local people goes back into the community, to the plumbers, hairdressers, solicitors and dentists, whereas money given to Tesco winds up hundreds of miles away in Tescoland, wherever that is.

Source: Simon Hoggart, *The Guardian*, 25 February 2006

Document C: Total number of independent retailers, 2000–2004

2000 = 34,250
2001 = 33,787
2002 = 32,900
2003 = 29,030
2004 = 26,873

Source: IGD Convenience Retailing Report

We could select from a number of choices about responding to the growth of large supermarket chains. The selection may be influenced by a number of criteria (such as the impact on local employment). Evaluate one choice by reference to three appropriate criteria.

- Local shops – under threat?

Comment

◼ You should spend quite a bit of time on this activity – it is important that you practise tackling this kind of question.

◼ Before starting, read through Chapter 2 once more to remind yourself of the sort of points you should be making.

◼ Identify a choice, and evaluate it by three appropriate criteria, including the one provided.

◼ Once you have finished the activity, make sure you study the more detailed guidance provided on the Student CD-ROM.

◼ Be sure to study carefully the Exam Café section.

Summary

You should now be able to:

◼ understand how evidence will help in framing a series of choices in response to a particular issue

◼ understand and explain how important it is to identify and apply relevant criteria in helping us to make decisions

◼ understand and explain some of the problems we might come across in applying criteria

◼ use criteria to evaluate choices in the context of evidence provided.

Learning objectives

- Examine what we mean by the term 'dilemma'.
- Identify and explain some dilemmas.
- Set out and explain a dilemma.

Chapter 3 extends a process we started in Chapter 1 and developed in Chapter 2. Let's recap what we have done so far. We have:

◼ used evidence to explore some problems of definition

◼ used evidence to help us to identify and explain factors that might influence how people react to issues or problems

◼ identified appropriate choices in response to issues of concern

◼ identified and evaluated criteria which could be used in deciding upon courses of action

◼ used criteria to evaluate choices made.

What is a dilemma?

Questions 3 and 4 in the Unit 3 exam will consist of discussing an issue in which it is difficult to decide between two or more choices. On some occasions, this issue may be presented in the form of a **dilemma**.

For our purposes in Unit 3 we will define a dilemma as arising from a situation in which we need to:

◼ make a decision – we cannot simply avoid or ignore a dilemma

◼ choose between alternatives, each of which has good reasons against it. The reasons against one alternative may consist of failing to achieve the benefits which the other alternative would bring.

◼ the subject of a dilemma is always important: a matter of life and death or something which seriously affects the quality of life. The choice between two brands of breakfast cereal, for example, could not pose a dilemma, because it is trivial.

◼ in most cases dilemmas involve conflicting criteria. For example, the case of giving the morning-after pill to girls who are under age might meet the criterion of being easy to implement but may not meet the criterion of parental approval. However, both sides of some dilemmas involve harm by the same criterion, e.g. public acceptability in cases where one section of society disapproves of one alternative and a different section of society is offended by the other.

Expressing and explaining a dilemma

In the exam you may be required to identify and explain a dilemma that arises from the issue covered in the Resource Booklet. Therefore, it is important that you learn how to express a dilemma clearly. If you do not express your dilemma clearly, you will find it more difficult to suggest ways in which it might be resolved. Alternatively, the dilemma may be stated in the question paper, and you may be asked to explain why it is a dilemma.

Before moving on to look at some real-life situations which throw up dilemmas, here are some useful tools that can help you when you are thinking about dilemmas:

◼ the harm test

◼ identifying where the interests of the individual conflict with the collective

◼ identifying conflicting criteria.

KEY TERM

Dilemma ◼
A situation where a difficult and important choice has to be made between two conflicting options, each of which will result in some undesirable consequences.

The harm test

One way of checking whether or not you have identified a dilemma is to apply what we might call the harm test: are the options you are putting forward in your dilemma each going to result in some kind of harm being done?

If the answer is 'yes', then you are likely to be on the right lines in terms of framing your dilemma.

For example, if a housing authority allocates accommodation on the basis of 'first come, first served', emergency needs will not be met, which will cause serious hardship to some people, but if they give priority to the people who have the most pressing needs, some people who need housing will remain on the waiting list for longer and perhaps even never reach the top of it.

Identifying where the interests of the individual conflict with the collective

Many dilemmas revolve around the problem of trying to reconcile the interests of the individual with those of the various groups that we as individuals belong to.

We all, as individuals, have our own needs, demands and expectations, but there are many occasions when these will conflict with the requirements of the **collective**.

For instance, we all value our freedoms or what we can call our civil rights, such as freedom of speech and the right to be tried by a jury. However, there are times when the government might think it necessary to over-ride some of our civil rights in order to preserve public safety.

For example, if you decide to detain suspected terrorists indefinitely, innocent people might be held against their will and deprived of their civil liberties. If you don't take this course of action, you may run the risk of releasing a terrorist, leading to a serious attack and loss of life.

Identifying conflicting criteria

We have seen in Chapter 2 that when making choices we need to identify and apply criteria. However, the criteria we use to evaluate these choices might well produce conflicting results. Consider the following situation:

> It is your duty as a school governor to decide whether or not to give permission for a school visit that involves outdoor activities such as rock-climbing and pot-holing. What do you decide?

In order to help you make your decision, you would need to apply some criteria:

- one criterion we would have to apply here is that of risk
- another criterion could involve a consideration of personal development.

So in deciding whether or not to allow the visit to go ahead we need to strike some kind of a balance between conflicting criteria: let the visit go ahead on the basis that students will learn something about themselves and the importance of teamwork but accept the risk that they might get hurt; or stop the visit on the basis that we do not want to run the risk of accidents, and therefore deny students a valuable experience.

KEY TERM

Collective

Refers to situations where groups of people are affected as a whole rather than just on an individual level.

■ Rock climbing – a suitable activity for school children?

In other words, what we have here is something of a dilemma:

> Should the school governor give permission for outdoor activities that might involve health and safety risks or refuse permission and in the process limit possible personal development for the children?

Look back to worked example 5, which we discussed in Chapter 1, pages 25–26. The situation which is described and discussed in the resource documents poses the following dilemma:

> Do we provide the morning-after pill in schools even though it might encourage under-age sex, with all the problems that can bring in terms of health and parental disapproval; or do we decide not to provide it and run the risk of a rise in under-age pregnancies, with all the unfavourable consequences which would follow?

WORKED EXAMPLE 8

Look at the following evidence about the medical drug Herceptin.

- Herceptin targets the HER2 protein which can increase the growth of breast tumours.
- About a fifth of breast cancers are HER2 positive.
- Breast cancer is the the most common single cause of death for women aged 35–54.
- 41,000 cases of the disease are diagnosed each year.
- At the moment (May 2006) Herceptin is only licensed for women with advanced disease, where it has spread in the breast or to another organ.
- It is estimated 2000 British women suffering early breast cancer could die before Herceptin is available on the National Health Service.
- The cost of one year's treatment with Herceptin is £19,500.
- In 2006 an NHS Trust was taken to court by a patient because she had been denied Herceptin on the grounds of lack of evidence of its effectiveness. (NHS Trusts are responsible for running the National Health Service in each area.)

1 **What choice does the NHS Trust have to make? Do not summarise one alternative as 'or not', but identify both choices in full.**

2 **Would both alternatives cause negative consequences? If so, what are they?**

3 **Do both choices satisfy different criteria?**

Comment

The NHS Trust is clearly faced with a dilemma here because of the following points.

- As the body responsible for the running of the NHS in its area, the Trust has to make the decision whether or not a new and expensive drug should be freely available on prescription.

- There are clearly negative consequences either way. Denying a patient free treatment could be seen as discriminatory and even cruel in terms of the pain and suffering that could result. But spending large amounts on providing an expensive, and as yet possibly unproven, treatment might result in other patients being denied treatment, on the basis that there is not an unlimited budget for drugs.

- Conflicting criteria could include cost versus the welfare of individual patients.

In the exam, you may be asked either to:

- suggest and explain a dilemma, or

- explain why a named choice is a dilemma.

In order to identify and explain a dilemma, you need to identify the choice clearly and in full and show that each alternative would cause adverse consequences. In order to explain why a named choice is a dilemma, you need to show that a choice needs to be made (you cannot choose both alternatives, or neither) and to identify the reasons against each alternative.

WORKED EXAMPLE 9

Now look at the following report of a court case involving a vicar and his council tax.

Vicar who refuses to pay council tax is sent to jail

A retired 71-year-old vicar yesterday became the first pensioner in England to be jailed for failing to pay his council tax on a point of principle.

He arrived at court carrying his toothbrush after refusing to comply with a court order that he repay the arrears on his council tax. He and his wife had paid an increase of 2.5% on their previous bill to cover inflation, leaving them only £63 in arrears, but with court and bailiff costs the amount now owed was £691.15. He was jailed for 28 days.

'We have been very patient with you,' the magistrate told him. 'As you have failed to pay we have no alternative but to enforce the suspended prison sentence.'

The vicar replied by saying: 'The council tax has risen by 76% in the last few years. I am not paying it because it is an illegal tax.'

Afterwards the national anti-council tax pressure group Is It Fair? said: 'It is a really wicked tax, and an upside-down world when a man goes to prison for withholding a portion of his council tax when you can hit someone over the head with a bottle and get a caution.'

The vicar's son said that his father was 'a man of principle and he might well go through all this again when he comes out. It all depends on how he finds the next 28 days.'

The vicar's wife said: 'The state of the council tax is a very serious issue. The Government needs to listen and put things on a basis of people's ability to pay.'

The Director of the Prison Reform Trust said: 'The average cost of keeping someone in jail for a month is more than £3000. Surely there must have been a cheaper way of dealing with the £63 originally owed?'

The Local Government Association said: 'We have consistently argued that council tax needs fundamental reform. This debate, however, cannot be used as an excuse for non-payment of council tax.'

Source: Fran Yeoman, *The Times*, 8 September 2005

Comment

In this case there are three main participants:

- the vicar
- the magistrate
- the local authority.

On one level or other, each of these participants in the case has decisions to make. It could be argued that in each case, whatever course of action is chosen, it will cause problems for those making the decision. In other words, each participant is faced with a dilemma. Let us examine the position of the vicar.

The vicar chooses to go to prison rather than to pay what he calls an 'illegal tax'. His son refers to him as being a 'man of principle'. Later on we will be examining the use of this word 'principle', but it is sufficient now to indicate that this issue of the council tax is more than just about the money as far as the vicar and his supporters are concerned. Either way, the vicar is faced with an awkward choice: 28 days behind bars with some potentially not very nice people; or pay up and risk losing the argument. Admittedly he is in a situation of his own making, and in a way he seems pleased enough to be going to prison in order to make his point and get plenty of good publicity. However, having got to this stage of being up before the magistrate, he now has a clear choice to make. He cannot decide both to go to prison and not to go to prison. Whatever he chooses to do, there will be some negative consequences. He is clearly faced with a dilemma.

ACTIVITY 10

a) **Suggest and briefly explain a dilemma facing the local council in worked example 9 on page 49.**

b) **Suggest and briefly explain a dilemma facing the magistrate in worked example 9 on page 49.**

ACTIVITY 11

On the basis of work you have done in earlier chapters, suggest a dilemma arising from each of the following situations and subjects:

a) **Activity 2: The use of Anti-Social Behaviour Orders (page 16)**

b) **Activity 5: The gender pay gap (pages 27–28)**

c) **Activity 9: Supermarket expansion (pages 41–43)**

Summary

You should now be able to:

■ explore what we mean when we talk in terms of facing a dilemma

■ identify and explain a dilemma – how we frame a dilemma

■ explain why a particular situation requiring a choice to be made is a dilemma.

4 Applying principles to make difficult decisions

Learning objectives

● Define and explain what we mean by 'principles'.
● Explore how we might best apply some principles in attempting to resolve an issue or dilemma.

By this stage you should be feeling more confident when it comes to identifying and explaining dilemmas. Next you need to examine how we might attempt to resolve issues or dilemmas – the single most important thing you will have to do in the Unit 3 exam.

Faced with the sort of difficult decisions we have been examining earlier, such as the Herceptin case in worked example 8 (page 48), we might be tempted to feel that there is no solution. And you can argue that by its very nature a dilemma cannot, in truth, be satisfactorily resolved. (Think here in terms of conflicting criteria – see page 46.)

However, a dilemma, also by its very nature, is a situation wherein a choice needs to be made. Whether the issue you have to discuss in question 4 of the exam is set out in the form of a dilemma or not, it will be one where a choice must be made between two or more possible courses of action but there are good reasons against all of them. In Unit 3 we need to demonstrate how we can attempt to resolve a contentious issue through:

- identifying relevant principles. What we mean when we refer to 'principles' will be explained in some detail, but remember that we are looking at general rules that will apply to more than just an individual case and in a variety of contexts. For example, the rule against killing, which philosophers usually express as something like '*You should never directly kill innocent bearers of moral standing*', can be applied to a wide variety of issues, including abortion, euthanasia, suicide, war and capital punishment, and should therefore be regarded as a **principle**.

- assessing the extent to which principles might be useful in helping us to make the sort of difficult decision posed by a dilemma.

Some suggestions about how to resolve an issue or dilemma after discussing both alternatives are given at the end of Chapter 5.

Principles

- A principle is not merely a rule. '*You are not allowed to cycle on motorways*' is a rule.

- A principle is a general rule which can be applied in a range of different contexts. '*You should avoid acting so as to cause unnecessary harm to others*' is a principle.

Let's look back at the case of the vicar who would not pay his council tax (worked example 9, page 49) and see how we can use this to illustrate the nature of principles.

- You must pay your council tax: this is the rule, or law, which the court is upholding when the magistrate tells the vicar that 'we have no alternative…'.

- The rule the magistrate is applying is based on the principle that you should pay your fair share of the cost of providing public services.

- The vicar's 'point of principle' can be expressed as a general rule: you should not be forced to pay a tax which you consider to be a bad one.

- The vicar's wife is assuming that a tax should be based upon 'people's ability to pay'.

- The Local Government Association seems to be recommending that the law be upheld in this case based upon the principle that you should pay your taxes (even if you think they are unfair).

Identifying relevant principles

As you might expect, certain principles are likely to be more useful in some cases than in others. A business, for instance, will base its operations on the principle that we should manage our time as effectively as possible. A television executive might operate on the principle that we should give the public what it wants and not what we think they should want.

The word 'principle' is often used in the context of **morality**. In attempting to resolve a dilemma, we might very well adopt the approach that our best way forward is to examine the **ethics** of the situation. The words 'moral', 'morality', 'ethics' and 'ethical' all refer to making judgements and choices on the basis of what is good or bad, right or wrong.

Ethics consists of thinking systematically about what is morally good and bad, what is the best way to live a good life and how we make moral choices. When we refer to ethical principles, we are talking about ideas and concepts to do with whether a course of action is considered morally good or bad. If you refer to them as 'moral principles', it will mean more or less the same thing.

Consider the following opinion:

> I believe it is wrong to take a life. So for me, abortion cannot be an option, unless pregnancy endangers the life of the pregnant woman.

It is clear that the general principle, '*It is wrong to take a life*', has been used as a reason to justify decision-making in the specific case of abortion. This is clearly an ethical principle because it refers to the taking of a life as *wrong* (or morally bad).

Whatever line of work you become involved in, you are likely to come across an ethical dimension to what you are doing. There are medical ethics, legal ethics and business ethics, to mention just a few.

Using ethical principles in the Unit 3 exam

- Some of the principles you apply to the issue may not be specifically ethical. For instance: in making decisions about nuclear power we have to consider the practical principle that tells us that whatever form of energy we invest in has to be one that we can afford.

- However, there will be few issues that do not have a moral aspect. For instance: in making decisions about nuclear power we need to consider the problem of nuclear waste that will be inherited by future generations. Do we have a moral duty to consider the well-being of people in the not-so-distant future? Do we have a moral duty to our planet as a whole?

- Unit 3 of the A2 exam in Critical Thinking is entitled 'Ethical reasoning and decision-making'. So the issue you will be asked to resolve will be concerned with deciding on the morally right course of action to take, and most or all of the principles you apply should be ethical principles.

Why do we use ethical principles?

An ethical principle is a decision-making tool which can help in a variety of both personal and public issues. It can provide a basic guide, which avoids working out each decision from scratch.

- *It saves time*: if an ethical principle is true, it should be true in all situations. Once accepted there can be no debate about whether or not it should be followed. Establishing a principle should, therefore, cut down the time taken in discussion about public issues.

- *Persuasion*: an ethical principle can also be an effective method of persuasion since if a recommendation is based upon a commonly held principle, such as *resources should be distributed equally*, then those who uphold the principle would need to agree to the recommendation or rethink their belief in the principle.

- *Rational response*: an ethical principle provides the opportunity for consistency in decision-making, as opposed to being guided by feelings which might be simply reactions to family, social or cultural influences.

Choosing ethical principles

When we come to resolving an issue, it is important that we try to identify principles which are relevant to the problem we are discussing and which will help us to resolve it. These will be principles which we can readily apply to the situation we are dealing with and which will help us to come to a decision about the best course of action to take.

Some ethical principles can be described as 'simple' or 'free-standing', while others are part of ethical theories, which have been put forward by various philosophers. You can use either or both kinds of principles in the exam, but because ethical theories offer more scope for development they may make it easier to achieve the higher marks. We will look at simple principles in this chapter, and ethical theories in Chapter 5.

In this chapter and the next, we will look at lots of cases in which a choice needs to be made. Some of these will be dilemmas, but the skills of choosing appropriate principles and applying them to an issue are the same whether the question is a dilemma or not.

Deontological and consequentialist ethical principles

Ethical principles can be roughly divided into two types. The first kind, which dominated discussions for several hundred years until the nineteenth century, consists of applying rights, duties or rules to a case. The rights, duties or rules exist before a particular situation arises, and the task for ethics consists of deciding which ones apply and then relating them to the specific features of the case. These are known as **deontological** principles (from the Greek *deon*, meaning duty). Theories of this kind evaluate actions themselves as right or wrong, irrespective of the consequences.

For example, some deontologists might argue that the principle *'It is wrong to take a life'* should be accepted because it is intrinsically right (simply right in and of itself). They would claim that this principle is true regardless of any consequences that might result from its application: for example, even if it caused the prolonged suffering of someone with a terminal illness.

> **KEY TERM**
>
> **Deontological**
> Making moral choices and judgements on the basis of rights, rules or duties, irrespective of consequences.

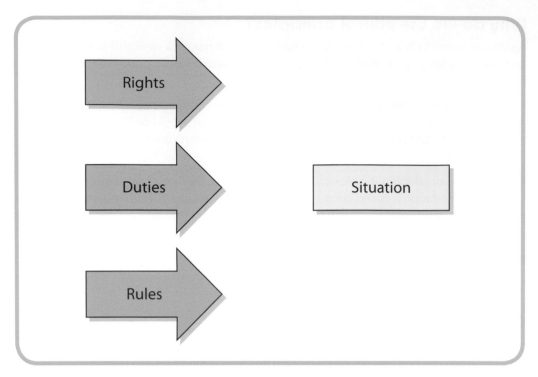

- Deontological approaches to ethics apply rights, rules or duties to a situation.

When an absolute principle of this kind leads to unconvincing results in particular cases, deontologists may revise the principle, to make it more complex. The full rule against killing, as generally accepted by ethicists, is '*It is always wrong directly to take the life of an innocent bearer of moral standing*'. This implies that killing may be justifiable if the killing is indirect, or if the victim is not innocent, or if the victim lacks moral standing (a right to life). Many people claim that abortion (especially if performed early in pregnancy) does not infringe the rule against killing, because an embryo or foetus does not have moral standing (a right to life).

In the exam, you may simply assert that certain rights, rules or duties are true and then apply them to the issue under discussion, but an argument of that kind may be quite flimsy by comparison with one based on principles which are more widely accepted or derived from an ethical theory.

The second approach, which has dominated debates in the last two hundred years, evaluates actions by their consequences, and theories of this kind are known as **consequentialist**. According to this view, actions are not good or bad in themselves, but are judged to be good or bad only according to whether they produce good or bad results. Many people who discuss ethical issues without having studied Moral Philosophy adopt a consequentialist approach without realising that there is any other way.

KEY TERM

● **Consequentialist**
Making moral choices and judgements on the basis of consequences only.

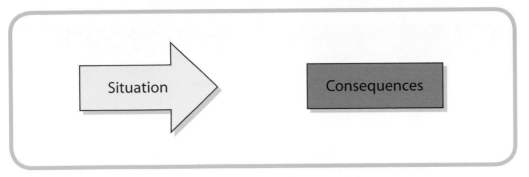

- Consequentialist approaches to ethics evaluate the consequences of alternative responses to a situation.

Consequentialist theories are sometimes called 'teleological'. Strictly speaking, 'consequentialist' and 'teleological' mean different things, but the difference is minor. In this textbook, we prefer to use the term 'consequentialist', and we advise you to do the same in the exam because it is a clearer and more accurate term.

In the exam, you may approach the issue from a consequentialist perspective without committing yourself to any particular consequentialist theory. In such a case, you would need to compare the consequences of the alternatives with regard to such aspects as:

■ short- and long-term consequences

■ the value used, e.g. happiness, love, money

■ and consequences for whom – self, others, everyone.

Moral standing

Some issues which might feature in the exam raise the question of whose interests should be considered when applying principles to resolve an issue or dilemma. For someone's (or something's) interests to be counted in an ethical analysis is usually referred to as having 'moral standing'.

The word 'person' is used in philosophy to denote a being which has full moral standing. It is generally agreed that only persons have a right to life.

Most non-philosophers would probably say that all human beings, and no members of any other species, have full moral standing. Many philosophers, however, claim that species is not a moral category, and that moral standing should be based on relevant criteria, such as consciousness, the ability to be aware of one's own existence, or being a moral agent. The implications of that approach are that some humans who have not yet achieved rationality (such as babies and foetuses) or who never will (because they have profound learning difficulties) do not qualify as persons and do not have a right to life. This approach also raises the possibility that moral standing and a right to life should be attributed to animals with developed mental capacities, such as dolphins and chimpanzees. However, other ethicists disagree strongly with both these suggestions.

STRETCH AND CHALLENGE

Most discussions of moral standing regard it as a matter of 'all or nothing'. On this basis, animals should be regarded either as the moral equal of humans or as morally negligible: no intermediate position is possible. Similarly, a human foetus should be treated as either the equivalent of a born child (so abortion is wrong except in extreme cases) or morally insignificant (so abortion should be freely available at the request of the pregnant woman). This approach gives no basis for claiming that abortion should be allowed for good reasons, but not for trivial ones, which is what many thoughtful people judge to be the right policy.

One philosopher, however, has plausibly suggested that we should recognise three levels of moral standing: all living things have some moral standing and some right to life; beings that can feel pain have higher moral standing and a stronger right to life; beings that are conscious of their own existence and can think rationally have full moral status and a full right to life; only the last of these three should be regarded as persons.

- Do dolphins have moral standing?

Most of the contentious ethical issues which occur both in real life and in the Unit 3 exam refer to human individuals or human communities, and most ethical theories refer only to questions of that kind. In the last generation or two, however, people have become increasingly concerned about the environment, including animals and topics of that kind could occur in the Unit 3 exam.

There are three general reasons why it might matter morally how we treat the environment.

1 We might have a duty to future generations of persons to hand on the world to them in as good a condition as we can.
2 We might be responsible to God for the way we use his creation.
3 Some people consider that the environment itself has some kind of moral standing.

WORKED EXAMPLE 10

Several times in recent years, some Members of Parliament have suggested that we should change the law on abortion by reducing the number of weeks of a pregnancy at which abortion would be allowed. Such a reduction would not apply to abortions where the foetus has been diagnosed with a serious handicap or where the pregnancy seriously endangers the life or long-term health of the pregnant woman, since there is no time limit for abortions on those grounds.

Members of Parliament have had to choose whether to reduce the age of foetuses at which abortion is permitted, even though that would prevent some women from having abortions, or to keep the age at 24 weeks, even though that causes the death of some foetuses which may have achieved moral standing.

Comment

How might the application of a deontological principle help us here?

The number of weeks into a pregnancy might be viewed as irrelevant according to deontological principles. We might oppose the suggestion on the basis that there is a duty to do what is good and that doing good involves the preservation of life. Merely limiting the number of weeks when abortion is allowed does not, therefore, address the issue that all life should be preserved even if it is in the womb. This would not be very helpful to those who want to limit the number of abortions rather than banning abortion altogether.

However, the issue could well revolve around a definition of independent life. When do we classify a foetus as possessing life on the same terms as a baby? The answer to some people might be not until it is actually born, while at the opposite extreme some people attribute full personhood to the developing embryo and foetus from the moment of conception.

Probably the majority of people think that the moral status of the foetus should be defined in terms of how many weeks have passed since its conception. If we accepted this view, then an application of deontological principles might still allow abortion under a certain number of weeks. Another way of expressing this point is to say that a foetus does not acquire moral standing, and thereby come under the full rule against killing (see page 56) until a certain age.

An application of principles

In the exam you will be dealing with an issue which the examiner will have selected from a wide range of possibilities. You will need to be skilled at selecting relevant principles to apply to whatever problem is raised by the evidence in the Resource Booklet.

With this in mind, let us examine a situation where principles play an important role: the courts and divorce.

The following extract concerns guidance given by the Law Lords to the lower courts on how they should decide on divorce settlements.

In their judgement, the Law Lords refer closely to what they see as being the relevant principles which should be applied in the difficult matter of deciding property settlements between a divorced couple.

Balancing fairness and compensation

How can the courts achieve fairness when dividing property after a divorce? As Lord Nicholls explained, in his leading judgement, that was the 'intractable' problem that the Law Lords were trying to solve in their ruling.

Married couples committed themselves to sharing their lives: 'When their partnership ends, each is entitled to an equal share of the assets of the partnership – unless there is a good reason to the contrary. This principle is applicable as much to short marriages as to long marriages.'

Lady Hale, the only Law Lord to have specialised in family law reform, stressed the need for consistency and predictability in payments on divorce. She identified three principles that might guide courts in future cases: 'need, compensation and sharing'.

She stressed, too, that conduct could not be taken into account by the courts unless it was both 'obvious and gross'. This approach, Lady Hale said, 'was not only just, it was the only practicable one.'

Source: Joshua Rozenberg, *The Daily Telegraph*, 25 May 2006

Judges in divorce settlement cases can be faced with having to make some difficult decisions. The situation they face shares at least some of the elements which will face you in the exam:

■ the judge has to make a decision

■ whatever is decided, one partner or the other will receive less than they want or think they deserve

■ the competing claims of both partners are likely to be based on conflicting criteria.

We can see, too, how judges formulate principles to help them to resolve such disputes. Phrased fully, the three principles identified here are:

■ division of property should be determined by need

■ division of property needs to take into account elements of compensation

■ division of property should be determined by equal share.

WORKED EXAMPLE 11

Use the principles identified by the Law Lords to help you to try to resolve the following case.

> Mr and Mrs Persimon were married for four years. When they got married, Mrs Persimon gave up her £70,000 a year job because they intended to start a family straightaway. However, they were unable to have children.
>
> The marriage broke up after Mr Persimon confessed to seeing another woman. He has since remarried and has one child with his new wife.
>
> Mr Persimon had just started setting up a new business when he first met his ex-wife. This business is now worth £15 million. He has other assets of about £10 million.
>
> His ex-wife is now claiming she should receive a settlement worth at least £5 million. Mr Persimon is prepared to offer only £2 million.

Comment

The Law Lords defined three principles upon which post-divorce property settlements should be based, as follows.

- *Division of property should be determined by need*: Mrs Persimon gave up her job to try to have a family. She will need to recover at least some of that lost income from her ex-husband's assets. Mr Persimon could claim that he now has the greater need as he has a new wife and child to support. He does, however, have assets totalling £25 million.

- *Division of property needs to take into account elements of compensation*: Mrs Persimon has lost earnings of at least £280,000 during the period of her marriage. Not working for that time might also have affected her future earning power through lost opportunities for promotion and experience. However, Mr Persimon could claim that his offer of £2 million represents ample compensation.

- *Division of property should be determined by equal share*: the Law Lords stated that when a marriage ends each partner is entitled to an equal share of the assets of that partnership. They also stated that this principle is applicable as much to short marriages as to long marriages. On this basis, the ex-Mrs Persimon's claim to at least £5 million would appear to be justified in law.

Verdict: Using the principles defined by the Law Lords, Mr Persimon should give his ex-wife the settlement of £5 million she is claiming. This would still leave him with enough assets to provide for the needs of his new family. It would provide the ex-Mrs Persimon with ample compensation. Mr Persimon should perhaps reflect that a strict application of the principle based upon sharing assets might well have cost him more. He should settle.

The principles of equality, need and desert

Remember that in the Unit 3 exam you are required to identify principles to help you resolve an issue or a dilemma. You will obviously not know the issues you will be dealing with until you see the Resource Booklet in the exam. It will be very useful, therefore, if you have knowledge and understanding of the sort of principles you could apply to a range of cases.

One approach you can take is to look at principles based upon those referred to by one of the Law Lords in their divorce settlement judgement. We will now develop these in terms of looking at the concepts of *equality*, *need* and *desert*. Principles based on these concepts could be particularly useful when dealing with problems of distribution.

Equality

We could express this principle as:

> Every individual is of equal value and should therefore be treated equally.

This principle could be used to establish that:

> A basic retirement pension should be paid to everyone over the age of 65, irrespective of their financial position.

How might using a principle based upon equality be useful?

- It could be easy to apply as there can be a clear decision about how much each person gets.

- It can speed up decision-making and cut down on administration and fraud.

- Decisions made on this basis can easily be defended against complaints.

What problems might there be in using this principle in this case?

- It may lead to a lack of motivation as you will never merit any more than anyone else.

- It will be more expensive than providing only for the people who need help.

- In many practical ways, people are in fact not equal. To use Aristotle's quaint example, if you are going to distribute flutes, you should give preference to flute players.

- Giving the same to everyone does not produce equality (some people need more help than others to reach the same state).

Need

We could express this principle as:

> We ought to distribute to each person according to their need.

This recognises that all humans have equal worth but don't all start life on an equal footing. This imbalance should be rectified.

This principle can be used to establish that:

> We should provide free care in the community for those elderly people who are less well-off.

In the UK, the welfare state uses the tax system to establish funding to help those with particular needs.

How useful might such a principle be in helping us to make decisions?

■ It could help us to allocate our resources in an objective and measurable way.

■ It could be seen to be a humane and fair principle to adopt.

■ It could help to prevent potentially damaging social divisions between the poor and the better-off.

What problems might we have in applying this principle in this case?

■ It could prove to be very expensive to provide such free care as the number of elderly people is increasing.

■ The elderly who would still have to pay for their care might complain that they were being penalised for working hard and saving up when they were younger.

■ The government might then have to decide whether or not to provide free care for all.

■ You could argue that this would be a better way to achieve equality of outcome – more people get free care and are therefore happier with the situation – but not equality in terms of the personal resources available to elderly people.

It is useful at this stage to consider the principle of desert.

■ Free care could prove very expensive as the number of elderly people rises.

Desert

We could express this principle as:

> We ought to reward only those who merit (or deserve) it.

This principle could be used to establish that:

> Expensive medical care should be provided first to those who have worked hard and looked after their bodies the best.

How useful might such a principle be in helping us to make decisions?

- It would be seen to reward people for working harder and thereby encourage them to do so.

- It could lead people to take more responsibility for their own lives and to see the connections between what they do now and what happens to them later.

- It could encourage people to try to lead healthier lives, with benefits to society all round.

- It could turn out to be very cost-effective as people who look after themselves tend to need the NHS less than those who do not.

What problems might we have in applying this principle in this case?

- This could conflict with the principle of need.

- It would be difficult to assess who exactly are the most deserving.

- It could be seen to be discriminatory against groups such as smokers and drinkers.

- It could be argued that this principle supports inequality of opportunity, since some people cannot compete for the reward as well as others. This could be because of low incomes, lack of facilities, inadequate education, etc.

- It might widen the gaps in society, which could be seen as promoting injustice and resentment.

ACTIVITY

Should the government give Child Benefit to all families, even though some of them do not need it, or should they give it only to families with low incomes, even though parents who have slightly more money because they work hard and act responsibly may feel that such a policy is unfair to them?

Apply the principles of equality, need and desert to this dilemma.

Some ethical principles

Three more principles which are often used in ethical discussions are **autonomy**, **non-maleficence** and **beneficence**. It would be very acceptable for you to appeal to any of these in the exam.

The principle of autonomy can be stated as follows:

■ Sane adults should not be prevented from deciding for themselves in matters affecting their own lives.

The principle of non-maleficence can be stated as follows:

■ Everyone should avoid harming other people.

The principle of beneficence can be stated as follows:

■ Everyone should do good to other people.

KEY TERMS

Autonomy ●
Being able to make decisions concerning one's own life.

Non-maleficence ●
Not harming other people.

Beneficence ●
Doing good to other people.

ACTIVITY

Apply the principles of autonomy, non-maleficence and beneficence to the following choice facing a government.

If avian influenza ('bird flu') reaches the UK and if the virus mutates so that it can be transmitted between humans, the government will have to decide whether to make immunisation compulsory or voluntary. To make it compulsory will involve forcing some people to be immunised against their will, but making it voluntary will cause some people to die of the disease and the mutated virus will not become extinct, thereby continuing to pose a threat.

Truth-telling

Some hard moral choices facing individuals involve deciding whether to lie or to tell the truth. The duty to tell the truth can be regarded as an ethical principle, but most people feel that there are some circumstances under which it is better to lie, or at least to hide the truth.

ACTIVITY

Which one of the following principles do you most closely agree with? Compare your answer with those of other students.

a) **You should always tell the truth.**

b) **You should normally tell the truth, but in rare, extreme cases it may be better to lie.**

c) **You should tell the truth unless doing so will hurt yourself or other people.**

d) **You should say whatever you think is the kindest thing to say, whether it is true or not.**

e) **You should say whatever you think will benefit you most, whether it is true or not.**

ACTIVITY 15

At times of national financial crisis, it is sometimes necessary for the government to devalue the currency. On one occasion, when the government was considering whether to devalue the pound, the Chancellor of the Exchequer was asked in Parliament whether the government was proposing to devalue. If he had said 'Yes', companies and individuals would have quickly transferred their wealth into other currencies, thereby making the national financial crisis worse. By saying 'No', he would be lying, which broke his personal moral principles and lessened his credibility for the future. A refusal to answer would have been interpreted as meaning 'Yes'.

Apply appropriate ethical principles to the choice he faced between telling the truth and lying.

Special rights and duties

Some rights and duties are based on the roles which particular people perform in society. Some of these are imposed by law, while others are voluntarily accepted as a condition for entering a career, and others are not enforceable but are nevertheless generally agreed.

The moral demands of family life

It is widely accepted that both entering a relationship and choosing to have children create moral obligations. Few would disagree, for example, that parents have a duty to house, feed, clothe and educate their children. If children have duties towards their parents, they do not originate from their own choice (as teenagers sometimes say, 'I didn't ask to be born!') but are the expected response for the benefits they have received from their parents.

The duties of parents towards their children are linked with rights. There can be little doubt that parents who seriously fail to fulfil their duties thereby forfeit their rights and that the state should intervene for the sake of the children. Moral dilemmas often arise in particular cases, however.

WORKED EXAMPLE 12

Members of some religious groups reject certain kinds of medical treatment. Medical staff treating children of such people may be faced with the dilemma of whether to respect or overrule the wishes of the parents. If they respect the wishes, the patient will suffer and may die, but if they go against the wishes of the parents they will infringe family autonomy, distress the parents and – according to the parents – commit an intrinsically wrong act.

Comment

The most important principles which should be used on one side of this discussion are the duties of doctors and other medical professionals to save life and to cure disease. These duties are fundamental to codes of medical ethics. Although it is generally agreed that the most fundamental duty of medical staff is not to harm, the harm to the parents in this case is minor and an unavoidable consequence of saving the life of the child.

On the other side come the rights of autonomy and religious freedom. In cases involving competent adults, these rights are generally considered to be decisive. People who are capable of making decisions about their own medical treatment can, if they wish, refuse treatment and no one has the right to go against their wishes. The situation is, however, rather different in the case of children. The autonomy and religious commitment of parents do apply to their children, but in a secondary and rather weakened sense and it is, therefore, easier to justify over-riding them than it would be if the parent were the patient.

A consequentialist approach to this issue produces a clear result. The distress and reduced quality of family life which would be caused by over-riding the wishes of the parents – and even the possible long-term harm to family life in general – are far outweighed by the benefits of saving the child's life. On this basis, it is quite clear that the medical staff should act according to their professional judgement.

ACTIVITY 16

Apply appropriate ethical principles to the following dilemma.

> Should the government make it compulsory for children to attend school, even though that may reduce opportunities for individuals to develop their own values and interests, or should they continue to allow parents to educate their children at home if they wish to do so, even though children educated in that way may be less well equipped to choose a worthwhile career?

Professional ethics

Certain jobs are recognised as professions; they have a higher status than other occupations. One of the characteristics which can mark out an occupation as being a profession is that it has a code of ethics which all practitioners are expected to follow. The duties which professionals owe to their clients include:

- competence: professionals should maintain their expertise in their subject and give advice based on that expertise
- loyalty: professionals must act in the best interests of their clients
- diligence: professionals must work hard on behalf of their clients.

Professional codes of ethics typically also emphasise duties which professionals owe to their colleagues. These duties include:

- professionals must not persuade clients of colleagues to transfer to them ('poaching')

- professionals must not criticise colleagues

- professionals must not bring the profession into disrepute.

WORKED EXAMPLE 13

If professionals discover that a colleague in the same practice has been giving misleading and inaccurate advice to clients, should they report the colleague to the professional body even though doing so will probably end the colleague's career and harm professional relationships, or should they keep quiet, even though doing so will harm the interests of future clients?

Comment

In cases of this kind, consideration should be given to the duties of professionals towards colleagues, their profession, clients and the general public.

The duty of loyalty towards colleagues implies that their privacy should not be breached. From this perspective, professionals who become aware by chance that a colleague is practising incompetently should ignore it and the most they might legitimately do in response to a complaint from a member of the public is to have a quiet word with the colleague concerned.

The duty not to bring the profession into disrepute could be used in favour of either reporting or not reporting the incompetence of colleagues. If the incompetence becomes public knowledge as a result of the report, then the reputation of the profession will to some extent be diminished. Arguably, however, greater harm to that reputation may occur if incompetent practitioners are allowed to continue their course unchecked. The duty to the profession can also reasonably be considered to include a duty to improve standards of practice, part of which is to help to weed out incompetence.

Strictly, no duty to a client exists in the absence of a specific professional-client relationship. Professionals in shared practices may possibly have a secondary and reduced duty towards the clients of their partners. If a client moves on to a new professional, either by referral or because they have become dissatisfied with the service they were receiving, the new practitioner does now have an obligation to further the interests of their client, but it is doubtful whether that duty includes siding with the client against a colleague. Some professionals act on the principle that they should never take on clients who have left their last practitioner because of alleged incompetence, but that policy is arguably unfair to members of the public who have genuinely received poor service.

The professional's duty of beneficence towards the general public is too limited to justify informing on the incompetence of a colleague.

Overall, therefore, a duty-based approach to this issue is most likely to lead to the conclusion that a professional who becomes aware of a colleague's incompetence should keep quiet about it. This assessment confirms the fears of many lay people, who define professions as 'conspiracies against the public'.

A consequentialist approach to this issue would almost certainly lead to different conclusions. The benefits to the general public of eliminating incompetence would outweigh the harm caused to the individual whose licence to practise might be revoked, and would still be the most significant factor even if one were to take into account the stress caused to other professionals who might fear for their own future.

Confidentiality

The principle of confidentiality could be stated as follows:

■ No one should reveal information which they have agreed not to reveal or which they have come to know in their professional role.

This principle is included in most codes of professional ethics, but arguably it applies to other jobs, too. Certain exceptions have become built in to the duty of confidentiality – for example, professionals who become aware that a client is guilty of child abuse or planning terrorist offences are legally obliged to breach confidentiality and to inform the police. Many clients may not know that, and may have thought that their secret would be safe.

WORKED EXAMPLE 14

> When an engineer is servicing a computer, he notices that the owner has saved a large number of photographs of naked women on his hard drive. None of the photographs appears to be illegal, but the fact that the person has such an interest in soft pornography would be an interesting topic of gossip in the community if the engineer let it be known. Can the engineer speak freely to other people about what he has found, or should he preserve the client's secret?

What principles would you use to help the engineer decide what to do, and how would you apply them?

Would it make any difference to your assessment if the owner of the computer held a position of trust in the community, such as a teacher, doctor or vicar?

Comment

The ethical principle which immediately comes to mind is the duty of confidentiality, but it is not clear whether the engineer has such a duty or not. If he were a solicitor or a doctor, then it would be a clear breach of professional ethics to gossip about knowledge he had discovered in his professional role. The engineer is not bound by an explicit code of professional ethics as they are, and he does not have a professional organisation which would discipline him for breaking that code. Like them, however, the engineer acquired knowledge about a client through his work and the client has to waive his strict right of privacy in order to enable the engineer to do his work. So there is a strong moral obligation on the engineer not to talk about the client's secret.

By comparing consequences, the pleasure which the engineer and anyone he spoke to might take in gossiping about the customer would almost certainly be outweighed by the embarrassment and possible harm caused to the customer. Furthermore, in the long term the engineer might find that he would lose clients if it were to become known that he was breaching a client's confidentiality in this way. So it is probably in his own interest to respect client confidentiality.

If the client held a position of trust in the community, the public's right to know might perhaps outweigh his own right to privacy. The three examples given are subtly different in this respect. The work of doctors sometimes requires them to see their patients naked, and female patients might be less inclined to consult a doctor if they knew he gained pleasure from looking at women's naked bodies. Arguably, therefore, they have a right to know this about him. In the case of a teacher, there seems no basis for a public right to know – unless the images were of children, which would be illegal and is not the case in this hypothetical example. The reason for a possible public interest in the case of a vicar is not concerned with the content of his job, as in the case of a doctor, but is based on a belief that vicars are supposed to be holier than other people. Some people might accuse a vicar who enjoys soft pornography of hypocrisy, which might possibly provide some basis for a public right to know, but probably not a strong one.

ACTIVITY

a) **Choose some appropriate principles and apply them to the following dilemma.**

> Should a father who discovers a gun hidden in his teenage son's wardrobe inform the police, even though doing so will cause his son to be punished and probably disrupt family relationships, or should he keep quiet, even though doing so may prevent the perpetrator of a crime from being identified and the gun might be used in future crimes?

b) **Would it make any difference to your assessment if the father was a policeman?**

ACTIVITY 18

Apply appropriate ethical principles to the following dilemmas or situations requiring a choice:

a) the dilemma regarding provision of contraception to under-age girls in worked example 5 (pages 25–26)

b) the dilemma facing the retired vicar in worked example 9 (page 49)

c) the dilemmas you identified in answer to activity 9 (pages 41–43)

d) the dilemmas you identified in answer to activity 10 (page 50).

Summary

You should now be able to:

■ understand the term 'principles'

■ understand the difference between deontological and consequentialist principles

■ consider how various ethical principles might be used to help us to resolve a contentious issue.

Learning objectives

● Examine some ethical theories.
● Explore how we might best apply those theories in attempting to resolve an issue or dilemma.

GENERAL MEDICAL COUNCIL

Using ethical theories in the Unit 3 exam

The ethical principles we looked at in Chapter 4, such as equality, truth-telling and autonomy, were free standing. Other principles are part of theories of ethics which have been put forward by various philosophers. These theories are the focus of this chapter.

Some ethical theories (such as Hedonistic Utilitarianism) can be expressed as principles, while others (such as Divine Command ethics) are sources of principles.

This exam is based on practical ethics, not on Moral Philosophy (the theory of ethics). You will be awarded marks for applying major ethical theories to the issue and the documents, but not for your knowledge of the theories themselves.

If you happen to know more about ethical theories than is contained in this textbook (e.g. because you have studied Moral Philosophy or Religious Ethics at A Level), feel free to make use of that knowledge in the exam, but never forget that marks are awarded for the use you make of the theories, and not for knowledge of the theories themselves.

Some of the worked examples and activities in this chapter will tell you which principles to use. This is in order to practise the skills of resolving an issue or dilemma and to increase your familiarity with some ethical theories which may be useful in the exam. Do not forget that in the exam itself, you will be allowed to choose whatever principles you consider relevant to the issue and you will also be required to make appropriate references to the resource documents.

Some deontological theories

Divine Command ethics

Historically, most discussion of ethics has been based on religion. The simplest ethical principles of all are:

- ◼ 'God says you must…'
- ◼ 'God says you may…'
- ◼ 'God says you may not…'.

These deontological principles are expressions of **Divine Command ethics**.

Although religion is much less influential in Western Europe in the early twenty-first century than it was in earlier generations, Divine Command ethics is still relevant to some people and often features in political debates. If you happen to know some religious principles which could have a bearing on a topic set in the exam – perhaps because you follow a religion yourself or because you have studied Religious Ethics as part of a GCSE or A Level course – then you should feel free to make use of them.

Among the best known religious ethical principles are the Ten Commandments, accepted by Jews and Christians. These include the rules:

- ◼ You must not commit murder.
- ◼ You must not steal.
- ◼ You must not lie in court.
- ◼ You must not commit adultery.

> **KEY TERM**
>
> **Divine Command ethics** ◼
> Ethical principles which are obeyed because they are said to have been given by God.

Similarly, the 'Five Precepts', which are considered binding on all Buddhists, forbid killing, theft, sexual misconduct, lying and the consumption of alcohol.

They are usually expressed as follows:

■ I undertake the rule of training to refrain from harming any living thing.

■ I undertake the rule of training to refrain from taking what is not given.

■ I undertake the rule of training to refrain from a misuse of the senses.

■ I undertake the rule of training to refrain from wrong speech.

■ I undertake the rule of training to refrain from taking drugs or drinks which tend to cloud the mind.

Some principles of religious ethics refer to animals and the environment. The Jewish Scriptures (the Christian Old Testament) portray humans as having been appointed as managers, rather than owners, of the environment. Although humans are superior to animals, which they are entitled to use for both work and food, they are commanded to treat them with as much kindness as possible under the circumstances and also to avoid causing permanent harm to the environment. The Buddhist prohibition against intentionally killing living beings of course includes animals, although not all Buddhists are vegetarians.

Natural Law

One possible source for deontological ethics is nature. The principle could be expressed as follows:

■ We should act in accordance with nature.

The fact that an action is unnatural is often given as a reason against doing it. For example, this was the main objection made against transplant surgery when it was first introduced in the 1960s, and more recently it has been a major objection to the genetic modification of crops. In a simple (not always wholly serious) form, it has been raised as an objection against aeroplanes: 'If God had meant us to fly, he would have given us wings.' Against the latter, it can reasonably be replied, 'Instead of giving us wings, God gave us the ability to invent aeroplanes.'

If you think about particular examples of this kind of argument, you will probably realise that they are actually quite weak. Most of the things we do during the course of a day – beginning with living in a house – are unnatural, but we do not consider that to be a reason for not doing them.

The institution which makes most use of **Natural Law ethics** is the Roman Catholic Church. Building on the work of St Thomas Aquinas, a complex and developed system of rules and judgements has grown up, and reference books are now available in which answers can be found to a wide range of moral questions, all traced back to principles of Natural Law. Aquinas pointed out that all species other than humans automatically act in accordance with their own nature, without having any choice in the matter, but one of the unique things about humans is that we can choose whether to act in accordance with our nature or contrary to it.

KEY TERM

● **Natural Law ethics**
Ethical principles which are based on nature, especially human nature.

- Pope Benedict is leader of the Roman Catholic church, which makes use of Natural Law ethics.

According to Aquinas, the most basic and universal precept of Natural Law is survival: everything seeks its own survival. The second most fundamental precept is propagation of the species: all living things seek to produce the next generation. A third precept, which applies to all humans but not to other species, is society: it is natural for humans to display the qualities which enable them to live together in families and communities. As ethical principles, these precepts could be expressed as follows:

◼ You should act in such a way as to ensure your own survival.

◼ You should act in ways which will ensure the survival of your species.

◼ You should act in ways which will promote human community.

You may find that you can apply one or more of these fundamental principles of Natural Law to the topic chosen for discussion in the exam.

It is unfortunate that the applications of Natural Law which have become best known outside the Catholic Church relate to sexual ethics, because that approach leads to some judgements which most non-Catholics find very unconvincing. If nature teaches that the primary purpose of sex is procreation, or that the procreative and relational aspects of sex belong together, then it follows that contraception, masturbation and homosexuality are all seriously wrong acts, since they go against nature.

The Categorical Imperative

The most famous deontological theory of ethics came from the German philosopher Immanuel Kant. He believed that people should always perform actions which are right in themselves, and that the ethical evaluation of actions should take no notice of consequences.

Kant identified two fundamental principles, which he called the **Categorical Imperative** (by which he meant a command which applies universally, not just under particular circumstances).

- ■ The first form of the Categorical Imperative is that we should act only in ways in which we should like everyone to act.

This is sometimes known as the principle of universalisability. For example, we should not make promises which we do not intend to keep, because we would not like other people to make promises to us that they do not intend to keep.

Modern followers of Kant sometimes use the principle with greater reference to circumstances than Kant himself did. For example, we can be sure that Kant would have disapproved of euthanasia, because one of his reasons for condemning suicide was that it would be self-contradictory to want everyone to commit suicide. Some modern Kantians, however, suggest that one could reasonably want everyone suffering from intolerable pain in a terminal illness, with no hope of recovery, to be free to choose euthanasia or assisted suicide. If this subject were to occur in the exam, you could reasonably use both of these approaches, contrasting Kant's own argument with that of some of his followers.

- ■ The second form of the Categorical Imperative (sometimes known as the principle of ends or the principle of humanity) is that we should always treat persons (by which Kant meant human beings) as 'ends' in themselves (that is, as having their own value) and not only as a 'means' to our ends.

For example, stealing treats victims as the means of supplying our needs, and not as having their own needs. Some forms of sexual activity treat women or men as a means for satisfying our lust, rather than as persons with their own goals and life-choices. Murder treats the life of another human being as an obstacle in our way rather than as being valuable in its own right.

It is important to note that there is nothing wrong with using people as a means to our ends, provided we also recognise them as ends in their own right. For example, you use your teachers as a means to your end of gaining A Level passes and they use you as a means to their end of earning a living. But the way you behave towards one another, and especially your recognition of one another as persons with their own dignity, relationships and life-goals, shows that you are not using them *only* as a means.

These principles can be applied to many of the issues which may arise in the Unit 3 exam. The first version of the Categorical Imperative, *'Act according to that maxim which you can will to be a universal law'* could conceivably be applied to issues of animal welfare or the environment, although Kant himself did not do so. For example, one could ask 'Would you like every generation to use up natural resources so that there will be nothing left for the generations to follow?' or 'Would you like every generation to leave the planet to its descendants in a grossly polluted state?' If we are glad that our ancestors did not disadvantage us in either of those ways, then according to the Categorical Imperative we should not do so, either. Kant specifically excluded animals from the second version of the Categorical Imperative, which originally stated that we should always treat humans as ends, and not as means only.

KEY TERM

● **Categorical Imperative**

A command which applies universally, not just under particular circumstances. It is commonly associated with the philosopher Kant.

STRETCH AND CHALLENGE

The major objections which can be levelled against Kant's theory are that many people think he was wrong:

- to deny that duties sometimes conflict

- and to refuse to make any exceptions to his principles in the light of consequences.

Towards the end of his life, he gave an imaginary example which most people find very hard to accept:

If a friend fleeing from a murderer takes refuge in your house and the murderer then asks you if you know where his intended victim is hiding, you still have a duty to tell the truth, even though it will probably lead to the death of your friend.

Kant explained that it would be the murderer, not you, who was guilty of causing the death. Most people think that the issue of guilt is not the most important aspect of this case: what matters is that the friend dies.

Human rights

Another deontological approach which you may find useful in the exam is **human rights**. The most influential change in political philosophy towards the end of the eighteenth century was the recognition of human rights as central to politics. The American War of Independence and the French Revolution were both based on the conviction that humans had certain fundamental rights and that political systems must defend those rights. Despite the determined and frantic opposition to those revolutionary maxims in England, they eventually became accepted by almost everyone and it is now generally taken for granted that any government which deprives its citizens of their human rights is an unjust government, which can rightly be condemned by other countries. Since the passing of the Human Rights Act in 1998, human rights have taken a central place in ethical discussions in the UK.

The expression 'human rights' refers to those fundamental rights which exist whether a particular government recognises them or not. They are the most important kind of rights, and the most likely to be useful in a Unit 3 exam. Other kinds of rights do exist, however. 'Legal rights' are given by particular legal systems, while 'special rights' apply to particular categories of people; for example, if you have a right to borrow books from the library of your school or college it is a special right, although the right to education, from which it is derived, is a human right.

Several attempts have been made to identify the fundamental human rights.

Following the Second World War, the United Nations drew up a Declaration of Human Rights, which identified:

- life

- liberty

- security of person

as the fundamental rights.

- The European Court of Human Rights.

KEY TERM

Human rights ●

Fundamental needs of every individual person which, it could be argued, should be protected by their fellow citizens and government.

STRETCH AND ● **CHALLENGE**

A British philosopher, Sir David Ross, put forward a theory of duties which avoids these objections to Kant's theory, by being more flexible. Ross distinguishes between 'prima facie duties' (duties which apply in principle) and 'actual duties' (what it is right to do under particular circumstances).

In the case of Kant's example, although we have a prima facie duty to tell the truth, it is outweighed under these circumstances by the duty to preserve life: so the actual duty in this case is to lie.

Rights have been analysed and classified in various different ways, but the most useful division is between 'liberty rights' and 'claim rights'. If you have a liberty right to do something, then no one should prevent you from doing it, whereas if you have a claim right, then someone (e.g. the government) has a duty to help you do it. For example, the right of free speech is a liberty right, whereas the right to education is a claim right.

In recent years, liberty rights have tended to evolve into claim rights. For example, the right of procreative autonomy used to mean that no one, including the government, should be able to prevent couples from choosing whether to have children or not, but some people now argue that this right should include free access to new reproductive technologies for couples or individuals who cannot reproduce in the normal way.

ACTIVITY 19

As a group make a list of rights which you consider to be human rights. Can you relate them to fundamental rights?

In recent years, more and more human needs and desires have been identified as rights. These new rights can usually be explained as being derived from one of the fundamental human rights. For example, many people in the UK would claim that they have a right to free health care, which can be traced back to the right to life. The right of autonomy (your right to make choices affecting your own life) is an aspect of the right to liberty.

One example of an issue for which you would probably want to appeal to human rights if it were to occur in the exam is whether universities should be allowed to restrict entrance by reference to educational qualifications or should be required to admit anyone who wishes to attend (and can afford the costs). Since all political parties have clearly stated that they regard it as ethically unacceptable for secondary schools to practise selection on the basis of ability, sooner or later someone will probably apply the same principle to universities. If you were asked to discuss this issue, you would almost certainly refer to the human right to education. Ideally, you would mention that the right to education can be derived from the right to freedom and the right to the pursuit of happiness (since without education, one's choices in life are severely restricted).

Although everyone in principle has human rights, there are exceptional circumstances where they may not come into effect. Rights may be waived, forfeited or over-ridden. A right is waived if someone gives it up voluntarily; for example, the right to autonomy is (at least to some extent) waived by people who marry, join the armed services or become nuns. Criminals may be judged to have forfeited their right to liberty (so they may be imprisoned) or even their right to life (so they may be executed). Under exceptional circumstances it may be necessary to over-ride some human rights; for example, in war-time the government may introduce restrictions on freedom of travel and of speech.

Opinions vary widely as to what rights – if any – animals have. Some people believe that all living things have a right to life, and they try to avoid killing even insects, while at the other extreme some people believe there is no moral objection to killing any animal. Most of us probably take a view between those two extremes. Very few people nowadays would disagree with the view that animals have the right not to be caused pain unnecessarily.

How useful are deontological principles in making decisions?

- ■ *Bring clarity to decision-making*: such principles may be considered to be right regardless of the consequences. Therefore, you do not have to consider exceptions or weigh up or predict the consequences of an action guided by such a principle.

- ■ *Universal standards*: as everyone is expected to follow the principle, anyone breaking the principle should be relatively easy to identify.

- ■ *Public knowledge*: this can be relatively easy to achieve, as the rules can be kept simple. Exceptions do not need to be set out or defended.

- ■ *Cannot be refuted*: this is provided that their overall justification is accepted. For example, if the principle *'It is wrong to take a life'* is considered to be right because God has commanded it, then there can be little argument, provided that those involved believe that God exists and what God says is right. Similarly, there might be agreement about the duty to protect the right to the freedom of speech if this is considered to be a basic human or social right.

What limitations might be met when applying deontological principles?

There are some significant limitations to this approach.

- ■ *They do not take into consideration harmful consequences*. Some deontological principles do not allow exceptions where the consequences are negative. Strict deontological ethics considers that actions such as killing, stealing and lying are always wrong, even though in some circumstances they do more good than harm. However, not all deontological theories present this problem.

- ■ *If two principles conflict, there may be confusion over which should be followed* (unless a hierarchy of principles is established – where if two conflict, the higher order principle should be followed).

- ■ *Where there is a conflict of interest, there may be confusion*. For example, in the National Health Service where funds are limited, it might be difficult to decide who should have the right to treatment.

Applying deontological principles to particular issues

> **WORKED EXAMPLE 10 (CONT.)**
>
> **Let's look again at the issue of reducing the number of weeks of pregnancy at which abortion is allowed (see worked example 10, page 59).**
>
> **How might deontological theories help us to resolve this dilemma?**

Comment

Natural Law has been used to oppose abortion in the following two ways:

- Abortion is wrong because it frustrates the purpose of sex, which is deemed to be procreation (or procreation and the marital bond together). The weakness of this argument is that it forbids contraception for exactly the same reason; in other words, it ignores the difference between a foetus which already exists and one which might hypothetically come into existence. The gestational age of the foetus is irrelevant to this argument.

- It is wrong to kill a being which has a soul. Reducing the age at which abortion is permitted might make it less likely that abortions will infringe this principle.

Kant might well have judged, as some of his followers do, that a foetus should not be regarded as a person, because it is not (yet) rational. In that case, the second version of the Categorical Imperative would not apply to it. However, if a foetus does count as a person, then abortion is forbidden by the second version of the Categorical Imperative (the principle of humanity), since the foetus would be being used as means to the woman's end. If a foetus becomes a person at some stage during gestation, then the principle of humanity implies that late abortions are more objectionable than early ones.

It is possible to defend abortion on the basis of a less strict version of Kant's theory, by claiming – for example – that every woman whose health is threatened by a pregnancy should have the choice to abort it, or that every foetus which is diagnosed as suffering from a handicap should be aborted.

The abortion debate has often been expressed in terms of a conflict of rights between a pregnant woman's right to choose (or procreative autonomy) and the foetus's right to life. There is no doubt that women – like men – do have a right to choose whether to become parents or not, but some people would argue that once a woman has become pregnant, she has already exercised that choice and cannot change her mind.

This way of interpreting the abortion debate assumes that a foetus is the kind of being which has a right to life – that is, a person. Once again, the issue of the age of the foetus is relevant, since a late foetus may be more likely to have a right to life than an embryo or early foetus.

WORKED EXAMPLE 15

Read the following passage about assisted suicide.

We are all likely to be faced with having to make some difficult decisions about death, either our own or that of someone close to us. If suffering from a terminal illness – or watching somebody for whom we care suffer – we might hope that a doctor would respect our wish that they withhold any treatment that would prolong life. We might even hope that a doctor might decide to treat our pain in such a way that it helps us to die more quickly. Both of these options are legal and occur frequently, but it is illegal for doctors deliberately to cause the death of patients or to assist them to kill themselves. Should we change the law in some way so that people can be helped to end their lives in cases of terminal illness?

What would be the result of applying deontological principles to this issue?

Comment

The most likely result of applying deontological principles to this issue is that we should oppose any attempt to change the law in order to make it easier for us to help people to end their lives in the case of terminal illness. We can explain this as follows.

Deontological principles insist that some actions are right or wrong regardless of the consequences. Such a principle could be that there is a duty to preserve life regardless of the consequences. This would include taking your own life, or helping someone to take their life. These principles could be derived from the Categorical Imperative, Natural Law, Divine Command or human rights (the right to life).

ACTIVITY

Apply appropriate deontological theories to the following case.

In the campaign leading up to local elections, a political party promised that it would not raise the council tax in any area where it controlled the council. Soon after the election, the national government announced a reduction in the grants which would be paid to local councils from central funds. Some local councils had to decide whether to increase council tax, which would involve breaking their promise to the voters, or keep council tax at the same level, which would involve reducing expenditure on such services as welfare for the elderly, sanitation and leisure.

Some consequentialist theories

Utilitarianism

The best-known consequentialist theory of ethics is **Utilitarianism**, which was invented by Jeremy Bentham in 1781. Many people nowadays who have never studied Moral Philosophy follow Utilitarianism without knowing it. A slogan which is often used to express Utilitarianism is that moral choices and actions should seek 'the greatest good of the greatest number'.

Bentham's theory was based on these three principles:

■ Actions should be judged by consequences and nothing else.

■ The consequences which matter are the increase of pleasure and decrease of pain.

■ No one's pleasure or pain counts more or less than anyone else's.

Bentham believed that when a moral choice has to be made, the consequences of the alternatives should be calculated, and the one most likely to produce the greatest amount of pleasure should be chosen. He claimed that different outcomes could be compared by means of the 'Hedonic Calculus', whereby the pleasure produced by an action could be calculated according to factors such as: intensity (how much pleasure it makes you feel), certainty (how likely it is that pleasure will be produced), and extent (how many people will be affected).

■ Jeremy Bentham, who invented Utilitarianism, the best known consequentialist theory of ethics.

Bentham's follower, John Stuart Mill, agreed with these three principles, but he adapted them in two important ways. First, Mill did not agree that pain and pleasure should be judged only by quantity. He believed that intellectual pleasures, such as reading poetry, were of a higher quality than physical pleasures, such as eating and drinking, and should therefore count for more in the Hedonic Calculus. Second, Mill thought it was unrealistic to judge every case individually, as Bentham had urged. He thought that moral rules, such as the laws of the land, gave generally good guidance as to the actions which would produce the best consequences and so they should normally be followed. He described such rules and laws as 'landmarks and direction-posts' on the road to pleasure.

The view that the consequences of every situation should be assessed individually is known as *Act Utilitarianism*. The theory that rules and laws are the best way to achieve the greatest good of the greatest number is *Rule Utilitarianism*. A middle approach, which says we should usually follow rules and laws but should depart from them on the rare occasions when they will fail to produce the greatest good of the greatest number, is known as *2-level Utilitarianism*. Bentham was an Act Utilitarian and Mill a 2-level Utilitarian.

Act Utilitarianism can be expressed as:

- In each situation, everyone should choose the option which will lead to the greatest happiness of the greatest number.

Rule Utilitarianism can be expressed as:

- Everyone should obey laws and rules which typically lead to the greatest happiness of the greatest number.

2-level Utilitarianism can be expressed as:

- Everyone should obey laws and rules which typically lead to the greatest happiness of the greatest number, except in cases where it is very probable that doing so will not lead to the greatest happiness of the greatest number.

WORKED EXAMPLE 16

Use Utilitarianism to discuss the following question.

> Should researchers be allowed to perform medical experiments on animals in the hope of developing cures for human diseases, even though they will cause suffering and death to animals?

Comment

The only major ethical theory which explicitly includes animals is Utilitarianism. Since animals are capable of experiencing pleasure and pain, they are included in the Hedonic Calculus. Bentham himself argued that:

> The question is not, 'Can they reason?' nor, 'Can they talk?' but, 'Can they suffer?' Why should the law refuse its protection to any sensitive being?

Utilitarianism claims that the morally correct action is that which will maximise pleasure and minimise pain. In this case, the possible pleasure and freedom from pain of patients who might be cured from painful and deadly diseases in the future must be weighed against the certain pain which will be experienced by animals that are used for experimentation.

One of the items from Bentham's Hedonic Calculus which are most relevant to this case is Certainty: the uncertain and speculative nature of the pleasure and freedom from pain caused to patients in the future by comparison with the certain pain suffered by animals probably implies that they should not be used for research.

Intensity is a significant element of the Hedonic Calculus, but it is not easy to compare the level of pain experienced by animals with what human patients may be spared in the future. It seems likely that human pain is more intense, since it includes a psychological and rational element, but some people would point out that we do not know how much pain animals feel. Many people feel that there is more moral objection on this basis to testing on primates than on rodents.

A third element of the Hedonic Calculus which is significant in this issue is Extent. Unless a real medical breakthrough is achieved quickly through a research project, almost certainly many more animals will suffer pain than humans will be spared it.

Since pain is so important to Utilitarianism, the possible use of anaesthesia is a very significant aspect of this issue. Most research projects are not invalidated if the animals are anaesthetised: so this should happen.

Because Mill included quality in the calculation, he claimed that the pain or pleasure of animals – though not to be overlooked – should count as less than those of humans. He would probably have concluded that the potential benefit to humans of using animals for medical research outweighed the pain caused to the animals. However, he would also have insisted that wherever possible anaesthesia should be used to minimise the pain to the animals.

ACTIVITY 21

Use Utilitarianism to discuss the following issue.

The body responsible for distributing charitable grants from the National Lottery has given regular grants to opera companies, thereby keeping the cost of tickets down to an affordable (although still very expensive) level. Some people have complained that the Lottery should not be subsidising the leisure activities of the rich. If the committee were to discontinue those grants, financial pressures would probably force some opera companies to close. Should they continue to give grants to opera companies, or should they divert them to a more popular leisure activity, such as football?

ACTIVITY 22

Use Utilitarianism to discuss the following dilemma.

Should a doctor tell a terminally ill patient that he has only a short time to live, even though the knowledge will distress him and prevent him from enjoying the last few weeks of life, or should she tell him that he will soon recover, even though that will deprive him of dignity and of knowledge which he wants to have and will prevent him from putting his affairs in order before becoming too ill to do so?

How useful are consequentialist principles in making decisions?

■ *Relevant*: almost everyone would agree that increasing the sum total of pleasure is a good thing, and that we should be concerned for the well-being of everyone, and not just of ourselves.

■ *Realistic*: they recognise that in some situations a degree of harm is inevitable and they use reasoning to achieve the best possible outcome, sometimes as the lesser evil.

■ *Practical*: they can offer a solution when there is a conflict of principles or conflict of interest.

■ *Speed up the assessment of the consequences*: past situations can be used as a guide in decision-making.

What problems might be met when applying consequentialist principles?

There are some significant limitations to this approach.

■ Assessing the consequences to find out what is the right thing to do might make decision-making *complex*, *confusing* and *time-consuming*.

■ There may be disagreement as to whether *short-term* or *long-term consequences* should be assessed.

■ It might be *difficult to weigh up the options* in that both quality and quantity are often involved.

■ Despite Bentham's optimism, when hard decisions have to be made, it is very difficult to compare the likely outcomes of alternative courses of action and impossible to predict with any certainty which of them will produce the greater amount of pleasure. It is a little easier to do it after the event, when we know how things turned out: as a wise person once observed, Utilitarianism is better at telling us what we should have done than what to do. For example, going to war might end atrocities quickly or lead to long, drawn-out reprisals from the country being invaded.

■ Although it is good to give some consideration to the welfare of strangers, it seems unduly harsh to rule out giving any preference to ourselves, our friends and members of our families. For example, one Christmas, a woman didn't give any Christmas presents to her best friend's children (aged 7 and 8), explaining that they would receive plenty of presents from other people and that she had sent the money to OXFAM instead. They were not at all pleased. She was very disappointed by their reaction, since her action was exactly what Utilitarianism required.

It is highly likely that Utilitarianism will be an appropriate theory to apply to the dilemma presented to you in the exam, butremember these criticisms.

Applying consequentialist principles to particular issues

> **WORKED EXAMPLE 10 (CONT.)**
>
> **Let's look again at the issue of reducing the number of weeks of pregnancy at which abortion is allowed (see worked example 10, page 59).**
>
> **How might consequentialist theories help us to resolve this dilemma?**

Comment

Let's look for the last time at the issue of reducing the number of weeks of pregnancy at which abortion is allowed. How might consequentialist principles help us here?

In principle, a consequentialist would say that abortion should be permitted if the harmful consequences of not allowing abortion would outweigh the harm which abortion would do to the foetus. The main harm to the foetus consists of depriving it of the life it would have had if it had been born. In very exceptional circumstances, it may be that this life would contain more pain than pleasure, in which case it would be better for the foetus never to be born. A minor additional point is that it is possible that the abortion procedure itself might cause pain to the foetus. The foetus's pain or loss of pleasure has to be compared to the pains and pleasures which continuing the pregnancy and becoming a parent would cause to the pregnant woman.

Is reducing the number of weeks at which abortion is allowed likely to lead to more harm or less harm overall?

The loss to the foetus of never being born is not affected by the gestational age at which abortion occurs, although some people have suggested that some recognition should be given to the additional development which a later foetus has 'invested' in its own life.

It might be possible to argue that the further the foetus develops, the more it may suffer as a consequence of the abortion. It could also be argued that the risks of abortion to the pregnant woman, in terms of physical and emotional well-being, might increase the longer the pregnancy continues. Both reasons may give us cause to consider reducing the number of weeks at which abortion would be allowed.

However, lowering the number of weeks of pregnancy at which abortion is allowed would reduce parental choice as well as significantly increasing the number of unwanted births. In this case, the sum total of harm to the community as a whole may increase.

WORKED EXAMPLE 15 (CONT.)

Re-read the passage on assisted dying in worked example 15 (page 81).

What would be the result of applying consequentialist principles to this issue?

Comment

Applying consequentialist principles to this issue is more likely to result in some support for a change in the law in order to make it easier for us to help people to end their lives. We can explain this as follows.

Consequentialist principles involve weighing up the consequences – or effects – to work out the right course of action. Consequentialist ethics involve us in deciding on a course of action on the basis of the amount of 'goodness' produced. It is recognised that there are situations in which a degree of harm is unavoidable. Thus the best possible outcome is one which, in other circumstances, we might not normally choose. Helping a terminally ill person to die could therefore be seen to be justified, even though in general we believe that taking another life is wrong, because the amount of pain and suffering will be reduced.

ACTIVITY **23**

Use the results of worked example 15 (page 81 and above) to:

Write an argument that attempts to resolve the issue of whether or not we should allow terminally ill people to choose when they should die. You should apply deontological and consequentialist principles to this issue and you should comment on the extent to which each of these principles might help you to resolve the issue.

STRETCH AND CHALLENGE

As you have read these brief accounts of major ethical theories, you may have noticed that some are rigid, while others are flexible. For example, the theories of Kant and Bentham are rigid, whereas Ross and Mill take more flexible approaches.

The advantage of rigid theories is that they give clear guidance, with no room for disagreement or misunderstanding, but the disadvantage is that in exceptional circumstances (such as Kant's example of the murderer seeking his victim) these clear answers seem to many civilised people to be wrong.

The positive and negative aspects of flexible theories are the opposite of these. Their strength lies in being able to produce convincing answers in hard cases, while their weakness consists of failing to exclude disagreement and uncertainty.

Bear these possible strengths and weaknesses in mind when you discuss ethical principles in the exam.

Political theories

Some of the topics which are chosen for the Unit 3 exam are concerned with public policy. Three of the principles which could be applied to issues of that kind are the principles of *liberty*, *paternalism* and the *Social Contract*.

The principle of liberty

We have already seen that **liberty** is generally regarded as a fundamental human right. However, liberty (or freedom) is a more complex concept than one might guess. Most politicians and members of the general public nowadays accept the principle of John Stuart Mill that the only consideration which can justify a government or other body in restricting the liberty of a citizen is to protect someone else from harm. On this basis, a government is not entitled to restrict our liberty because they think it will be for our own good.

Although politicians do frequently introduce proposals to restrict the liberty of citizens for their own good, it is noticeable that they almost always seek to justify such restrictions in terms of preventing harm to others. For example, when Parliament agreed to force drivers and passengers in cars to wear seat belts and riders and passengers on motorbikes to wear crash helmets, they defended those decisions, not on the grounds that they would save those people from serious injury, but on the basis that anyone seriously injured in a road accident would take up a bed in an intensive care unit and thereby cause someone else's routine operation to be postponed.

Paternalism

The principle of **paternalism** states that some people are incapable of making life decisions for themselves and that someone else must therefore make those decisions for them. Some cases of paternalism are not controversial. Most people would agree that parents should make certain major decisions on behalf of their children, although many parents nowadays allow their children much more autonomy than was the practice in previous generations. Similarly, very few people will disagree with the claim that adults with severe learning difficulties need someone to make decisions on their behalf.

Various aspects of the relationship of parents to teenagers could appear in a Unit 3 exam, since examiners would expect students to find such issues interesting. You might then want to discuss whether teenagers should be regarded as children or as mature enough to take responsibility for their own lives.

The point at which this principle becomes controversial is when it applies to adult citizens in relation to the government. Evidence from opinion polls, for example, may show that a proposed policy is unpopular. Should the government press ahead with it, on the basis that they know best, or would that be exceeding their authority?

The principle of paternalism could be stated as follows:

■ Ordinary citizens are not competent to make major decisions concerning their own lives: so the government or professionals should make decisions on their behalf.

ACTIVITY 24

Apply the principles of liberty and paternalism to the following issue.

Should the government discourage smoking by greatly increasing the tax on cigarettes, even though some people who want to smoke will be unable to afford to, or should they keep the tax at affordable levels, even though many people who choose to smoke will suffer ill-health and die prematurely?

Social Contract

The **Social Contract** is the name of a number of theories which seek to explain why governments have authority over citizens and why citizens are morally obliged to obey governments. The central idea is that citizens have tacitly agreed to give up some of their freedom to the government in exchange for being protected from harm. Some defenders of this understanding of political philosophy (especially Thomas Hobbes) have claimed that the authority of the government is absolute, and that citizens must obey it at all times, whereas others (such as John Locke) have argued that citizens retain the right to dismiss a government which abuses its authority.

KEY TERM

Social Contract ■

A theory that the authority of governments is based on the consent of the governed and that citizens must therefore obey the laws which those governments impose.

WORKED EXAMPLE 17

Apply theories of the Social Contract to the following issue.

Should citizens who disapprove of the introduction of a National Identity Card scheme co-operate with it, or should they try to make the scheme unworkable by refusing to co-operate with it?

Comment

Different theories of Social Contract would to some extent evaluate this issue differently, but the outcome would probably be the same.

On the basis of Hobbes's version of the Social Contract, citizens who disapprove of the introduction of a National Identity Card scheme must co-operate with it whether they agree with it or not, because it has been introduced by the government in order to increase national security.

John Locke would not have objected in principle to the idea of refusing to co-operate with an unpopular decision by a government, but in this case – since the declared aim of a National Identity Card scheme is to improve national security – it would be hard to argue that the government had exceeded the authority which had been voluntarily given over to it. So Locke would probably have agreed with Hobbes, that citizens must participate in the National Identity Card scheme, whether they agreed with it or not.

The veil of ignorance

In the late twentieth century, John Rawls produced an influential Social Contract theory, based on asking what choices we would make if we did not know what position we would occupy in society (e.g. whether we would be rich or poor, male or female, talented or untalented, successful or unsuccessful). Rawls named this imaginary position 'the veil of ignorance'.

You may find that you can apply Rawls's approach to the issue which is presented to you in the exam, asking which option we would choose if we did not know what position we would occupy in society. You can think of this approach as an alternative version of Kant's principle of universalisability, and you may find that you prefer to use it in the exam in place of Kant's own principle; or you may choose to approach issues from three perspectives, namely deontological, Utilitarian and Rawlsian.

In any issue related to health care, you might argue on the basis of Rawls's theory that if we did not know whether we would be healthy or sick, rich or poor, we would choose to pay quite high taxes for health care just in case we might need what they would buy without being able to afford to pay for them ourselves.

In relation to the issue of abortion, you would have to choose a policy without knowing whether you were a pregnant woman or an unwanted foetus (or possibly her male partner). If you decided that your chances of leading a happy life if you were not aborted outweighed the inconvenience of continuing an unwanted pregnancy, you would opt for a fairly restrictive abortion law.

WORKED EXAMPLE 18

Apply appropriate ethical principles to resolve the following issue.

> Should the government raise the rate of tax charged to people with high incomes and use the money to help low-paid workers and unemployed people, even though doing so will deprive rich people of what they have earned or inherited?

Comment

These comments try to apply several ethical theories to the issue. This is done to show you how as many theories as possible might be applied. In the exam you would not be expected to write as much as this nor would you have time to do so. You would need to choose about three or four of these theories and explain how they could be applied to each choice.

Divine Command ethics, as expressed in the Hebrew Bible (Christian Old Testament), accepts that some people will be richer than others, but lays a responsibility on rulers to mitigate the natural process whereby the rich become richer and the poor become poorer. These principles support a policy of limited redistributive taxation, but it is likely that existing levels of taxation more than meet the expectations of Divine Command ethics.

Natural Law does justify the state in levying taxes on its citizens, but focuses on raising the taxes needed to pay for public services. Redistributive taxation is rather different, and comes into direct conflict with the principle of private property, which Natural Law accepts. The principle of survival (the most fundamental and far-reaching principle of Natural Law) implies that poor people should not be allowed to starve, but current redistributive taxation achieves that and it would be hard to justify an increase by reference to Natural Law.

As in the case of most issues which might occur in the exam, Kant did not actually discuss this question. It would be ridiculous to argue that everyone should give part of their capital and income to everyone else, but a slightly less rigorous version of the principle of universalisability (first version of the Categorical Imperative) could be used to argue that everyone who has more money than they need should share it with those in need.

Either increasing redistributive taxation or keeping it at its current level could be interpreted as using persons as means only and thereby infringing the second version of the Categorical Imperative. Arguably, redistributive taxation treats the rich as means only – a source of money to be used to subsidise the poor. Conversely, it could be argued that by forcing rich people to share their resources with poor people (whose labour may be the direct or indirect source of their wealth), redistributive taxation prevents the rich from treating the poor as means only.

An obvious human right which needs to be considered in a rights-based approach to this issue is the right to private property. The justification for over-riding this right, by depriving wealthy people of some of their capital and income, is that it is outweighed by the need to use the money to defend the right to life of poor people. Important though the right to private property is, the right to life 'trumps' it.

Utilitarianism would in principle favour a policy of large-scale redistribution of wealth, since that would cause the greatest amount of happiness overall. The benefits gained by the recipients of this redistribution would far exceed the cost to those who have some of their wealth taken away from them. However, political parties which have indicated support for a policy of that kind have discovered that the rich have many ways of preventing them from implementing it. If parties want to take office so that they can make the world a better place, they have no choice but to abandon any policy which is going to prevent them from being elected, however fervently they believe in that policy. Furthermore, it is very easy to remove money from a country with a harsh tax regime and relocate it where it will be less vulnerable, thereby increasing unemployment and depriving the government of large amounts of tax revenue. Behaving in that way or threatening to do so is not just, but Utilitarianism judges actions only by their consequences and not by their intrinsic quality. In practice, therefore, a policy of increased redistributive taxation would probably fail to achieve the greatest good of the greatest number.

Rawls claimed that although most people would hope to succeed in life and to enjoy the rewards of their success, behind the veil of ignorance they would be prepared to restrict those rewards, just in case they turned out to be losers. If Rawls was right, it follows that the government should set taxation and unemployment benefits at fairly high rates, since that is what the population wants (whether they know it or not). Other writers have disagreed with Rawls's judgement, and suggested that most people would prefer a lower safety net combined with the possibility of achieving great riches.

ACTIVITY 25

You have already applied appropriate free-standing ethical principles to the following issues. Now apply appropriate deontological and consequentialist theories to them.

a) **Activity 11 (page 50)**

b) **Activity 12 (page 64)**

c) **Activity 13 (page 65)**

d) **Activity 15 (page 66)**

e) **Activity 16 (page 67)**

f) **Activity 18a (page 71)**

g) **Activity 18b (page 71)**

h) **Activity 18c (page 71)**

i) **Activity 18d (page 71)**

REMEMBER

In the exam, you will be expected to refer to the resource documents in addition to identifying and applying ethical principles.

Referring to documents in discussing difficult issues

Some of the marks for question 4 are awarded for your use of the resource documents. Try to support every point you make by a brief reference to something in one of the documents, but those references must be *relevant* and *critical*.

REMEMBER

Critical comments about documents in this question may be positive ('The document is reliable because…') or negative. They may refer to any of the following:

- credibility criteria
- plausibility of claims
- the support for the conclusion given by the evidence
- flaws, weaknesses or strengths in the reasoning.

WORKED EXAMPLE 19

Read the following document outlining a research proposal involving animals. If you wanted to refer to this document to support a claim that research on animals causes the greatest good for the greatest number, what brief critical comments about the document could you make? In a group, list as many comments as you can. Do those comments weaken the support which the information gathered from the document can give to the claim?

> **An extract from a research proposal involving animal testing**
>
> A significant number of babies are born with brain damage resulting from problems with oxygen supply and/or the presence of infections at the time of childbirth. We hypothesise that treating the mother with statins during the last stages of pregnancy may help to reduce the degree of brain damage in the new born.
>
> Statins are a class of drugs routinely used to lower cholesterol concentrations in the blood. They also have many other beneficial effects on both the blood vessels and the nerves.
>
> Statins are not licensed for use in pregnant women. Before we can test our hypothesis we therefore need to determine if treating pregnant animals in late pregnancy has any adverse effect on either the mother or the babies. We have chosen to use rats as these are the lowest vertebrate that we can administer the statins to orally in the most controlled but least stressful manner. We will give the mother rats statins in the last few days of pregnancy so that we can determine where in her and her babies' bodies the statins go. Following birth some of the rat pups will be killed and their brains prepared for

examination. The remaining pups will be observed daily for the first 3 to 4 weeks of their life to determine if their exposure to statins during the last few stages of pregnancy has had any obvious adverse effects on their development. The mothers' health will also continue to be monitored through this period. At approximately 3 weeks after the birth the experiment will be concluded and both the mother and the remaining pups will be killed.

Brain damage occurring around the time of childbirth has a large emotional and economic cost for society. Treating mothers in late pregnancy with statins may be a cost effective method to reduce the extent of brain damage occurring in children around the time of birth. This study is the first step in determining if this is a feasible treatment.

Source: Home Office, www.homeoffice.gov.uk

Comment

The publisher of this proposal is the Home Office, which has high credibility in relation to expertise, ability to see and vested interest to represent facts accurately and fairly.

However, the proposal itself comes from the institution or company wishing to undertake the research, the identity of which is not stated. The credibility of these proposers may be significantly different from that of the Home Office. Since they want to undertake the research, they have a vested interest to emphasise the scale and likelihood of the possible benefits and to minimise the risks, in order to obtain permission. This vested interest is especially strong if the proposers are a pharmaceutical company, which would hope to expand even further the market for statins.

On the assumption that the proposers are professional and specialised researchers, they presumably have appropriate expertise and the ability to see the details of the proposed research and the likelihood that it will actually achieve the benefits outlined in the final paragraph of the document.

The proposal is heavily affected by bias. The possible eventual benefits of the research are emphasised, but – although the speculative nature of the proposal is not concealed – it does not admit explicitly that the possibility of success is very low.

The vested interest and bias of the proposal severely affect the support it can give to the claim that research on animals causes the greatest good for the greatest number. If this document occurred in the exam, any candidate who made use of it to support this claim without recognising its shortcomings would not achieve a very high mark.

How to resolve an issue

Whether question 4 is expressed in the form of a dilemma or not, it will require you to use principles to argue in favour of at least two courses of action and to decide which you prefer.

To achieve Level 3 or above for 'Resolution of issue', you must both:

■ give at least one argument in favour of two alternatives and

■ attempt a resolution.

In relation to some issues, it is easy to argue in favour of both sides, but harder to decide between them; in other cases, you may find it easy to make a choice, but harder to defend more than one side.

We will now look at some of the ways you might resolve an issue and illustrate them by reference to the following question:

> Should the government make it compulsory for cyclists to wear protective helmets, even though it will restrict their freedom and cost them money or should they continue to leave it to individual choice, even though some cyclists who choose not to wear helmets will suffer unnecessary death or serious injury?

■ There may be more principles in favour of one side than the other. In the case of the cycle helmet dilemma, most of the arguments which could be used favour making their use compulsory. Consequentialists would see saving people from death or serious injury as outweighing the loss of freedom; other relevant consequences would be the use of National Health Service resources by people seriously injured in accidents. The principle of paternalism and the government's duty of care would both support the government in legislating on this matter. The right to life and the principle of survival (the most fundamental principle of Natural Law according to Aquinas) would also support such legislation. Behind the Rawlsian veil of ignorance, most would probably opt for making the helmets compulsory. Hobbes's version of the Social Contract would support the legislation, although Locke's version might see it as going beyond the government's remit. It is really only the right of autonomy and the principle of liberty which support the other side.

■ The principles on one side may give stronger support than those on the other. In this case, someone might argue that very few lives would be saved or that the estimated number of deaths and injuries avoided would be speculative, but a stronger case could probably be made that the inconvenience of wearing a helmet would be minimal, whereas the benefit of not dying or being seriously injured would be huge, albeit for only a few people.

■ The principles in favour of one side may be more fundamental and important than those on the other side. For example, it is generally accepted that the principle of non-maleficence is more important than the principle of beneficence (in other words, it is more important to avoid harming people than it is to do them good). The right to life is normally identified as the most important principle, and Natural Law identifies survival as the most fundamental good; both of those principles favour making cycle helmets compulsory.

■ You may have a personal commitment to giving priority to certain principles, such as Divine Command ethics or Utilitarianism. Those who oppose making the use of cycle helmets compulsory are most likely to do so because they have a particularly strong commitment to autonomy.

■ It may be possible to reduce the harm caused by one side of the dilemma. In this case, the government could subsidise the cost of cycle helmets, so that at least people who did not want to wear them would be spared all or part of the cost of buying helmets. It may be possible to resolve other issues by compensating the people who suffer harm.

The conclusion of your answer to question 4 does not need to be very long. You will have already explained how various principles or ethical theories can be applied to justify each side of the issue, so you should need no more than one paragraph to bring that discussion together into a resolution.

Chapters 4 and 5 of this book have included a number of dilemmas and other situations in which a choice needed to be made. You have already decided which principles and theories could be used in support of each side and how they could be applied. To practise the skill of resolving an issue, Activities 26 and 27 now ask you to go back to those exercises and decide between the alternatives.

ACTIVITY 26

Review your use of ethical principles and theories in relation to the following dilemmas and situations requiring choices, and write a one-paragraph conclusion for each, deciding between the alternatives and giving a reason for your choice.

a) **Activity 18 (page 71)**
b) **Activity 20 (page 81)**
c) **Activity 21 (page 84)**
d) **Activity 22 (page 85)**
e) **Activity 23 (page 87)**

ACTIVITY 27

Review your use of ethical principles and theories in relation to the dilemmas and situations requiring choices which you discussed in Activity 25 (page 92), and write a one-paragraph conclusion for each, deciding between the alternatives and giving a reason for your choice.

After reading this chapter and tackling the activities, you should feel that you are well equipped to use principles to help you to resolve an issue or dilemma. It is important for you to feel confident in this, as it will be allocated at least half of the overall mark for the Unit 3 exam.

Summary

You should now be able to:

- ▨ understand the main points of some influential ethical theories
- ▨ consider how those theories might be used to help us to resolve a contentious issue.

Exam Café
Relax, refresh, result!

What the exam will look like

The basic structure will be as follows.

- The Unit 3 exam will last for 1 hour and 30 minutes and you need to attempt all the questions.
- The format will consist of a *Resource Booklet* and a *question paper*. You will answer the questions in the separate answer booklet provided.

The Resource Booklet

The Resource Booklet gives several documents relating to the topic or issue that will provide the context for you to demonstrate your Critical Thinking skills in a decision-making process. This topic could come from any one of a wide range of contemporary issues.

Make sure you take time at the beginning of the exam to study the Resource Booklet carefully. Read each document to get an idea of what it is about. The instructions on the front of the paper will advise you to spend 15 minutes doing this. This should be enough time, because it is important that you leave yourself a full hour and a quarter to answer all of the questions. This reading and thinking time is part of the exam and you should make full use of it.

The Resource Booklet will consist of between three and five documents providing:

- information – explanations, instructions, guidelines; facts and figures, tables and graphs
- opinion – the views of experts, scientists, politicians, newspaper columnists, religious leaders, judges: people whom we might refer to as 'opinion formers'.

Do not worry if you don't know much about the issue covered by the documents in the Resource Booklet. No specialist knowledge of the topic is required. It is how you use the evidence provided that will be assessed in the exam.

The questions

It is likely that the number and wording of the questions in the exam will follow a pattern and process very similar to that explained in this book, that is:

- two questions which will require you to examine evidence, information and views presented in the Resource Booklet (approximately 20 per cent of the total marks); aim to spend between 5 and 10 minutes on each of these questions
- a question which will require you to identify and discuss choices and criteria relevant to issues raised by the evidence provided (approximately 20 per cent of the total marks); aim to spend about 15 minutes on this question
- a question which will require you to state and defend a solution to a contentious issue arising from the resource documents. In addition to arguing in favour of one choice, you will be expected to show why some people might favour a different choice and the grounds on which you have rejected it. Probably more than 50% of the marks will be allocated to this question, and you should spend about 45 minutes on it.

However, the format of the question paper may vary slightly from session to session. You should read the instructions and the allocation of marks carefully, in order to ensure that you do what is actually being asked of you on this occasion, whether it is exactly what you expected or not. A short question may ask for one or three answers instead of the usual two (in which case you should give the amount of detail required for the number of marks allocated). There may be an extra short question. Question 3 may have 18 marks allocated instead of the usual 12, in which case you will probably be required to refer critically to the Resource Documents in support of your answer. Question 4 may be divided into two parts and the marks divided between them.

Refresh your memory

What the exam will assess

The examiner will assess your work on the basis of the three Assessment Objectives (AO1, AO2 and AO3) which are applied to all the Critical Thinking Units. These assessment objectives require you to:

- AO1 Analyse critically the use of different kinds of reasoning in a wide range of contexts.

- AO2 Evaluate critically the use of different kinds of reasoning in a wide range of contexts.

- AO3 Develop and communicate relevant and coherent arguments clearly and accurately in a concise and logical manner.

Important points to note

- Nearly half the marks in the Unit 3 exam are allocated to AO3, Develop and communicate relevant and coherent arguments clearly and accurately in a concise and logical manner.

- Nearly a third of the marks are allocated to AO2, Evaluate critically the use of different kinds of reasoning in a wide range of contexts.

The quality of your written communication will be assessed as part of AO3. For your work in the exam to be considered to be of a high standard in terms of written communication it should:

- show that you can use a form of writing appropriate to a complex subject matter

- show that you can organise relevant information in a coherent manner

- be legible and contain few errors in terms of spelling, grammar and punctuation. The meaning should be clear.

Presenting your answers

You should be careful to set out your work in a way that makes sense and is relevant, coherent and easy to follow. In questions 3 and 4, aim to put each point in a separate paragraph, leaving a blank line after each paragraph. This will help the marker to see exactly what you are doing and to give you all the marks you deserve. If you use bullet points, make sure that they are detailed enough for the marker to be able to understand what you wish to say.

Quality of Argument

Marks are available for Quality of Argument in questions 3 and 4. To gain a good mark, you should:

- make each point lead into a well-supported intermediate conclusion

- use hypothetical reasoning ('if...then...') wherever it is appropriate

- use relevant counter-arguments, analogies, evidence or examples wherever they will strengthen your argument.

Using a particular document to identify and explain factors affecting opinions

You may find it useful to think in terms of the different sorts of factors as outlined in Chapter 1: economic, political, social, health, and so on.

However, it is more important to remember to select a relevant piece of evidence from the source you have been referred to. You will probably find it better to approach questions of this kind by finding points from the document and drawing inferences from them, rather than beginning from a list of points and trying to find evidence in the document to support them.

Exam tip

▷ Ensure that you manage your limited time effectively. It is vital that you leave at least 35 minutes for the final question.

Identifying and explaining problems of definition

Think about factors such as the following.

- Context: who is using the words you are discussing? Where are they using them? Who is the likely audience? What is the nature of the topic or issue under discussion?

- Ambiguity: are terms being used in such a way as to be taken a number of ways? This can happen accidentally or be done quite deliberately.

- Specialist versus non-specialist use of language.

- The different ways in which different groups or societies might use key words and phrases, depending perhaps on different ethnic/political/religious/cultural perspectives.

- The use of certain words and phrases in such a way as to perhaps unduly/unfairly influence policy or public opinion to alter the terms of debate. (Here you might consider the impact of emotional and rhetorical language.)

Problems in using information from a particular type of source

Depending on the document and the topic under consideration, relevant problems might include the ones below.

- Statistical information may be insufficient to justify the inference being drawn from it.

- On its own the source might provide a one-sided/unbalanced view; bias might be conscious or unconscious in nature.

- The authority of any views presented might be disputed or not clear.

- The views expressed might lack clarity.

- Such views might be contradictory.

Advice on answering questions 1 and 2

Chapter 1 gives guidance on the kind of short questions which are likely to occur at the beginning of the question paper.

It is likely that 6 marks will be available for each of these questions. You will probably be told how many separate points to make (most likely two). If you are asked to 'identify' or 'suggest', 'briefly explain' and 'refer to', then those prompt words will show you how the marks are allocated. The instruction 'identify' normally means you should find something from one of the documents, whereas 'suggest' normally means you should think of something for yourself.

Treat each factor/problem separately – you may find it appropriate to present your answer in bullet-point style. If you present the answer in a single paragraph, the examiner may fail to recognise that you have made the correct number of separate points.

Numbering your answers in these short questions will help the examiner to see that you have made the right number of separate points.

These questions will normally ask you to explain as well as to identify. If you merely produce a list of relevant problems/factors then the most you can expect is 1 mark each. (However, even if you are not sure how to explain the relevance of a point, you will still gain a mark for listing it.)

If you are instructed to refer to a particular document or documents, you should ensure that you are seen to use the source referred to. This only needs to be done briefly – using a fact or figure from a source as evidence, or lifting a short phrase from it. You cannot hope for a really good mark if you fail to do this.

Advice on answering question 3

Using criteria to evaluate choices

The key section of the book here is Chapter 2, which guides you through the process of applying relevant criteria in order to help evaluate choices that could be made.

This type of question will probably carry the same number of marks as questions 1 and 2 together. So aim to spend the same amount of time on it (about 15 minutes).

When answering this type of question, bear in mind the following points.

▷ Make it clear from the start which choice(s) you are going to evaluate. Express the choice precisely.
▷ A good response to this question will require you to use more than one criterion.
▷ If you are asked to identify and evaluate one choice, select one that is likely to let you apply three or four criteria in a solid and sustained manner.
▷ If you are asked to compare two choices, evaluate them by the same criteria (two criteria will probably be all you have time for).

Response levels

This question will be marked in terms of which level of response the examiner thinks your answer belongs to.

There are four levels of response. A Level 4 (L4) response will be one that deserves to be credited with a mark between 10 and 12. Answers which receive a L4 mark will exhibit some or all of the following qualities.

▷ Sound and perceptive application of several well-chosen criteria to one clearly defined choice or two well-chosen criteria to two clearly defined choices (depending on which the question asks for).
▷ Firm understanding of how criteria might support and weaken the case for the selected choice(s).
▷ Cogent and convincing reasoning, very well structured to express/evaluate complex ideas/materials.
▷ Accurate use of relevant terminology.
▷ Few, if any, errors of spelling, grammar, punctuation.

Advice on answering question 4

Identifying and attempting to resolve a contentious issue

This question will carry the most marks. A close re-reading of Chapters 4 and 5 is the key to doing well in this question.

Most of the marks for this question are given for AO3 – in other words, on the basis of how well you develop and communicate your argument.

Exam tip

▷ It is possible that in one of the short questions or as part of question 4 you may be asked to suggest and explain a dilemma or just to explain it. If you are asked to suggest a dilemma, you must do so carefully (see Chapter 3). Remember that a dilemma occurs where someone has to choose between two alternatives but there are good reasons against both of them. Your explanation should consist of identifying the reasons against each side.

Question 4 will ask you to present an argument in which you apply some relevant principles to the issue. You will need to consider more than one principle, though a very good treatment of two clearly defined and appropriate principles can access the higher marks. The principles you apply may be based on ethical theories, but self-standing principles may be equally suitable for your purpose. The principles you choose must be relevant to the issue.

Using principles

▷ You should avoid using ethical theories in a formulaic manner. For example, it would not be enough to merely state the Utilitarian point of view; in order to gain a good mark, you also need to demonstrate how this might help you to resolve the issue you are discussing.

▷ Apply sufficiently different principles. For instance, you could apply a principle which judges an action on the basis of its consequences and a principle which puts more stress on our duty to do what we consider morally right regardless of the consequences. In many cases, however, a consequentialist approach itself can be used to support more than one choice, and in such cases one way of resolving the issue might be to estimate and compare the consequences of both alternatives.

▷ Assess the extent to which the principles you are using are helpful in trying to resolve the issue you are discussing.

▷ Check that the reasoning you are presenting is logical and not flawed or based upon too many questionable assumptions.

▷ Ensure that you refer to the documents in a selective and critical manner. If you do not show the examiner that you are using the documents critically, you will limit the marks available to you for this question.

▷ Ensure that you reach a conclusion in which you show how you might at least attempt to resolve the issue. This conclusion might well be based upon intermediate conclusions arising from the application of different principles to the issue.

Do not focus too closely on the number of principles needed for Level 4. The point of mentioning three principles or two ethical theories in the level descriptor was mainly to discourage candidates from producing long lists of theories in preference to discussing a small number in greater detail. Free-standing principles are things such as equality of opportunity, the right to life or confidentiality. 'Two major ethical theories' might consist of one deontological theory (such as Divine Command or Kantianism) and a form of Utilitarianism.

Response levels

A Level 4 answer is one that will be credited with between 28 and 36 marks. It will display some or all of the
following qualities.

▷ Perceptive, relevant and accurate use of resource material.
▷ Sustained and confident evaluation of resource material.
▷ Skilful and cogent treatment and application of at least three principles or at least two major ethical theories.
▷ Clear and purposeful exposition of how the principles might be more or less useful in resolving the issue.
▷ Confidently expressed support for a clearly defined choice in the light of rejection of at least one alternative.
▷ Cogent and convincing reasoning.
▷ Well-developed suppositional reasoning.
▷ Communication very well suited to handling complex ideas.
▷ Meaning clear throughout.
▷ Frequent and very effective use of appropriate terminology.
▷ Few, if any, errors in spelling, grammar and punctuation.

Get the result!

Practice Unit 3 exam paper

Allow yourself 1 hour and 30 minutes to tackle this sample exam paper. Then compare your answers with the sample answers provided on the CD-ROM. This sample paper is not necessarily in exactly the same format as the OCR paper you will take, but it is based on the same assessment objectives and should resemble the actual exam.

There are two parts to this activity: resources and questions. As in the exam, you should allow time to study the documents carefully. In the exam you should spend 15 minutes studying the Resource Booklet before answering the questions.

Resources

Document 1

How far would you go?

Victoria, 50, from Hampshire, has four daughters aged between nine and 18:

'You're not a good parent if you don't know what your kids are doing. In what other part of their life do you just sign off responsibility and leave them to cope on their own? In a casual way, I check their Bebo sites, their mobiles and look in their address books in their mobiles to make sure that everything is OK and that things are not getting out of hand. I am pretty good at teen speak now and I can tell any parent who wants to know.'

'My kids are aware that I do a bit of light monitoring and seem pretty used to it by now. I can reassure parents who wouldn't dream of prying and have a much higher ethical code that most of what goes on is pretty dull. At first I was really shocked by the pouting photos they put up and then I realised that, particularly on MSN and MySpace, they create wilder, more interesting personas that often bear little relation to who they are and what they are really doing. It's often quite funny and creative and they really listen to each other's music and poetry. On MSN, which is used by the younger teenagers, they do relate to each other in this very casual, sexual style, which actually doesn't mean that they are having sex left, right and centre. One boy who seems to be the most wild online is actually a bit of a geek. If anything, I find it reassuring.'

George, 39, from Leeds, has two daughters aged 15 and nine:

'I am not ashamed of what I did. I am Greek-Cypriot and had a much more traditional upbringing than my children. My wife is English and she is much more relaxed about our two kids than I am. My 15-year-old daughter stopped talking to us and was spending so much time on MySpace that I got really suspicious about it. She wasn't doing her homework and the school were going mad at us and she had GCSEs looming, so one day at work I signed up.'

'I pretended to be a boy of her age and got to know her over the course of a couple of weeks. I found out that she was having a relationship with a man in his 20s and that they were sleeping together and planning on going away for a weekend in the summer. She boasted to me (or the boy I was pretending to be) that she was going to tell us that she was staying with her best friend, who had agreed to lie for her.'

'Of course I confronted her! I wasn't going to stand by and let her do this to herself and us. What kind of father would that make me? Both my daughter and my wife seem to think that what I did was worse than sleeping with a man five years older and lying to your parents, but that's just rubbish.'

Source: *The Guardian*,
www.guardian.co.uk

Document 2

Paedophile warning over teen websites Bebo and MySpace

Schoolgirls are putting intimate details of themselves on the Internet in increasing numbers and are at high risk of falling victim to paedophiles, a headmistress has warned. The grammar school headmistress has alerted parents to the danger of new 'online networking' websites after finding 700 pupils at her school alone had signed up to a single website, with many attaching revealing pictures of themselves and personal details.

Yet despite the alert from the headmistress, pupils from the school were still last night showing inappropriate pictures of themselves online. In moments our reporter found pictures of one 16-year-old girl at the school posing in a swimsuit and on her bed, and she had given enough details for her address and phone number to be discovered minutes later.

The headmistress wrote to all parents after investigating her pupils' use of the Bebo website. Bebo specialises in creating virtual communities around particular schools, and like the similar MySpace website enables individuals to create their own webpages free of charge within minutes. Users can write anything they like on their sites, and can post dozens of pictures of themselves for anyone in the world to see. Viewers can then write to the children anonymously, and try to arrange to meet them.

The headmistress said last night: 'We've just been monitoring it, going onto the site occasionally and keeping an eye on what was going on, what girls were doing and saying and the way they were presenting themselves. Some were putting on photographs which had them in perhaps quite strappy tops, reasonably short skirts and so on, and they could come across really as soft pornography in the hands of the wrong person. What an 11-year-old girl views as being perfectly innocent isn't necessarily what some more unsavoury characters would view as innocent.'

Source: *Daily Mail*, 3 July 2006,
www.dailymail.co.uk

Document 3

Parents urged to monitor children's surfing

Relying on a 'verbal agreement' is not enough, warns report
Ian Williams, vnunet.com, 28 September 2007

Parents are too trustful of their children when it comes to safe Internet use, according to new research from BroadbandChoices. The broadband comparison service found in a recent survey that 84 per cent of UK parents rate 'verbal agreement' with their children on safe Internet use as their number one means of monitoring online activity.

'It is surprising that so many people rely heavily on their child doing what they ask. It is not going to happen in most cases and the government's research proves this,' said Michael Phillips, product director at BroadbandChoices. 'However, there are a few simple steps parents can take to bolster protection for their child when online. Rather than relying on a single approach, they should use parental control and security software, combined with education, to stop inappropriate material, and people, reaching their child.'

The survey found that 63 per cent of parents use parental control software, 62 per cent restrict the amount of time children spend online, and 59 per cent manually check the computer to monitor online activity.

The poll also asked children aged 11–16 to list their online activities during the school holidays. The most popular activities were downloading music and photos (48 per cent), joining in with chat rooms and making new friends (45 per cent) and using social networking sites (40 per cent).

The report offers five tips to help concerned parents monitor and protect their children online:

1 using parental control software
2 educating children on why they need to be careful on the Internet
3 keeping the family computer in the living room
4 using antivirus and firewall software
5 monitoring downloads and setting alarms when limits are neared.

Source: www.computing.co.uk

Questions

1. Refer to Document 2. With reference to Document 2, identify and briefly explain two problems in defining the term 'inappropriate pictures' in the context of the monitoring of children's use of the Internet. [6]

2. Some parents monitor their children's use of the Internet up to the age of 18 and tell them they are doing so. Suggest two alternative choices that parents might make about monitoring their children's use of the Internet. [6]

3. Evaluate one choice that parents might make about monitoring their children's use of the Internet. In your evaluation you should use three criteria (such as safety). [12]

4. Write an argument supporting one choice which parents might make about monitoring their children's use of the Internet. In your argument you should use some relevant principles and explain why you have rejected at least one possible alternative. Support your argument by referring critically to the resource documents. [36]

Unit 4 Critical reasoning
Analysing different forms of real-life reasoning

Learning objectives
- Revise how to identify arguments.
- Identify and analyse a wide range of forms of reasoning.

Real-life texts

When you are trying to decide what to believe about important issues in the world, newspaper and magazine articles are important sources of information, opinion and argument. They can help you to form your own thoughts and opinions. It is important, however, to take a critical stance. You can evaluate the credibility of the source (the publication, the author, the author's sources, the particular claims that are made), applying the skills you developed in Unit 1. In addition to this, it is also important to ask:

■ What am I being persuaded to accept (what is the conclusion)?

■ How am I being persuaded to accept this (what sort of reasoning is being used)?

■ On what grounds am I supposed to accept this (what are the main reasons)?

■ How effective is this persuasion (is this reasoning strong)?

This chapter will guide you through the first three steps in analysing different forms of reasoning which occur in real life. The focus will generally be on written reasoning, which can be found in newspapers and magazines, but the skills you gain can also be applied to spoken reasoning.

Reasoning

Reasoning is a thread of thought, connected in a logical manner.

■ Reasoning can refer to the way the evidence, reasons, assumptions and conclusions are connected in an argument.

■ Reasoning can also refer to the overall train of thought in a piece, which includes arguments and other strategies to persuade the audience to adopt a point of view.

Real-life texts tend not to be as clear cut as, for example, a multiple choice question in an AS exam. It is not always clear what kind or kinds of reasoning they are using. They tend to be made up of passages of opinion, narrative, report, argument, explanation, emotive persuasion and reasoning which contains argument but which never quite reaches its conclusion. In this chapter you will first revise your AS skills of identifying argument, and then extend them to identifying a wide range of forms of reasoning, sifting passages of argument from articles which are not in themselves an argument, and identifying sections of text which are not part of an argument.

How will these skills be tested?

You may be asked a question such as:

> 'Consider Document 2. Is this an argument? Justify your answer,'
> 'Consider paragraph 5 of Document 1. Is this an argument? Justify your answer.'

Your justification may include an analysis of the kinds of reasoning that are in the passage. For example, your answer might be:

> 'This is not an argument as it doesn't come to a conclusion, but it does contain an argument in paragraph 2. This is fairly emotive reasoning and the reader is expected to draw the conclusion that...'

EXAM TIP

One of the best ways to prepare yourself for the OCR A2 Unit 4 Critical Reasoning exam is to read as many newspapers and magazines as you can.

Try to read articles from newspapers like , the , the and the , and from magazines such as , the , the and .

Use Internet searches to add other reliable, high-quality sources to your list. Another good way to prepare yourself is to listen to current affairs shows on television or radio such as or the .

'Yes, this is an argument, which concludes that ... but it also contains an explanation used as a reason and reports facts to set the context for the argument.'

Another form of question you might be asked is:

'Analyse in detail the reasoning in paragraph 4.'

Your answer might include an understanding that parts of paragraph 4 are, for example, setting the context rather than actually supporting the conclusion. (We will cover the skill of analysing in detail in Chapter 8).

In addition, you are likely to be asked to evaluate the reasoning in one or more documents. If you can analyse the reasoning, and tell what sorts of reasoning are being used, you will find it easier to evaluate it, and say how effective it is. (We will cover evaluative skills in Chapters 9–11).

Identifying an argument

REMEMBER

An argument is an attempt to persuade others to accept a conclusion on the basis of reasons which support that conclusion.

One of the most important forms of reasoning that we work with is argument. Even at A2 candidates make mistakes about what is and isn't an argument, so it is worth revising the skill of identifying an argument. An argument is an attempt to persuade others to accept a conclusion on the basis of reasons which support that conclusion. The reasons should give rational support to the conclusion. For example:

We want to go away next year. We should go to the theme parks in Orlando in February. I get winter depression, which would be eased by a trip to somewhere sunny and warm. The average temperature in Orlando in February is 23°C and it is generally sunny. Also, my daughter will be 14 then, and if we leave it much longer she will not want to go to theme parks with her mother. At the moment we both enjoy sharing scary rides.

This is a simple argument to support the conclusion that 'we should go to the theme parks in Orlando next February'. It is not a conclusive argument; it would certainly be possible to weaken it by arguing that we don't have enough money or that a trip to southern Argentina would be warm and sunny, but would also give my daughter Spanish practice and allow us to see penguins and seals, which would be better than going on scary rides. However, this passage uses reasons to persuade us to accept the conclusion in a rational way. Let's look at a similar text:

> We have decided to go to the theme parks in Orlando next February. I get winter depression, which will be eased by a trip to somewhere sunny and warm. The average temperature in Orlando in February is 23°C and it is generally sunny. Also, we wanted to do this trip before my daughter was too old to enjoy theme parks with her mother. We still enjoy scary rides together.

In this passage the reasoning is similar to the first example, but it is not an argument. There is no element of persuasion that we should accept the conclusion. Instead, this passage is explaining why we have made a decision – it is an explanation. In the first example, the decision had not been made, so it still made sense to use persuasion to affect the decision.

> **REMEMBER**
>
> An explanation tells us how or why something is the case.

Argument and explanation

An argument persuades us to accept a conclusion. It is possible to argue against the conclusion, to persuade us not to accept the conclusion. For example,

> Argument: The theme parks in Orlando are the best in the world. They have a great mix of thrill rides, zoos, water parks and film tie-ins.
>
> Argument against the conclusion: The theme parks in Orlando are not the best in the world. Ohio theme parks have a much greater concentration of thrill rides, and there are theme parks in Hong Kong and Japan, which look even better.

In this example, the first argument is trying to persuade us that the theme parks in Orlando are the best in the world. The second argument is arguing against this, by persuading us that there are theme parks which are better. There is a real debate about where the best theme parks in the world are, and it is, to a certain extent, a matter of opinion, so there is room for persuasion.

An explanation tells us how or why something is the case. The claim being explained is not normally open to persuasion. It is possible to challenge the explanation and suggest that there are different reasons why this claim holds true. For example:

> **Explanation**: Rainfall during the monsoon has decreased in India since the 1950s, despite predictions that global warming would increase it. Although surface temperatures are increasing near the equator, further north the ocean is not warming. It is possible that sunlight is being absorbed by pollution.
>
> **Challenge to explanation**: The reason that rainfall has decreased in India is not that pollution has absorbed sunlight. It is that predictions about global warming were wrong in the first place.

In this example, there is no debate about the claim that 'rainfall during the monsoon has decreased in India since the 1950s'. This is a matter of fact that can be established. The disagreement is about why that fact is the case – about how to explain it.

It is worth noting that there are some explanations where the claim being explained is not certain. When scientists are testing a hypothesis, for example, they may explain how their theory might work, even though they are not sure that their theory is right.

■ Rainfall during the monsoon season has decreased since the 1950s.

Interpretation

Sometimes it is not clear whether a claim is factual and being explained or a matter of opinion, which we are being persuaded to accept. An explanation can have a structure very much like an argument. There is a grey area where arguments and explanations overlap. In these cases there is room for interpretation. You will need to use your judgement and justify your decision. For example:

> Clones would be different ages. Clones would be brought up in different contexts. So clones would be less alike than twins.
>
> Source: Very short extract from OCR Unit 4 Section B June 2009, taken from resource material, McLachlan, *New Scientist*, 21 July 2007

Here it is unclear whether there are two reasons supporting a conclusion (which may or may not be the case and is open to persuasion) or whether this is an explanation in which the first two claims tell us why the third is the case. To a certain extent it depends on the context of the argument, and on scientific information that cannot be researched in exam conditions.

So, what does this mean in terms of how the skill will be tested in the exam? Let's work through an example.

WORKED EXAMPLE 1

Clones would be different ages. Clones would be brought up in different contexts. So clones would be less alike than twins.

Is this an argument? Justify your answer.

Answer A
It's an argument which supports a conclusion.

Answer B
It's an argument which uses two reasons to support the conclusion that clones would be less alike than twins.

Answer C
It is not an argument. It is an explanation of why clones would be less alike than twins, based in science.

Answer D
It is unclear whether this is an argument or an explanation. It depends on whether it can be firmly established whether clones really would be less alike than twins. At the moment it is unclear whether this claim is something we are being told about or persuaded to agree with. It's probably an argument because the author is making a prediction in an area where there is little evidence, so we need to be persuaded that clones would be less alike than twins.

Comment

Answer A is very weak. It is a stock answer, which merely states part of the definition of a conclusion. It looks more like a guess than a thought-through answer. It would be regarded as, at best, basic in the exam.

Answers B and C are reasonable. Both show clear understanding and have provided some justification for the answer in terms of the text in question rather than simply generic terms. Either is a reasonable interpretation of the reasoning.

Answer D is sound, thorough and perceptive. It shows awareness of the need for interpretation, and justifies its interpretation in terms of the reasoning in question. This sort of answer would get high marks in the exam – but only if it really were uncertain whether the reasoning was argument or explanation.

ACTIVITY

For each of the following texts answer the question, 'Is this an argument? Justify your answer.'

A   Art should be beautiful. Some works of art only make us think. Too many works of art are ugly.

B   Light bulbs normally blow when they are first switched on rather than after being used. When it is cold the filament (thin tungsten wire) has less resistance, so the electric current surges up it with a higher than normal voltage when you flick the switch. This spike of electricity breaks the filament.

C   Brain imaging technology should not be used in the courts or by the police or security services. This technology is developing fast. The relationships between brain images and thoughts are very complex.

D   The average temperatures between 2000 and 2005 rose despite an increase in cloud cover. Low-lying clouds bounce sunlight away from the earth, whereas high-level clouds trap heat. There have been increasing amounts of high-level cloud.

E   Scientific research into the paranormal is useful and valuable. Although this research has not come up with a convincing, reproducible explanation of the paranormal, it has produced some interesting findings about the way the brain works.

F   London is a multicultural city. More than two million of the eight million total population are from ethnic minorities. There are 370,000 black Africans, and 437,000 Indians. 58% of Londoners describe themselves as Christians, 8.5% as Muslims, 4% as Hindus, 2.1% as Jewish and 1.5% as Sikhs.

Identifying a wide range of forms of reasoning in real-life texts

Real-life texts of the sort used in the OCR A2 Critical Reasoning exam are generally not 'pure' argument or explanation. They generally use a range of forms of reasoning including:

- setting the context for an argument, defining terms, narrating a story or course of events and reporting on facts

- arguing

- explaining

- expressing opinion, using rhetoric and persuading with emotion.

These forms of reasoning can occur in the same passage at the same time and this is not a complete list. It is possible to express opinion or use rhetoric and still be using argument. Setting the context for an argument might include expressing opinion or using emotive language to sway our views. An argument might contain all these forms of reasoning.

Equally, a passage might contain all these forms of reasoning (including argument) but not be an argument overall if it doesn't have a main conclusion. Your task as a critical thinker is to work out which kinds of reasoning are being used and to be aware that an author can be using two or more kinds of reasoning at the same time. We will discuss how you can do this during the rest of the chapter.

Considering the purpose of a passage

When you are considering what sort of reasoning is being used in a passage, you can ask yourself:

What is the purpose of this passage?

- To give me information?

- To persuade me to accept something?

- To tell me how or why something is the case?

- To share a view?

- To make me react emotionally?

- Any other purpose?

The purpose of some passages is to give you information, to report on events or to tell a story. Although they may include opinion, they do not intend to persuade you to agree with anything. You do not need to be able to tell the difference between a report and a narrative, for example, but you do need to be able to identify passages which are not arguments. Using common, non-specialist words like report or narrative can be helpful to you. Let's look at an example:

> **Version One**
> England's cricketers are once again facing a storm of criticism after their most recent failures against Australia. The jubilant Aussies beat England by 7 wickets, taking the series to 4-0. Under fierce pressure to resign in favour of a younger man, England's captain, Rama Ball, has identified three specific weaknesses in the team's game: the batting, the bowling and the fielding.

> **EXAM TIP**
>
> When you are talking about different forms of reasoning, don't worry about finding the right label. Apart from argument and explanation, you don't need to use technical terms, you just need to use your own language to explain what the reasoning is doing. You may think, for example, that an author is making predictions or testing a hypothesis. These could be acceptable answers.

> He says, 'My greater experience will help me guide this young team to success next season. Rome wasn't built in a day and nor is a winning team.'

Here, the purpose of the text is to report on the cricket and to tell us about the England team's loss as well as the effects of this loss. It is not trying to persuade us to agree to anything. Although the language does allow the author's view to show, the author is not persuading us to accept this view.

Some passages contain reasoning and may be persuasive, even though they are not, strictly speaking, arguments as critical thinkers understand the term (with reasons supporting a conclusion). Let's look at an extended version of the report we considered above:

> **Version Two**
> England's cricketers are once again facing a storm of criticism after their most recent failures against Australia. The jubilant Aussies beat England by 7 wickets, taking the series to 4-0. Under fierce pressure to resign in favour of a younger man, England's captain, Rama Ball, has identified three specific weaknesses in the team's game: the batting, the bowling and the fielding. He says, 'My greater experience will help me guide this young team to success next season. Rome wasn't built in a day and nor is a winning team.' But Pollock was out for 0 (again), Mantis for 3 and Darkwood for 6 (his best test innings this year). My Gran could have bowled better than Panther, who didn't seem to know where the wicket was, he bowled wide so often, and Gilbert looked like he was wading through treacle. Does this sound like a winning team in the making? Or should we get a new architect and a construction team that knows its adze from its elbow?

The purpose of this passage is now a little different. It is still reporting on the match, but it is also expressing opinion and sharing the author's view. It is starting to be a persuasive piece of writing, aiming to get the audience to share the author's view. It is not, however, an argument, because it does not state a conclusion. We are clearly intended to come to the conclusion that the team captain and several of the players should be replaced, but we are being persuaded with emotive language and leading questions rather than by reasons which support a conclusion.

Some passages combine argument with emotive language and opinion. Let's have a look at a different version of the report we have been considering:

> **Version Three**
> England must surely now replace the tired, ageing captain, Rama Ball. After another crushing defeat by Australia, taking the series to 4-0, Ball has shown himself to be a weak captain. The players are unmotivated and often badly placed in the field. Pollock was out for 0 (again), Mantis for 3 and Darkwood for 6 (his best test innings this year). My Gran could have bowled better than Panther, who didn't seem to know where the wicket was, he bowled wide so often, and Gilbert looked like he was wading through treacle. Ball took no action. These are all players with potential, who could do well with the right leadership.

This text is still reporting on the match, and it is still expressing opinions, sometimes using emotional language, but it is also providing an argument to support the claim that 'England must surely now replace the tired, ageing captain, Rama Ball'. Some of the reasoning is implied or suggested rather than being stated, but there is a structure of reasoning here which can be paraphrased roughly as follows:

England has lost, *and* this can (partly) be explained by Ball's poor captaincy, which is *shown* (supported) by the poor performance of the players (results, motivation and placing) *and* they are potentially good players (implication – *so* their poor performance can't be explained by their being poor cricketers but can be blamed on the leadership) *so* England should get a new captain.

The words 'and' and 'so' are highlighted here so that you can see logical links between the parts of the argument. This kind of use of paraphrase to find a structure of reasoning is not tested in itself in the exam, but it can be a useful tool for you to decide whether there is an argument, which is a skill that is tested. Be aware also that you should not confuse this way of understanding a loose argument structure with the skill of analysing reasoning in detail, where you should use the author's words. The skill of analysing reasoning in detail will be covered in Chapter 8.

EXAM TIP

Paraphrasing reasoning as a part of investigating what form of reasoning you are dealing with is a different task from analysing reasoning in detail, which you will cover in Chapter 8.

ACTIVITY 2

Read the following passages. For each passage, answer the question:

Is this an argument? Justify your answer with reference to the different kinds of reasoning used.

A In order to be mathematically beautiful, a piece of work must have certain qualities. It must use the minimum number of assumptions, provide an original and important insight or cast new light on existing understanding.

B Only a small proportion of people with schizophrenia are violent. People in the early stages of the disease are more likely to be charged with murder than people in the later stages. A research project looking at statistics from around the world found that people having their first episode of psychosis are 20 times more likely to kill someone than in later years. This may be because people in the early stages of the disease have not yet learned to recognise delusions that drive them to violence as symptoms of their illness.

C Fathers are currently not allowed to stay the night in hospital with their partner and new baby. Nor are fathers encouraged to attend antenatal classes or classes that give information about stopping smoking, breast feeding and parenting skills. Midwives and nurses take every opportunity to tell the mother about her new responsibilities, but fathers are given the message that baby is nothing to do with them. Midwives should be trained to engage with fathers as well as mothers. Evidence suggests that more mothers quit smoking and continue to breast feed if fathers are informed and encouraging. If fathers were encouraged to feel responsible and important, there would be benefits for baby, mother and father for many years.

D It is of vital importance to our society that people have a strong sense of moral right and wrong at work. Too many people leave their values at home when they enter the cut and thrust of the workplace. This leads to people being treated like machines. It leads to money and power taking over as the supreme values. This is bad for society as we need proper moral values to help us function.

How am I being persuaded?

Authors of real-life texts use a number of ways of persuading us to accept claims, as we have seen in the discussion above. Sometimes they persuade us rationally with reasons and sometimes they persuade with language, implication, opinion and emotion. Often, they mix these methods. We are now going to look more closely at some different kinds of persuasion.

Rational persuasion

Rational persuasion relies on logical links between reasons and a conclusion. The technical term for this link is inference. Drawing a conclusion or making an inference is to see the next logical step in an argument, to see what follows. We can use the word 'follow' to mean 'come as a logical consequence of'. If B follows from A, then B can be inferred from A.

Rational persuasion based on inference can be divided into two main categories: deductive reasoning and inductive reasoning.

Deductive reasoning

Deductive reasoning is a process of coming to logically certain conclusions by the use of logic on the basis of what we already know. It often (but not always) involves applying principles or general statements to specific instances, as in 'It is wrong to steal. John is stealing. Therefore John is doing something wrong'.

A deductively **valid** argument is one in which the conclusion must be true if the reasons are true. That is, the reasons **entail** the conclusion. For example:

> Every member of the McCulloch family can play a musical instrument. Callum is a member of the McCulloch family. Therefore Callum must be able to play a musical instrument.

Be aware that an argument can have a valid structure even if the reasons are false. For example, 'All teachers have wings. Mrs Leonard is a teacher. Therefore Mrs Leonard has wings.' If it were true that teachers had wings, and that Mrs Leonard were a teacher, then the conclusion would have to be true.

KEY TERMS

● **Valid**

In a valid argument, the conclusion must be true if the reasons are true.

● **Entail**

To have as a necessary consequence.

A deductively invalid argument is one in which the conclusion is not entailed by the reasons, even if they are true. For example:

> All dragons have teeth. My kitten has teeth. Therefore, my kitten is a dragon.

The examples we have been using whilst discussing deductive reasoning are **syllogisms**. Syllogisms are a traditional deductive argument structure that began over 2000 years ago with a philosopher called Aristotle. This form of argument uses two reasons to support a conclusion.

Inductive reasoning

Most of the reasoning used in real-life articles is inductive reasoning. It deals with inferences where the reasons do not entail the conclusion. That is, reasons give logical support to a conclusion and make the conclusion plausible, but do not mean that it must be true.

One special form of induction is the process of inferring a general law or principle from the observation of particular instances. For example, 'All the crows I (and everyone I know) have ever seen are black. So crows are generally black.' This form of reasoning often predicts a specific instance on the basis of the inferred general statement, 'So the next crow I see will be black.' It isn't certain that the next crow will be black – there may be an exception somewhere, but the more evidence we gather of crows being black, the more probable it seems that crows are generally black. This sort of reasoning underlies observational science and has led to some important knowledge and understanding.

Emotional and linguistic persuasion

As we saw in the discussion about the reports on cricket, there are different kinds of emotional and linguistic persuasion. Emotional and linguistic persuasive devices include but are not limited to:

- giving opinion
- relying on a claim about emotions
- using language which can affect our emotions
- dealing with concepts which are generally connected to our emotions
- expressing opinion forcefully
- attacking and insulting opponents
- making forceful, sweeping statements in emotional language which ignore the facts and distort opposing views
- some or all of these combined.

Part of your task when analysing how you are being persuaded to accept a claim will be to consider whether a passage is using some emotional or linguistic devices in the context of a reasoned argument, combining some reasoning with some emotional and/or linguistic persuasion, or persuading emotionally at the expense of reasoned argument. One term which can help you here is rhetoric.

KEY TERM

Syllogisms

A traditional deductive argument structure that began with Aristotle. It involves a format that relates two reasons and a conclusion.

EXAM TIP

You need to be able to recognise syllogisms and valid and invalid reasoning if you come across them. However, most of the reasoning you will come across in the OCR Critical Thinking Unit 4 exam is likely to be inductive reasoning.

STRETCH AND CHALLENGE

Can we know anything by reason?

Do we need experience of the world in order to gain knowledge?

Find out more about deductive and inductive reasoning and their uses. Make sure you use your credibility skills to help you find reliable sources, as there are some fairly suspect websites on this subject. University websites aimed at first-year undergraduates, are often accessible and accurate.

- Expressing opinion forcefully.

Rhetorical persuasion

Rhetoric is a complex concept which is used in everyday language and academic study in different ways, which include:

- the study of the effective use of language

- the art of making persuasive speeches

- the art of influencing the thought and conduct of an audience

- the study of writing or speaking as a means of communication or persuasion.

These uses clearly cover some of the emotional and linguistic devices we have been discussing, but they also cover a lot more ground than is needed for Critical Thinking. For the purposes of OCR's Critical Thinking Unit 4 exam, you should think of **rhetorical persuasion** (rather than rhetoric) as the use of linguistic and emotional devices in persuasive argument. You should think about how these affect the nature and strength of the reasoning. You do not need to know specific technical terms from the formal study of rhetoric, but you should be able to make comments such as:

> This is an argument because it gives some support to a main conclusion that…. However, it is fairly rhetorical, relying heavily on emotional persuasion, loaded language and leading questions. The logical links are rather tenuous.

> This is an argument which supports the conclusion that … using the reasons that… It includes some rhetorical persuasion, especially in the choice of emotional language.

KEY TERM

Rhetorical persuasion

An attempt to persuade or to get us to agree with a claim, or to adopt an attitude through use of words and emotive language, rather than good reasons.

WORKED EXAMPLE 2

Read the passage below.

New technology may be changing the human brain

Neuro-biologist Baroness Susan Greenfield has made a speech in the House of Lords, asking: is technology changing our brains? The context is the clicking, beeping, flashing world of screens. There has been a change in our environment that is so all-embracing that we barely notice it. In just a couple of decades, we have slipped away from a culture based essentially on words to one based essentially on images, or pictures. This is probably one of the greatest shifts in the story of modern humans but we take it almost for granted.

There are the icons of the iPod or Windows, those cute and reassuring little pictures that perform the role of Chinese ideograms rather than Western culture's words. Then there are the winking corporate mini-logos which are more familiar to children than national flags or famous authors. Just watch a teenager navigate, with thumbs or fingertips, a world of instructions, suggestions, offers and threats, scrolling through songs, adverts, film clips and software.

My children communicate by text and computer messaging, using the post-grammar, post-spelling shorthand that everyone under 30 finds normal and everyone over 40 finds menacing. There can be little doubt that the structures, never mind the surface form, of the English language are changing fast.

Baroness Greenfield wades straight into the dangers posed by this culture. A recent survey of 8–18-year-olds suggests that they are spending 6.5 hours every day using electronic media and multi-tasking is rocketing. Greenfield asks whether this could be having an impact on thinking and learning.

Greenfield points out that 'the human brain is exquisitely sensitive to any and every event: we cannot complacently take it as an article of faith that it will remain inviolate and that consequently human nature and ways of learning and thinking will remain consistent'. She argues that there should be more government funding for research into the impact of the digital-picture world on how children learn to think.

Politicians should be seriously concerned about these changes in the way we think. Parliamentary democracy has depended on a citizenry prepared to think logically about policies and to follow arguments, such as a politician's justification for charging higher university fees. Because Greenfield's feared world without context will lead to unthinking citizens it will therefore also be a world more prone to political illogic and fad. Politicians should take a valuable ten minutes to read and reflect on Baroness Greenfield's fine speech.

Source: Jackie Ashley, *The Guardian*, 24 April 2006

Is this an argument? Justify your answer with reference to the different kinds of reasoning used.

Answer

This is not really an argument, although it contains both reasoning and argument. It starts as a report of Baroness Greenfield's speech. Its purposes include telling us about the speech, sharing views with us and considering the implications of the changes in technology that the speech mentions. There are two main strands of reasoning*. One relates to whether changes in technology are having a negative effect on culture and learning. There is a train of thought here, but there is also a lot of assertion, emotional language and some illogical leaps. There also isn't a stated conclusion that is supported in this strand of reasoning. The other strand of reasoning concludes that, 'politicians should take a valuable ten minutes to read and reflect on Baroness Greenfield's fine speech'. It is supported by a train of reasoning as follows: Greenfield has written a speech about changes in the way we think and learn; we have moved quickly from a culture based on words to a culture based in images and these changes might be affecting the way we think and learn, so this culture poses dangers. Therefore, politicians should be concerned and so they should read Greenfield's speech. Most of the passage does not support the only stated conclusion (regarding politicians) so, overall, it is not an argument.

* See Chapter 7 for a discussion of strands of reasoning.

ACTIVITY 3

Consider the following passages. For each passage answer the question:

Is this an argument? Justify your answer with reference to the different kinds of reasoning used.

Passage A: Packed lunches

A packed lunch raid has left children in tears after their crisps and biscuits have been confiscated. The school says it has repeatedly asked parents not to send their children to school with crisps and chocolate, in order to improve the learning environment. Step-dad Sean puts his arm around 8-year-old Shawna and says, 'I don't like the way they've done it, Shawna was upset. But it's like that Jamie Oliver said, kids have got to have good food if they're going to be healthy and do the best they can in life.' Most parents, however, are up in arms, claiming that teachers should not tell them what their children should eat. Mother Debbie Warton said her children were terribly upset at having their food taken away. 'They want to control our lives. I give my girls a balanced lunch. They go dancing and they're not fat. The teacher's taken half their lunch away and not replaced it with anything.' Dad Kieran May adds, 'My boy would've had sausages and chips in the canteen. Seems like it's all right for the school to provide junk dinners, but it's not alright to have crisps in your packed lunch. Doesn't make sense.' Granddad Keith said his granddaughter Charlene had been in tears. 'Seems like the school and the government want to tell us what's best. Where's it going to end? Are they going to tell us what to eat at home?'

Passage B: Selfish, smug, self-righteous, unbearable two-wheeled idiots!

1   Cyclists are a danger to us all. They're aggressive, foul-mouthed oafs, a far cry from the virtuous saints they'd have us believe they are. Once cyclists symbolised the slow, gentle pace of genteel rural life. Now they are a menace to the public and should not be allowed on our roads.

2   Gentility and modesty have been replaced with arrogance and aggression. Brimming with hostility, utterly indifferent to those around them, they appear to think they're above the law. As if laws about red lights, pavements or one-way streets applied to them! These lycra monsters ooze contempt for pedestrians and motorists, and have made travel around London a nightmare.

3   Worse, they behave as if they were somehow morally superior to the rest of us. They flaunt their politically correct badge of greenness as if it allowed them total freedom of action. Swear at motorists? Why not! Bowl pedestrians over? Abuse them for getting in the way! A green outlook is supposed to be based on a concern for your surroundings, but cyclists routinely abuse their surroundings.

4   This is all the more infuriating, as their environmentalism is, in any case, mostly posturing. Half of them have a car driving behind them with their briefcase; most of them jet off for trendy weekend breaks, oozing smugness as their planes belch noxious gases into the clouds. They do not question whether their ghastly lycra was made by exploited 6-year-olds in third world countries, or whether their trendy bicycle was manufactured in a low-wage factory in China.

5   These people don't even pay road taxes – they get to use the roads we pay for without contributing a penny, yet they abuse us for the privilege. These people should be made to pay and they should be licensed and they should be punished if they do not abide by the regulations of the road.

6 Cyclists make us law-abiding citizens foam at the mouth and dream of slashing their tyres and jamming sticks in their spokes to bring them down to earth and the realities of motoring. We need a return to a gentler era, when cyclists were well-mannered and young men were routinely locked up for cycling without lights. Then it might become clear that moral superiority does not come from owning a bicycle.

▪ These lycra monsters ooze contempt for pedestrians and motorists.

Summary

You should now:

- have revised and extended your understanding of how to identify an argument

- have a clear idea about how to identify a range of forms of reasoning using technical language such as argument, valid, conclusion, and everyday language such as report, narrative and opinion.

Learning objectives

- Revise and extend AS understandings of (some) AS analysis skills.
- Analyse the framework reasoning in a longer passage, identifying elements of reasoning.
- Analyse strands of reasoning.

NATIONALGEOGRAPHIC.COM/MAGAZINE

NATIONAL GEOGRAPHIC

CHASING
TORNADOES
A TALE OF SCIENCE, GUTS, AND LUCK

Framework reasoning

This chapter will guide you through the skills you will use when analysing **framework reasoning**. By framework reasoning we mean the main structural outline of reasoning in an article. In a long article there is likely to be quite a lot of detailed argument, as well as other kinds of reasoning. In many passages there is a conclusion supported by two or three key intermediate conclusions, which are, in turn, supported by more detailed argument.

KEY TERM

Framework reasoning

The main structural outline of reasoning in an article.

Gist and precision

In Chapter 6 you used the skill of summarising the gist of an argument in order to help you to decide whether it was an argument. In this chapter, you will focus on elements of reasoning precisely as the author has used them, as you did at AS.

Giving the gist of an argument is sometimes useful. It shows you have some understanding of a line of reasoning. When you are analysing reasoning, however, it is normal to use the author's own words. The task is to identify the author's reasons and intermediate conclusions as the author wrote them. This will help you later when you are evaluating; if you give gist versions, you might accidentally make the argument stronger or weaker – and your task is to work with the author's argument as they wrote it.

Revising AS understanding

The skill of analysing reasoning should be familiar from AS, but at A2 the emphasis is generally on broader tasks in which you have to select appropriate skills. The following quick revision exercise will make sure that you are moving on from a sound basis.

┌─ ACTIVITY ────────────────

Test yourself. Write a short definition of each of the following terms from your AS Critical Thinking course:

Conclusion	Reason	Intermediate conclusion	Assumption
Explanation	Argument	Counter-argument	Counter-assertion
Analogy	Evidence	Hypothetical reasoning	Principle

Extending AS understanding to A2

At AS the emphasis in analysis was on being able to find and state elements of reasoning. The texts you work with were structured so that each element had a clear function in the argument. At A2 there are several differences:

■ you will be working with more complex texts

■ you will learn about nuances, ambiguity and grey areas relating to familiar terms

■ you will be working with elements of argument which have a less clear-cut function in the structure of reasoning, so you will need to interpret.

Argument elements in the framework structure of complex texts

Remember that the first thing to do when analysing a text is to decide whether it is an argument or a different form of reasoning – perhaps a report that contains an argument. If the text is an argument, you must then identify the main conclusion. At A2 Critical Thinking, when using real texts, the task of identifying the main conclusion may be complicated. The argument may have a complex structure, with a number of strands of reasoning and more than one intermediate conclusion. If the article ends with an intermediate conclusion, it can be tempting to pick that instead of the main conclusion. Remember to test your decision by checking whether the element you have decided on is actually supported by all the other elements of the reasoning.

Identifying the reasons in a longer text

When you are doing a framework analysis of a passage, you need to identify the most important grounds – the main reasons – given to support the conclusion. Remember that these main reasons are often supported by other reasoning. In the context of a framework, or outline (analysis) we call them reasons, but in the context of the whole passage of reasoning, many of them will be intermediate conclusions.

> **REMEMBER**
>
> A reason which gives support to the main conclusion in the framework structure is usually supported by evidence and other reasons, so it is often an intermediate conclusion. You can refresh your memory on this in Chapter 8 of *AS Critical Thinking for OCR*.

WORKED EXAMPLE 3

Public art – a powerful and positive image

▪ Marc Quinn's sculpture of Alison Lapper.

Read the article below.

1 Marc Quinn's sculpture of Alison Lapper, officially unveiled on the fourth plinth of Trafalgar Square yesterday, is now one of the most striking sights in London. Ms Lapper was born with no arms and shortened legs as a result of a congenital disorder. In Quinn's sculpture, she is depicted eight months pregnant and naked. It is a powerful and positive image. As the artist himself puts it: 'It is so rare to see disability in everyday life – let alone naked, pregnant and proud.'

2 Those perplexed by the notion of a disabled person on a pedestal might bear in mind that Nelson, whose own monument adorns the same square, had one arm. The sculpture is also a clever echo of those revered icons of antiquity such as the Venus de Milo and the Apollo Belvedere, neither of which is considered ugly because of its missing limbs. The sculpture provokes thoughts on heroism too. According to the Mayor of London, Ken Livingstone, whose office underwrote this project: 'This square celebrates the courage of men in battle. Alison's life is a struggle to overcome much greater difficulties than many of the men we celebrate and commemorate here.'

3 Not all will agree with this. But the virtue of the sculpture is that it encourages people to address such issues. Some have taken issue with Quinn's workmanship, calling Alison Lapper Pregnant a 'concept' rather than a sculpture. But this is a side issue. It is true that Quinn's work was created with moulds. But so were the bronzes of Henry Moore, which adorn many a public space. And we must be careful not to be drawn into a sterile debate about the merits of conceptual art.

4 Regardless of whether people like this artwork aesthetically or not, it has generated a welcome debate about public sculpture and what it is for. From Antony Gormley's iron figures in Liverpool to Millennium Square in Bristol, public art in Britain is capturing the imagination. Giancarlo Neri's sculpture of a giant table and chair on Hampstead Heath has become a focal point for the local community in a way that few anticipated.

5 Controversy was recently generated over a rock sculpture called Monolith and Shadow commissioned to stand outside a new London hospital. It was described as a '£70,000 pebble' by the down-market press. But this only served to demonstrate their knowledge of the price of everything and the value of nothing. Public art, whether commissioned by the public or private sector, has the capacity to enhance our cities and our quality of life. Alison Lapper Pregnant is a welcome addition to our capital's collection of artistic riches.

Source: *The Independent*, 16 September 2005

Let's ask three of the questions we considered in Chapter 6:

- What am I being persuaded to accept (what is the conclusion)?

- How am I being persuaded to accept this (what sort of reasoning is being used)?

- On what grounds am I supposed to accept this (what are the main reasons)?

We are being persuaded to accept that 'Alison Lapper Pregnant' is a welcome addition to our capital's collection of artistic riches. The author is reporting a recent event and trying to persuade us to accept their opinion about this event. Much of the persuasion is done by reporting and by juxtaposing and suggesting ideas, rather than by giving reasons. For example, paragraph 2, gives examples of other statues without arms to persuade 'those perplexed by the notion of a disabled person on a pedestal' that 'images of people who lack limbs (and therefore images of disability) can be beautiful'. Although this is only implied, it is an important reason for the main conclusion (an assumed reason). Other main reasons given are:

- It [the statue of Alison Lapper] is a powerful and positive image.

- The sculpture provokes thoughts on heroism too.

- The virtue of the sculpture is that it addresses such issues (disability, beauty, heroism).

- It [the statue] has generated a welcome debate about public sculpture and what it is for.

- Public art has the capacity to enhance our cities and our quality of life.

Comment

Note that we have used the author's own words for the stated reasons *almost* exactly. Where a sentence in the author's own words doesn't make sense out of context it is good practice to fill in the context with a couple of words so that it does make sense. For example, 'It is a powerful and positive image' makes sense only if you know what 'it' is. So it is good practice to include the words '[the statue of Alison Lapper]'. You will not, however, be required to do this in the exam when time is an issue.

Understanding the framework structure in an exam

In the exam you will be under time pressure. You will not necessarily have time to write out the framework structure in full – especially if the questions do not ask for this. However, you will find it easier to answer the analysis and evaluation questions if you do have a clear idea of the framework structure. You can think about this structure as you read.

When you are reading through the resource material, you might find it useful to annotate it, to help you remember what you have thought. You could use a number of methods – the key is to find a method that suits you.

WORKED EXAMPLE 4

The following text has been annotated to help a candidate remember the sorts of reasoning being used and to find key parts of the framework structure.

Consumer capitalism is making us ill – we need a therapy state

context

IC

1 (Britain is becoming unhappier as depression, crime and *MC or* alcoholism grow.) Government can and should intervene. *summary or signpost?*

2 Britain may have got very much richer in the past 40 years but it has not got happier. In fact, by measures such as epression, crime, obesity and alcoholism, <u>we have got very much unhappier.</u> *R*

3 Research has established more clearly than ever what the most likely predictors of happiness are, and there are now proven methods to treat unhappiness. Happiness is no longer an elusive, fuzzy feeling: a body of data gives us the tools to analyse what it is and what causes it. Happiness has gone respectable, and it's been tagged to intellectual disciplines – the science of happiness, happiness economics – <u>so it will be taken more seriously.</u> *IC*

4 But there is an even more pressing reason to take happiness seriously – <u>unhappiness is an expensive business.</u> Mental ill *R/IC* health is the biggest single cause of incapacity and costs the country an estimated £9 billion in lost productivity and benefits. The weight on the NHS is enormous.

5 Plus, there is a whole range of political issues which have roots *R?* in mental health, from obesity and alcoholism, to parenting, the respect agenda and anti-social behaviour among children and young people. *function?* { *report? opinion?*

6 <u>The old liberal concept that the emotional life of citizens is no</u> *R* <u>business of the state is crumbling.</u> This raises the prospect of a future politics where emotional well being could be as important a remit of state public health policy as our physical well-being. In 10 years' time, alongside 'five fruit and veg a day,' our kids could be chanting comparable mantras for daily emotional well-being: do some exercise, do someone a good turn, count your blessings, laugh, savour beauty.

7 We might also be discussing emotional pollution in much the way we now discuss environmental pollution. Top of the list would be advertising, which is bad for our emotional health. It induces dissatisfaction with its invidious comparisons with an affluent elite. There would also be a strong rationale to increase subsidies for festivals, parks, theatres, community groups, amateur dramatics, choirs and sports clubs.

use of laguage to persuade?

consequences/ prediction

emotion & language?

opposing view

8 To some, these kinds of interventions represent a nightmare scenario of a nanny state, an unacceptable interference in personal freedom. If people want to pursue their own unhappiness, then the state has no right to stop them.

9 But the problem is, as Richard Layard argues in his book *Happiness: Lessons from a New Science*, that the decline of both religious belief (a strong predictor of happiness) and the social solidarity movements of the 20th century has left a vacuum of understanding about what constitutes a good life and how to be happy.

unsupported

10 The church has lost sway, and the state has retreated behind the *R* single rationale of promoting economic competitiveness with its overtones of Darwinian selection (a major source of unhappiness in itself with its vision of life as a competitive struggle). That *IC* leaves the market a free rein to describe happiness – the new car, new sofa, new holiday – and to manipulate our insecurities around status.

11 Leave things as they are and the state will increasingly have to *IC* pick up the bill for how consumer capitalism effectively produces emotional ill health – depression, stress, anxiety. Leave things as they are and the state is part of the problem, promoting a set of *R/IC* market values that produce emotional pollution. (The state should *MC* resume a role in promoting the good life, not just chivvy us along in the global rat race, anxious and insecure.)

answer to opposing view

Source: Madeleine Bunting, *The Guardian*, 5 December 2005

Comment

Note that the candidate has used different colours. There are two claims underlined in blue: the candidate is considering that one of these might be the main conclusion. The annotations show that the candidate has thought of a number of functions for the first of these elements before finally deciding that it is an intermediate conclusion (IC) which is supported by most of the reasoning (R) and which supports the main conclusion. This is a reasonable decision: most of the reasoning supports the claim that 'government can and should intervene'. This claim can be seen as supporting the final sentence. *Because* it can and should intervene, 'the state should resume a role in promoting the good life, not just chivvy us along in the global rat race, anxious and insecure'. What is here seen as the main conclusion shown, *how* the government/state should intervene?

However, it would also be reasonable to make a different decision here. It would be quite possible to argue that, 'government can and should intervene' is the main conclusion, and that the final sentence is a more or less unsupported statement of the author's opinion about *how* this should happen. This claim is quite reliant on rhetorical persuasion, using emotionally charged language such as 'chivvy'. It's quite a leap from intervening in increasing unhappiness to 'promoting the good life', and the author is using opposite concepts to persuade us rather than really supporting this claim.

Reasons and intermediate conclusions have been labelled in green, and the candidate has labelled R/IC at times. This might reflect a changing view of what that element is, or an uncertainty about whether a claim is supported. For example, 'the state is part of the problem'. This is a key claim in the reasoning to support the (intermediate) conclusion that 'government can and should intervene'. If the state is part of the problem, then it should make changes such that it is no longer part of the problem. Whether it is an intermediate conclusion or just a reason depends on whether it is supported. It is a matter of interpretation whether this claim is supported.

It could be seen as supported by 'the state has retreated behind the single rationale of promoting economic competitiveness'. It could be seen as supported by [because it promotes] 'a set of market values that promote emotional pollution'. However, this could be argued to be summary, rhetorical persuasion and statement of opinion rather than reasons supporting an intermediate conclusion.

ACTIVITY 5

Consider how you might best annotate an article in exam conditions. Work with newspaper articles to practise. You need to find a method that works for you.

ACTIVITY 6

Read the following passage. Work out the framework reasoning and note the kinds of reasoning being used (You might want to practise annotating the text, but if the book does not belong to you, you should write the key elements out in full.)

Family holidays are best avoided as they have too many disadvantages. We plan a perfect escape from our everyday lives, only to find that we actually have to live through it. Parents still find their children selfish, ungrateful and demanding, and can't understand why the kids would rather text their friends than look around art galleries. Children still find their parents weird, annoying and embarrassing, and can't understand why they couldn't just go to Disneyland. And neither has anything to say that the other would find interesting. So we spend the whole holiday squabbling. Because we can't get away from each other, and because we feel the pressure to enjoy 'family time', but don't, we argue more.   1

In addition to this, being in a strange place takes us out of our comfort zone. This is tiring and makes us less tolerant of other people being difficult. So the holiday is actually more stressful than staying home. Because we set our expectations of a perfect, harmonious family idyll so high. This stress is unreasonably disappointing and makes us even more stressed. So the thousands we spend on family holidays are wasted.   2

You only ever see the resort you are staying in, not the country you are visiting. You'll speak the same language, see the same people, eat the same food and behave in the same way, so you may as well still be at home. Except, of course, that you will experience some interesting and different illnesses. If you do make it out of the hotel, you'll probably get heat exhaustion battling through the crowds of other fraught families to the sights. Unless you're in northern Europe, in which case you can try out a new variant of the cold virus. Wherever you are, you'll get the local stomach bugs and a chance to inspect the hygiene facilities more closely than you really wanted to.   3

And then there's the trip home, trapped in a small metal cage with all the people (and their irritating habits) you would most wish a million miles away.   4

Deciding what function an element has

As you have seen, an element might have different functions in a passage of reasoning, or it might be unclear what its function is. Don't worry about this. There are some strategies you can use to help yourself decide:

■ Always ask yourself: 'Is this part of an argument structure? Or is this element serving a different purpose in this text?'

■ Always ask yourself: 'Is this claim supported? Does it give support?'

■ Look out for argument indicators such as 'therefore' and 'because'.

■ If you are uncertain which is the main conclusion and which is an important intermediate conclusion, ask yourself: 'Does either of these give me a reason to accept the other?'

Strands of reasoning

At AS Level Critical Thinking we considered how reasons support a conclusion. At A2, however, we need to extend this understanding to **strands of reasoning**. For example, let's take the following argument:

> **R1** Walking to work is much better for the environment than driving.
> **R2** Walking is also much better for your health.
> **R3** As you live just a mile from work,
> **C** you should walk to work.

Here we have three simple reasons which support the conclusion independently. We can show this with a simple diagram:

If we wanted to develop the argument, we could make R1 and R2 into intermediate conclusions by supporting them with evidence, examples and additional reasons. This would give us two strands of reasoning as follows:

> Cars release pollutants such as carbon monoxide into the atmosphere, causing air pollution which leads to acid rain, deforestation and global warming. They also depend on a rapidly depleting stock of fossil fuels, so their use is simply not sustainable. **Walking has very little impact on the environment, so walking to work is much better for the environment than driving.**
>
> If you drive to work, you do not use your muscles much. If you walk, you exercise your muscles, get your blood circulating and strengthen your heart. This means you are less likely to suffer heart disease if you walk than if you drive. **So walking to work is better for your health than driving.** As you live just a mile from work, you should walk.

- Walk to work…

Now there are two strands of reasoning, one relating to the environment, the other to your health. If you wanted to analyse the argument, you would now have a choice. You could analyse the framework structure. This would produce the simple analysis and diagram we saw above. You might comment on the extra support given to two of the reasons, but would not show it in detail.

Applying your understanding of strands of reasoning

So how does this idea of strands of reasoning apply to the longer passages we have already worked with? Look back at worked example 2 on pages 121–22. In the comment, we said, 'There are two main strands of reasoning. One relates to whether changes in technology are having a negative effect on culture…. The other strand of reasoning concludes that, "politicians should take a valuable ten minutes to read and reflect on Baroness Greenfield's fine speech".'

Here you can see that an understanding of strands of reasoning can help you to analyse the kinds of reasoning in a passage. In this instance there were two strands of reasoning, one which was argument and one which was not, so we were able to decide that the whole passage was not an argument.

An understanding of strands of reasoning can also help you with the framework analysis of a passage. It is a way of dividing the passage into logical, easy-to-manage segments. It can help you to find the main reasons and how they are related to each other.

WORKED EXAMPLE 5

Comment on any strands of reasoning used by Bunting in the article 'Consumer capitalism is making us ill – we need a therapy state', pages 131–32.

Answer

Bunting's argument to support the claim that the government 'should resume a role promoting the good life' is supported by two main strands of reasoning. One strand shows that the government can intervene [in Britain's unhappiness]. The other strand shows that the government should intervene [in Britain's unhappiness]. This strand is more complex than the first strand and can be divided into further strands of reasoning; one which deals with expense, one which deals with our attitude to state intervention in our personal lives, and one which shows that there is a real need for state intervention. Because this is a journalistic piece using report, rhetorical persuasion and suggestion, there is no an intermediate conclusion at the end of each of these strands as there was in the example about walking to work [see page 135]. The strands are also entwined rather than neatly separated into paragraphs.

Gist and precision in strands of reasoning

When you are analysing strands of reasoning in a passage, you are likely to use a combination of gist and precision analysis. Where the author is using argument in a very clear and structured way, you should talk about a strand of reasoning relating to [topic], supporting the significant IC 'quote'. Where the author is using suggestion, implication, juxtaposition of ideas or rhetorical persuasion, you are likely to find that many of the significant ideas have not actually been stated or supported. In this case, you will need to use your own language to express some of the strands of reasoning. This may involve giving the gist of the strand of reasoning, and/or pinpointing as precisely as you can in your own words what the author wants to persuade you to accept, but has not actually stated.

▪ The cooling towers of a nuclear power station.

ACTIVITY 7

Comment on any strands of reasoning used in the article below.

Who says nuclear power is clean?

1 Three massive claims are being made for Britain building a new generation of nuclear stations: firstly, it is the only way that Britain can meet its ambitious targets for reducing carbon emissions; secondly, it is the only reliable option available if we are to fill the energy gap left by declining sources of fossil fuels; thirdly it is the best way of ensuring that our energy comes from 'secure' sources, rather than unstable oil-rich oligarchies.

2 These claims are at best specious, at worst untrue. Take carbon emission. There is a blithe notion that nuclear power is 'clean' – it emits no CO_2 and therefore does not contribute to global warming. This argument has been systematically taken apart over the past five years by two independent experts, one a chemist and energy specialist, the other a nuclear physicist. They have looked at the entire life cycle of a nuclear power station, from the mining of the uranium to the storage of the resulting nuclear waste. Their conclusions make grim reading for any nuclear advocate.

3   They say that, at the present rate of use, worldwide supplies of rich uranium ore will soon become exhausted, perhaps within the next decade. Nuclear power stations of the future will have to rely on second-grade ore, which requires huge amounts of conventional energy to mine it. For each tonne of poor-quality uranium, some 5000 tonnes of granite will have to be mined, milled and then disposed of. This could rise to 10,000 tonnes if the quality deteriorates further. At some point, and it could happen soon, the nuclear industry will be emitting as much carbon dioxide from mining and treating its ore as it saves from the 'clean' power it produces thanks to nuclear fission.

4   At this stage, according to an article by the energy writer Fleming, 'nuclear power production would go into energy deficit. It would be putting more energy into the process than it could extract from it. Its contribution to meeting the world's energy needs would become negative.' The so-called 'reliability' of nuclear power would therefore rest on the growing use of fossil fuels rather than their replacement.

5   Worse, the number of nuclear plants needed to meet the world's needs would be colossal. At present, about 440 reactors supply about 2% of demand. The Massachusetts Institute of Technology calculates that 1000 more would be needed to raise this even to 10% of need. At this point, the search for new sources of ore would become critical. Where would they come from? Not friendly Canada, which produces most of it at present, but places like Kazakhstan, hardly the most stable of democracies. So much for 'secure' sources of energy. We would find ourselves out of the oil-producing frying pan, right in the middle of the ore-manufacturing fire.

6   These arguments have to be met before other, more searching questions are answered about where we intend to store waste, what we are going to do to prevent radioactive leaks, and how we should protect nuclear plants against terrorism. The truth is that this form of energy is, in the end, no more safe, reliable or clean than the others. That does not mean turning our backs on it: it means confronting reality rather than myth.

7   The decision to go nuclear will make the case for renewable energy stronger rather than weaker. There has been a growing sense that the government has lost faith in wind, wave and tidal power, on the grounds that the public has turned against them and that their efficiency is doubtful. Wind turbines in particular have been subjected to sustained local campaigns and derisive columns from the pro-nuclear lobby. They have one great advantage, however – they are genuinely reversible. A wind turbine, unlike a

nuclear reactor, can be removed once it has come to the end of its natural life.

8   Nor, in comparison to nuclear power are they gravely inefficient. Of course, a wind farm depends on wind, which may or may not blow, and a wave machine is similarly weather-dependent. But both need to be part of Britain's energy jigsaw. It is absurd, for instance, that the government is withholding the £50 million investment that is needed to turn wave power into a commercial proposition. Experiments in the Orkney Islands have proved so promising that the Portuguese government has bought the technology.

9   The British government must not exclude options other than nuclear power. Nuclear is not trouble free, and the more you look at it, the more enticing the other choices become.

Source: Magnus Linklater, *The Times*, 23 November 2005

How might these skills be tested in the exam?

As you have seen, an element might have a very clear function in the structure of an argument. However, it might equally have two or more functions, or it might be unclear exactly what its function is. Don't worry about this – just remember to justify your interpretation in the exam.

Let's consider one common way in which understanding of the framework structure of reasoning is tested. We will first take an example of an element with a clear function.

'Family holidays have too many disadvantages.'

(Activity 6, page 134, paragraph 1).

Name this element and briefly explain its function in the structure of the reasoning. [2]

Answer A
Main conclusion. It sums up all the other reasons which lead into it.

Answer B
Intermediate conclusion. It is supported by reasons and gives support to another intermediate conclusion.

Answer C
Intermediate conclusion. It is an IC supported by most of the reasoning in the passage and giving direct support to the main conclusion that 'family holidays are best avoided'.

EXAM TIP

Where there isn't one clear 'right' answer, the examiners will give credit for a number of different possible answers.

Answer D
Straw man – distorting the argument in favour of family holidays by overstatement, missing out important evidence and emotive use of language which persuades us in all the wrong ways and just isn't true.

■ *Answer A is wrong*. This element cannot be interpreted as the main conclusion of the argument because it gives support to the claim, 'family holidays are best avoided'. It does not make sense to argue: 'family holidays are best avoided' *therefore* 'They have too many disadvantages'. The explanation does *not* make sense. Conclusions do not 'sum up' reasons, they follow from them. Summarising is a different skill from drawing or supporting a conclusion. This answer would be awarded no marks in an examination.

■ *Answer B*. The name of the element is accurate, but the explanation does not go much beyond a definition of IC. It is also inaccurate to say that it supports another IC – in this case the support is given directly to the main conclusion. This answer would be awarded one mark in an examination.

■ *Answer C*. This answer is accurate and precise. It shows precisely what this element does in the structure of this reasoning. It gains full marks here.

■ *Answer D*. This answer is doing the wrong task. 'Straw man' is a flaw (also known as straw person), not an element in the structure of reasoning. The answer talks about types of reasoning and even disagrees with the reasoning, but does not name the element or explain its function in the structure of the reasoning.

Now let's look at a similar way of testing your understanding of the framework structure, using a claim with a less clear function:

'The state should resume a role in promoting the good life, not just chivvy us along in the global rat race, anxious and insecure.'

(Taken from Bunting, 'Consumer capitalism is making us ill – we need a therapy state', page 132, paragraph 11).

Name and explain the function of this element in the structure of Bunting's reasoning.   [4]

Answer A
This is the main conclusion of the argument, flowing from all the other reasons.

Answer B
This is probably what the author intends as her main conclusion, even though it is only partly supported by the reasoning. It is somewhat supported by the important IC, 'The government can and should intervene (in Britain's unhappiness)'.

EXAM TIP

Note two differences from the previous question: 'explain' rather than 'Briefly explain', and 4 marks rather than 2. Both of these differences indicate that you need to think carefully and answer this question in more **depth** (not necessarily at greater length!)

Answer C
This is a rhetorical flourish which the author clearly thinks we should agree with but which hasn't been properly supported.

■ *Answer A* has shown a basic understanding. It is certainly possible to interpret this claim as the main conclusion – but it is vague to say that a conclusion 'flows' from reasons.

■ *Answer B* has shown a sound and fairly thorough understanding. It shows that the candidate is aware of the need for interpretation.

■ *Answer C* hovers between basic and clear understanding. It would be possible to develop this answer such that it was better than answer B – but as it is written, it could apply to any argument and doesn't quite show that the candidate has understood this particular reasoning rather than making a guess. It uses vague language rather than precise technical terms. Let's look at how this understanding could have been shown more clearly:

This is a fairly unsupported statement of the author's opinion about what the government should do, persuading us with language and emotion, ('resume', 'good life', 'chivvy', etc). The author has supported the claim that 'The government can and should intervene [in Britain's unhappiness]', and clearly intends us to accept the given claim as *how* the government should intervene. However, it's just too much of a logical leap from 'intervening' in unhappiness to promoting the good life' for this to count as a claim that is supported.

This form of question has come up many times in past Unit 4 exams. There are other ways to test your understanding of framework structure of reasoning. Some examples might be:

Identify the framework structure of reasoning in Document 2. Justify your answer (where appropriate).

Comment on any strands of reasoning in Document 1. Justify your answer (where appropriate).

Summarise the main lines of reasoning in Document 3 in your own words.

Answering the letter question would be a useful way for you to deal with articles which use strands of reasoning but which do not clearly state their argument. Even if it never comes up as an exam question, it can provide useful practice.

REMEMBER — ！

Always show an understanding of different strands of argument.

Summary

You should now be able to analyse the framework structure of an article:

- using your AS understanding of analysis

- applying and extending your AS understanding to longer passages containing different kinds of reasoning

- analysing strands of reasoning.

Learning objectives

- Analyse arguments into elements.
- Analyse the structure of reasoning, identifying joint and independent reasons.
- Use argument diagrams to show argument structure.

Analysing arguments into elements

The first step in a detailed analysis of an argument or part of an argument, is to break the reasoning down into its component parts: elements of argument (such as **reasons** and **conclusion**) and elements of **reasoning** which are not part of the argument (such as scene setting). You have done this in a broader sense when you looked at the different kinds of reasoning in a passage. When you are analysing in detail you are working with the detail of a passage rather than the framework or outline.

Let's look at a simple example:

> It is seven o'clock in the evening. I am hungry. It is time for dinner.

This can be broken down as follows:

> **R1**   It is seven o'clock in the evening.
> **R2**   I am hungry.
> **C**   It is time for dinner.

REMEMBER !

We use R to mean Reason, and C to mean Conclusion when we are analysing and annotating argument.

Remember that something subjective, such as 'I am hungry', can be a perfectly acceptable reason to support a conclusion. An argument which consisted only of opinions would come dangerously close to ranting instead of arguing, but opinions, preferences and subjective claims do have a place in argument.

Note that it is normal to show the main conclusion at the end of your analysis, whenever it occurs in the passage.

Now let's look at a slightly more complex example:

> There is an ongoing debate about whether it was right to give President Obama the Nobel Peace Prize after just nine months in office. It clearly was the right decision because Obama has changed the whole atmosphere of international relations. He has started from the basis that understanding between people is possible, and can be achieved through negotiation. We have therefore seen an increased willingness amongst other world leaders to negotiate rather than attack.

This argument can be analysed as follows:

Context: There is an ongoing debate about whether it was right to give President Obama the Nobel Peace Prize after just nine months in office.

R1: He has started from the basis that understanding between people is possible and can be achieved through negotiation.

KEY TERMS

Reason (R) ●

Normally a general statement, which supports a conclusion by giving us grounds or information which helps us to believe, accept or agree with the conclusion.

Conclusion (C) ●

A claim which is intended to persuade the reader and is drawn from a reason or reasons.

Reasoning ●

A thread of persuasive thought, connected in a logical manner.

EXAM TIP ○

A single sentence can have more than one argument element. Make sure you use argument indicators such as 'because' and 'therefore' to help you. If a sentence includes 'because' or 'therefore', check whether there is a reason and intermediate conclusion, for example.

IC1: We have therefore seen an increased willingness amongst other world leaders to negotiate rather than attack.

IC2: Obama has changed the whole atmosphere of international relations.

C: It [giving Obama the Nobel Peace Prize] was clearly the right decision.

Interpretation

Even in detailed analysis of argument, there can be some room for interpretation. In the first example we looked at, there was very little room for interpretation. You might want to argue that it was actually an explanation of why I am hungry rather than an argument to persuade us that it is dinner time, but in this case the order of the sentences probably indicates that it is an argument with two reasons supporting the conclusion, 'It is time for dinner'.

The second example is more open to interpretation. It could reasonably be seen as an explanation of how Obama has changed the whole atmosphere of international relations, supporting the conclusion. If we saw it like this, we would analyse it as follows:

Context: There is an ongoing debate about whether it was right to give President Obama the Nobel Peace Prize after just nine months in office.

Explanation: Cause – he has started from the basis that understanding between people is possible and can be achieved through negotiation.

Consequence: We have seen an increased willingness amongst other world leaders to negotiate rather than attack.

R: Obama has changed the whole atmosphere of international relations.

C: It [giving Obama the Nobel Peace Prize] was clearly the right decision.

During the rest of this chapter there will be very little emphasis on interpretation. Exam passages for detailed analysis are chosen to minimise the need for interpretation; you should try to find a clear analysis of the argument. If there are two different ways of interpreting the argument, the examiners will credit either.

Argument elements – extending your understanding

Evidence and examples

One way of strengthening an argument is to use **evidence** and **examples**. Facts, figures and statistics can support a general point if they are well used. Specific examples can illustrate a reason, making it seem more credible because there is a concrete example which links the reason to real life rather than just possibility. For example:

> London is a multicultural city. More than two million from the eight million total population are from ethnic minorities. There are 376,000 black Africans and 437,000 Indians. 58 per cent of Londoners describe themselves as Christians, 8.5 per cent Muslims, 4 per cent as Hindus, 2.1 per cent as Jewish and 1.5 per cent as Sikhs. Many individuals in London are themselves multicultural. Sabiha Cohen, for example, has a Muslim mother, who was born in Nigeria, and a Jewish father, whose grandparents came from Hungary. Eight out of ten Londoners think the city's cultural diversity is one of its most attractive features.

KEY TERMS

● **Evidence (Ev)**

Facts, figures, statistics and specific information that can be used to support a claim.

● **Example (Ex)**

A specific instance which is used to illustrate a claim. An example does not support a reason in the same way as evidence, although a counter example can be used to demonstrate that a claim is false.

In this passage, the evidence (taken from 2003) about the ethnic origins and faiths of Londoners gives us reason to accept the general claim that London is a multicultural city. The last piece of evidence about eight out of ten Londoners does not support this claim. The example of Sabiha Cohen illustrates how individuals are multicultural, and makes the idea seem more believable but does not provide logical support.

Assumptions

Assumptions are missing steps in the argument. They are unstated but must be accepted if the conclusion is also to be accepted. It is important to take the time to consider any assumptions underlying an argument. It is often precisely those steps in an argument which are not stated that weaken it.

When you are identifying assumptions, you need to be careful to phrase them precisely, to make sure that you are correctly stating the unstated step of the argument. You can think of assumptions as missing pieces in a jigsaw. You need to find the piece which precisely fills the gap rather than making a similar claim which is too strong or too weak. Let's look at an example:

> We have been listening for radio signals from intelligent alien life forms for decades now, but we have heard nothing. So there can be no other intelligent life apart from us.

This argument clearly makes an assumption about alien life forms and radio signals. We need to specify precisely what that assumption is. Let's look at some options:

'All alien life forms use use radio signals.' This is too strong. The argument is talking about listening for intelligent alien life, and it would still work if there were some primitive alien life forms which did not use radio signals.

'Some intelligent alien life forms might use radio signals.' This is too weak. The argument moves from us having heard no radio signals from other life forms to there being no other intelligent life forms. If only some intelligent alien life forms use radio signals, then our failure to find radio signals does not necessarily mean that there are no intelligent life forms.

'All intelligent life forms use radio signals.' This does have to be assumed to move from our failure to find radio signals to the conclusion that there is therefore no other intelligent life than us.

Here is another example:

> It is not a bad thing to allow children to work. If children work for their pocket money, they learn the value of both labour and money. They therefore gain more respect for both, and this helps them mature into responsible citizens. This is much more important than being politically correct.

The challenge with assumptions is to recognise a gap in the reasoning and to find a way of phrasing that missing part of the reasoning precisely.

EXAM TIP

When you are analysing in detail, it is normally possible to get full marks without mentioning assumptions. That is, you can concentrate on the elements of argument that are written down. However, there is more than one route to full marks. If you do accurately identify and state an assumption, you will get credit for doing so.

ACTIVITY 8

Analyse the following arguments in detail by identifying elements of argument.

A Research suggests that there is a sleep trigger, which slows down in adolescence. This makes it difficult for teenagers to go to sleep early. This is also why teenagers struggle to get up early. This means that it is unfair to expect teenagers to attend morning lessons, so schools and colleges should rearrange their working days to start after lunch and finish during the evening.

B Our attempts to recycle are counter-productive. The point of recycling is to reduce the litter that does not decompose. The recycling boxes, which do not have lids, are regularly blown over on recycling day. There is therefore an increase in damaging litter on the streets as a direct result of our attempts to recycle such litter. We should abandon this futile effort.

Counter-argument

At AS you learned that counter-argument was, 'An additional argument that is against, or counter to, what the conclusion seeks to establish. The writer normally presents the counter argument in order to dismiss it'.

At A2 you need to be aware that the term 'counter-argument' can be used in more than one way. 'Counter' means oppose or answer. So any argument which opposes or answers a claim, or argument, is countering that claim or argument. This opposing argument is then a counter-argument.

Let's look at an example that we first used in Chapter 6 (page 111):

Argument: The theme parks in Orlando are the best in the world, because they have a great mix of thrill rides, zoos, water parks and film tie-ins.

Argument against the conclusion: The theme parks in Orlando are not the best in the world. Ohio theme parks have a much greater concentration of thrill rides, and there are theme parks in Hong Kong and Japan which look even better.

Here, the 'argument against the conclusion' can be called a counter-argument. In a television or radio debate, for example, you might have several speakers, who each counter the argument (or part of the argument of the previous speakers):

Presenter:
There is an ongoing debate about whether it was right to give President Obama the Nobel Peace Prize after just nine months in office. Let's hear what the members of our panel have to say.

> **Peace activist:**
> Obama has made a huge contribution to international peace because he has persuaded warring nations to negotiate, he has committed to withdrawing troops from Iran and is looking for a way forward on Afghanistan. He has changed international relations.
>
> **Politician:**
> Obama might talk the talk on negotiation and peace, but he remains the leader of a nation at war. He isn't actually taking action – he's all spin. He does not deserve the Peace Prize.
>
> **Academic:**
> I disagree, there. I think he may well deserve the peace prize, but it's too early to know. The leader of a nation at war who is trying to end those wars is making a contribution to world peace. The question is whether he will succeed – and I think it is success that we should reward, not the attempt.

Here, the politician is countering the reasoning of the peace activist, and the academic is countering the reasoning of the politician: they are making counter-arguments.

You need to be aware of this broader use of the term 'counter-argument'. You should also be aware of – and able to identify – the ways in which counter-argument is used and countered (or responded to) in journalistic articles of the kind found in quality newspapers and magazines, that is, in the kind or reasoning you are likely to come across in the OCR A2 Unit 4 Critical Reasoning exam.

Many authors take a counter-argument – that is, an argument which opposes their own – and include a brief version (or part) of it in their own reasoning. They often also counter or respond to this brief counter-argument. These authors generally have word limits and they mostly want to put forward their own views and arguments, so they don't give equal coverage to their own argument and to the counter-argument.

Let's look at an example:

> Obama is a worthy recipient of the Nobel Peace Prize because he has changed the atmosphere in world international relations. Although some argue that he does not deserve the prize because he is all spin and no action, this is an unjust claim. Obama has taken action towards peace by withdrawing troops from Iraq. Furthermore, his calm talk is in itself making the world more peaceful.

Let's look at how we would analyse this argument into its elements. The main conclusion is that 'Obama is a worthy recipient of the Nobel Peace Prize'. The reasoning given for this includes a refutation of a claim from a counter-argument. So, the analysis looks like this:

> **R1** He [Obama] has changed the atmosphere in world international relations.

> ## REMEMBER
>
> As you learned in Unit 2, refute means 'demonstrate to be wrong'.
> A refutation is one form of countering an argument which opposes your
> own (a counter-argument).

Counter-argument:

R (of CA) He [Obama] is all spin and no action.

C (of CA) He [Obama] does not deserve the prize.

Counter to counter-argument/response to counter-argument:

R1 Obama has taken action towards peace by withdrawing troops from Iraq.

IC This [the claim that Obama is all spin and no action] is an unjust claim.

R2 His [Obama's] calm talk is in itself making the world more peaceful.

C Obama is a worthy recipient of the Nobel Peace Prize.

Principles

As you learned in Units 2 and 3, principles are rule-like claims which apply beyond the immediate circumstances of an argument and generally help us to decide what to do or think. For example, 'All people deserve equal opportunities.' A principle may function as a reason, intermediate conclusion or conclusion in an argument. Assumptions are often principles.

Hypothetical claims

Hypothetical claims consider the consequences that may happen if a particular event occurs. They usually take the form, 'if … then'. For example, 'If I don't bother going to work, then my boss will sack me.' Remember to distinguish hypothetical claims which consider 'what if…' from 'even if…' statements. An 'even if' statement, such as 'I'm going to the party even if you're not', defines conditions rather than considering consequences.

Analogies

Analogies work by saying that two situations are so similar that a conclusion, claim or reasoning that can be accepted about one situation should also be accepted about the other. The two situations are said to be parallel. For example:

> Identifying the structure of an argument is like looking at a skeleton. It helps you to understand how the structure works.

At AS you will have come across analogies which are very clearly specified. For example:

> New road building can have a negative social impact. Feeding our addiction to cars (which everyone knows are bad for us) by building new roads must be wrong in the same way that it has been proven that giving alcohol to an alcoholic causes health problems.
>
> Sourse: OCR Unit 2 exam June 2007

In real-life passages and in your A2 exam you will come across analogies where the reader is expected to do most of the work. The analogy above might be expressed in real life as:

> Building new roads can have a negative social impact. It would be like giving alcohol to an alcoholic.

The reader is then expected to fill in the gaps and understand that giving alcohol to an alcoholic is harmful for the individual and for society. The unstated expectation is that you would not give alcohol to an alcoholic because it would be harmful. Because the two situations are held to be significantly similar, people who depend on roads are cast as road addicts, and the implication is that you would not give them roads. The pattern of reasoning is the same whether all the parts of the analogy are specified or not.

ACTIVITY 9

Analyse the following arguments.

A Even if only a tiny percentage of all the billions of stars have planets which can support life, that's still billions of planets. Therefore, we are told, it's pretty conclusive that life exists somewhere else in the universe. But it just can't be there. If the chance of extra-terrestrial life in the universe is so overwhelming, it is surprising, on a fantastic scale, that absolutely no evidence exists of it. When we look up at the night sky at all those billions of stars, we simply see a cold, uneventful and – apart from natural phenomena – dead universe. If the chances of life were as abundant as the common theory suggests, there would be millions of different alien races out there, all at different levels of evolution. It's simply not plausible to believe that every one of them has decided to hide from us.

Source: www.wearealoneintheuniverse.com
(This website address is made-up and for illustration purposes only.)

B Freedom of speech is a fundamental part of our democracy. However, we should not abuse this freedom. Being entitled to carry a gun does not entitle you to kill and maim other people at random. So preventing people from persistently ridiculing a group of people, or prohibiting incitement to religious or racial hatred does not go against the principle of free speech. It merely puts civilised limits on its use.

C Undergraduates at the University of Oxford are outraged because University Proctors (who deal with discipline in the university) have used photographs posted by students on their Facebook profiles to discover the names of those misbehaving at end-of-term celebrations and fine them. These students claim that their privacy has been invaded and the press have joined in, talking about a surveillance society. However, this is nonsense. The students posted pictures of themselves in a public arena. Facebook is not a private, personal photograph album – it is open to everybody. If robbers and murderers posted photos of their misdeeds on the Internet, we would expect the police to use this valuable evidence. If students put pictures of themselves breaking university rules in a public place, we should expect proctors to use them.

D Some people argue that we should keep spending money to kick-start the economy because spending money would keep people in work. These people are misguided. Spending more money would be like telling a drowning man to take big gulps of air even though his head is under water. He is in such trouble because his frenzied attempts to continue breathing have led to his lungs filling with water. As the old fix won't work, we need a radical new solution to the current economic predicament. The government could therefore do worse than to consider communal ownership of property.

The structure of reasoning

You have identified the elements of reasoning or the component parts of an argument. But this is only part of analysing reasoning. These elements are the building blocks of argument and can be combined in different structures. When you are analysing reasoning, you need to consider the structure.

Let's consider two basic structures which can be used in simple arguments:

◼ reasons which operate independently

◼ reasons which operate jointly.

> **REMEMBER**
>
> Break reasoning down into its elements, label them and understand the structure.
>
> An 'argument element' is a term which refers to parts of the reasoning such as reason, conclusion, assumption and intermediate conclusion.

Reasons which operate independently

Reasons which operate independently support the conclusion in their own right – independently of the other reasons in the argument. Let's look at an example:

R1	Smoking causes cancer.
R2	Smoking is very expensive.
C	Smoking is not a very good idea.

In this example we can see that either reason would support the conclusion, even if the other were not there. So we say that they operate independently. The structure of this argument can be shown with a simple diagram, like this:

When you draw a diagram, a line with an arrow shows the direction of support. It is normal to put the conclusion at the bottom of a structure diagram.

Reasons which operate jointly

Reasons which operate jointly support the conclusion only if they are both present. If one of them were not present, the other would not count as a reason to support the conclusion. Let's look at an example:

> **R1** Karim and Annie live alongside a river which often floods.
> **R2** Sandbags help to defend your property from flooding.
> **C** Karim and Annie should get some sandbags.

In this argument, we need both R1 and R2 to support the conclusion. If Karim and Annie did not live in a place where flooding is a problem, R2 would not give them a reason to buy sandbags. So we say that these reasons operate jointly. The structure of this argument can be shown with a simple diagram, like this:

```
R1   +   R2
  ⌣___⌣
     ↓
     C
```

> **R1** Dom is intelligent and very practical.
> **R2** Electrical engineering requires intelligence and a great deal of practical skill.
> **IC1** So Dom would probably be a good electrical engineer.
> **R3** There is a shortage of electrical engineers at the moment.
> **IC2** So electrical engineers are getting very highly paid.
> **C** Electrical engineering would be a good career choice for Dom.

In this argument, R1 and R2 operate jointly to support IC1. R3 supports IC2. IC1 and IC2 work independently to support C. The argument is stronger with both of these intermediate conclusions to support the conclusion, but either of them alone would give some support to the conclusion. This argument could be shown with a diagram like this:

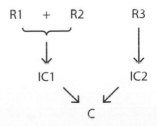

Bringing the skills together

You need to add your understanding of the structure of argument to your ability to break an argument or part of an argument down into its elements. You need to be able to show how the elements of an argument relate to each other.

Analysing the reasoning in detail

Once the framework of the structure has been identified, parts of the reasoning can be analysed in detail. Remember that a reason for the main conclusion will probably be supported by other reasons and evidence, and is therefore called an intermediate conclusion in a detailed analysis. Remember also that you may come across parts of the text that are not parts of the argument. Writers often set the context with some background information before they start the argument. In real-life reasoning you also find rhetorical questions or other devices which are not really part of an argument and passages of description and narrative. Let's analyse a relatively simple argument first.

> The world should celebrate the recent election of Barack Obama as President of the USA. Because he is of mixed ethnic origin, he will truly represent America's mixed population. Because he is intelligent, he will think through decisions before he makes them. Because he is humane, he will adopt policies to help people. So he is likely to be a good president.

This argument can be analysed as follows:

R1 He [Barack Obama] is of mixed ethnic origin.
IC1 He will truly represent America's mixed population.
R2 He is intelligent.
IC2 He will think through decisions before he makes them.
R3 He is humane.
IC3 He will adopt policies to help people.
A1 Representing the whole population, thinking through decisions and adopting policies to help people are characteristics of a good president.
IC4 He is likely to be a good president.
A2 It matters to the rest of the world how good the President of the USA is.
C The world should celebrate the recent election of Barack Obama as President of the USA.

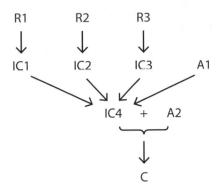

Let's look at paragraph 2 of the argument in Activity 6, page 134, about family holidays:

R1   Being in a strange place takes us out of our comfort zone.
R2   This is tiring,
IC1 makes us less tolerant of other people being difficult.

R1–IC1 is an explanation of why we are less tolerant on holiday.

A1   Being less tolerant is not outweighed by other factors such as being away from work.
IC2 So the holiday is actually more stressful than staying at home.

R3   Because we set our expectations of a perfect, harmonious family idyll so high,
IC3 this stress is unreasonably disappointing, and
IC4 makes us even more stressed.

This section (R3–IC4) is an explanation of why we become more stressed by the stress of holidays.

A2   The money we spend on family holidays is well spent only if we do not get stressed.
IC5 So the thousands we spend on family holidays are wasted.

IC5 is the conclusion of this paragraph. It acts as a reason to support the *further intermediate conclusion that 'they [family holidays] have too many disadvantages', which in turn supports the main conclusion, 'Family holidays are best avoided.'

* This occurs earlier in the passage, but it's later in terms of structure.

When you are analysing a paragraph or part of an argument in detail, it is important to identify the conclusion of that paragraph or part of an argument to show that you understand how the structure of support works. You should also understand how that conclusion fits into the framework structure of the whole argument.

We can use words to show the structure of the reasoning in this part of the argument. Explanations are given to support two intermediate conclusions, IC2 and IC5. IC2 supports IC5.

Alternatively, we can draw a diagram of the structure of the argument in paragraph 2 of the argument about family holidays:

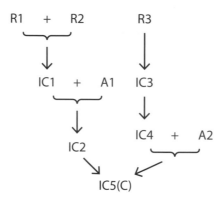

When you are drawing a diagram, you have to consider which elements support the others. Arguments are not always written with reasons first, then intermediate conclusions and the main conclusion at the end. For example, you may quite often find that an intermediate conclusion is written before the reasons that support it.

In a diagram, a reason is shown above an intermediate conclusion it supports, even if the intermediate conclusion is written first in the text. Arrows show the direction of support, so they should point from reasons to intermediate conclusions or from one intermediate conclusion to a further intermediate conclusion which it supports. If you find yourself drawing an arrow from an intermediate conclusion to a reason, stop and ask yourself if this is how relationships of support work?

ACTIVITY

a) **Analyse in detail paragraph 5 of the article about *Alison Lapper Pregnant* on page 129.**

b) **Analyse in detail the following short arguments:**

A   I should make a cup of tea now. I am thirsty, and I have stopped working productively. If I take a short break, I will be able to work better afterwards.

B   More and more women (and even some men) in their early twenties are paying hundreds of pounds for Botox treatment to prevent their skin from ageing, conceal the first signs of wrinkles and remain beautiful. These people are not simply wasting their money. A study of identical twins in America indicates that Botox injections can work to delay ageing in young women. One twin was given regular Botox jabs for thirteen years and her sister received none. The twin who had been treated showed no visible signs of wrinkles when she wasn't smiling, frowning or squinting. The other twin showed normal signs of ageing. This is because lines and wrinkles are caused by the muscle movements when we smile, frown, etc. and Botox stops these muscles working properly, so the skin is not being creased. It is easier to prevent wrinkles than to fix them, so these people will need less cosmetic surgery later in life.

Source: OCR Unit 4, January 2008

C Under new government plans, instead of using the courts, police could impose fixed penalty fines for crimes such as drunkenness, minor theft and assaulting a police officer. Improving the conviction rate for petty crime and reducing legal bureaucracy are worthy aims, but the government's proposals would undermine criminal justice in the UK. Imposing a fixed penalty fine barely counts as justice at all. These fines, like parking tickets, do not leave an offender with a criminal record or shame them in court, so there is nothing lasting to discourage them from offending again. Even minor incidents can have a lasting effect on the victim. They should have a lasting effect on the offender. Furthermore, although immediate payment of £100 ought to deter offenders, many people believe that fixed penalty fines do not have to be paid. In 2005 almost half the penalty notices issued by police were ignored. Fixed penalty fines send the wrong message to potential offenders: not only is assaulting a police officer equivalent to parking on double yellow lines, you can get away with it.

Source: OCR Unit 4, June 2007

D There is an urgent need for a radical shift in the drinking culture in this country. Our drinking culture is affecting our health. Admissions to hospital for drink-related diseases have almost reached an annual total of 50,000 and drink-related deaths have reached their highest level ever. The reasons for this are the availability of alcohol, the social acceptability of drinking, the increase in women drinkers and the falling price of alcohol. Drink-related violence has also escalated in recent years. For example, 20 per cent of murders and 25 per cent of serious head injuries occur under the influence of alcohol. Our attitude to drink is killing our country.

E Although licensing nurses to prescribe medicines ought to allow people easier access to routine medication, it is a disaster waiting to happen. It takes a doctor more than seven years to thoroughly understand how the human body works, and what effects various doses of drugs can have on it. Nurses do not learn in the same detail. They simply do not know enough to take charge of prescribing drugs. Furthermore, prescription is an unfair burden

EXAM TIP ●

You do not need to draw a diagram to show the structure of an argument. You can use words instead, but diagrams are a handy tool. Because they are visual, they help you to see what is happening, often more clearly than words.

If you are asked to analyse a paragraph or part of the reasoning in detail, you must show the function of every element and indicate the structure of the argument, including any strands of reasoning, using words or a diagram.

Practise identifying and analysing arguments you find in the newspapers, in your other subjects and even from AS Critical Thinking exam papers. This will improve your skills. Arguments can be found in many places.

of responsibility to lay on people who have chosen a caring rather than a diagnostic role.

F The UK's education system places great weight on very young children sitting still and learning to read. However, young children are more likely to learn to read well if we allow them to run around. Young children learn many important developmental skills through active play, for instance, lively pretending games often include basic language skills such as listening to and forming sentences. Active play also develops the child's basic motor skills, so it is an important foundation for learning to read.

So how will these skills be tested in the exam?

There are two common ways of testing detailed analysis in the exam. One of these is very similar to a way of testing framework analysis:

'Quotation'
Name and explain the function of this element in the structure of the reasoning.

When you are answering this kind of question, you will need to decide whether the element is an important part of the framework structure, or a detail from a part of the reasoning that supports (or possibly illustrates) the framework reasoning. Remember as well that the element might not be part of an argument, but might be a different kind of reasoning.

Let's look at an example of a claim taken from the detailed reasoning rather than the framework structure:

'At present, about 440 reactors supply about 2 per cent of demand'. (Taken from Linklater, 'Who says nuclear power is clean?', page 139, paragraph 5).

Answer A
Example of nuclear energy.

Answer B
Reason to support the IC that 'the number of nuclear plants needed to meet the world's needs would be colossal'.

Answer C
Evidence to support the claim that 'the number of nuclear plants needed to support the world's needs would be colossal'.

- *Answer A* has the name wrong. Although there is sometimes a grey area of overlap between evidence and examples, this is not one of those occasions. The explanation is too vague. This candidate has, at best, a limited understanding of the function of this element in the structure of the reasoning.

- *Answer B* gets the name wrong – something this specific is generally thought to be evidence. However, this answer has accurately understood the way this element supports the claim, 'the number…. colossal', so this answer gains some marks.

- *Answer C* is accurate.

The other common way of testing the skill of detailed analysis is:

> Analyse in detail the reasoning in [part of the passage] by identifying elements of argument and showing their relationships to each other.

In this type of question you need to make sure that you show the examiner that you have understood which claim is the main conclusion of this part of the argument (and is normally an IC in the argument as a whole).

Summary

You should now be more able to analyse reasoning in detail:

- by identifying elements of reasoning

- showing their relationships to other elements using words or diagrams.

Evaluating reasoning: structural strength and weakness in real-life reasoning

Learning objectives

Evaluate structural strength and weakness in reasoning by considering:
- how effectively reasons support conclusions
- how effectively evidence supports reasoning
- the effect of structural/logical flaws.

Evaluating reasoning – the context

In Chapter 6 we began to consider four questions that you can ask about a newspaper or magazine article. When you are trying to decide what to believe about important issues in the world.

- What am I being persuaded to accept (what is the conclusion)?

- How am I being persuaded to accept this (what sort of reasoning is being used)?

- On what grounds am I supposed to accept this (what are the main reasons)?

- How effective is this persuasion (is this reasoning strong)?

In Chapters 6–8 we considered the first three of these questions. In Chapters 9–11 we will consider the last of these questions. We will look at structural strength and weakness, other forms of strength and weakness, and then bring all your evaluative skills together to consider how different kinds of evaluative questions can be answered. It is, however, important to keep asking the first three questions; understanding *how* reasoning works is an important first step in deciding *how well* that reasoning works.

Moving on from AS

At AS you learned to evaluate reasoning by finding and explaining specific weaknesses (and occasionally strengths) in the reasoning. At A2 you will apply these skills in the context of a whole argument, and use them to decide how strong an argument is.

In this chapter we are going to concentrate on structural strength and weakness. We will consider:

- how effectively reasons support conclusions

- how effectively evidence supports reasoning

- the effect of structural/logical flaws.

> **EXAM TIP** ●
>
> Evaluation is not just about finding weakness in reasoning. It is about assessing how strong reasoning is. This means finding strengths and seeing weakness in the context of the whole argument.

How effectively reasons support conclusions

In Unit 2 you learned that reasons should be persuasive, give us good reason to accept a conclusion and be precisely focused on the conclusion. If all these conditions are met, then a reason gives strong support to the conclusion. For example:

> Being rude about people hurts their feelings. We shouldn't hurt each other's feelings. So it is better not to be rude about someone in their hearing.

However, if we are persuaded to agree to something similar but not precisely the same as the conclusion, then the reasoning gives weak support to the conclusion. For example:

> If you want to look good, you need to dress well. Celebrity X looked good at the Brit Awards. So you should buy the same dress as celebrity X.

■ Do you really need to look like this?

Here you are being manipulated to make you believe you need to buy a dress, but the conclusion does not follow from the reasons. It may be the case that dressing well helps you to look good and it may be the case that celebrity X looked good at the Brit Awards. However, this does not mean that the only way to dress well is to buy the dress that celebrity X wore, nor does it mean that you would look good in the same dress. This reasoning is imprecise and it also plays on our desire to be like celebrities.

Sometimes writers jump to conclusions without really supporting them, although on first sight their reasoning looks satisfactory. For example:

> Britons are spending more on leisure and less on food so we are likely to be getting thinner.

As we are generally richer, and as food is relatively cheaper than it was a hundred years ago, it is possible to spend less on food yet still eat more than we need. Leisure does not only mean physical activity, so the author has given us no rational grounds to accept that we might get thinner.

Understanding whether a reason gives precise support to a conclusion is a very important skill in analysing and evaluating an argument. In the short arguments we are dealing with, it may be obvious to you that some of the reasons have little relevance to the conclusion or that they offer weak support. In a longer argument, this lack of relevance may be hidden by the detail. This is one of the reasons why we identify the structure of an argument.

There can be room for interpretation when you are evaluating the extent to which reasons support a conclusion. Sometimes this depends on the assumptions and underlying beliefs that author and audience bring to an argument, as we will see in the worked example that follows.

WORKED EXAMPLE 6

'Suicide rates soar on Valentine's Day as lonely people watch others flaunting their gender success in love and succumb to despair. Others merely cringe as revolting members of the opposite sex plead for their attention. So we can see that Valentine's Day has greater negative effects than positive.'

How effectively do the reasons support the conclusion in this argument?

Answer A
Very effectively, they really show how horrible Valentine's Day can be.

Answer B
The reasons effectively support the conclusion, as nothing can outweigh the negative effect of increasing suicide.

Answer C
The reasons do not effectively support the conclusion that 'Valentine's Day has greater negative effects than positive', because they refer only to the negative effects. To fully support the conclusion the reasons would need to mention positive effects.

Answer D
As the argument stands, the reasons do not effectively support the conclusion that 'Valentine's Day has greater negative effects than positive', because the reasons only mention one side of the comparison. If we accept the assumption that 'nothing can outweigh the negative effect of increasing suicide', then the reasons do support the conclusion. But this assumption can be challenged – we might argue that the benefits of increasing love for many people outweigh the disadvantages of causing pain to a few.

Comment

Answer A shows a limited understanding of how the reasons support the conclusion. This response barely goes beyond agreement with the passage.

Answer B shows some, basic understanding, expressed as an opinion rather than as an evaluation.

Answer C shows clear understanding of a weakness in the support given to the conclusion by the reasons.

Answer D shows a sound, thorough and perceptive understanding of a weakness in the reasoning (one side of the comparison) and the effect of assumptions and principles on the strength of the argument. This candidate has awareness of ambiguity, nuance and the need for interpretation.

ACTIVITY 11

Do the reasons provide strong support for the conclusion in any of the following arguments?

> **A** We want our children to be safe, so we should publish lists of known paedophiles living in each community.
>
> **B** Anjuli eats at least six portions of fruit and vegetables every day, so she won't get ill.
>
> **C** The education of a child is too complex for a single teacher, so we should replace teachers with computer programs.
>
> **D** There is a great deal of suffering in the world and we have a duty to help those in need, so I should donate some money to a charity such as the Motor Neurone Disease Association.

Evaluating how reasons support conclusions in a longer text

Applying your understanding of syllogisms to everyday arguments

One of the oldest, and simplest, forms of argument is the syllogism. As you learned in Chapter 8, syllogisms often apply a general idea or principle to a specific situation. Most arguments you will come across in everyday life will not be written as syllogisms and they will not have conclusions that have to be true. The really interesting issues are often those where the conclusion cannot be shown to be true. They tend to be **inductive arguments**, in which reasons give support to a conclusion and make the conclusion plausible, but do not mean that it must be true. So, when you are evaluating the support given to an author's conclusion, you will need to look for reasons which give us grounds to accept the conclusion, rather than expecting authors to show that their conclusion must be true. However, during their arguments authors will often apply a general idea to a particular situation. This may be a statement which is claimed to be generally true, such as a principle, or a recommendation, which applies generally. In these cases you can use your understanding of syllogisms to decide whether an author has used a valid argument structure to support their claims or not. Let's look at an extract from the article in worked example 4, page 131:

> Happiness has gone respectable, and it's been tagged to intellectual disciplines – the science of happiness, happiness economics – so it will be taken more seriously.

This segment of the argument depends on an assumption that intellectual disciplines are taken seriously. We could re-write this argument in the form of a syllogism:

> **R1** Intellectual disciplines are taken seriously. (All As are B)
> **R2** Happiness is now an intellectual discipline. (C is A)
> **C**   So, happiness will be taken more seriously. (Therefore C is B).

This does have a valid structure, so if the reasons are true, the conclusion must be true. But there is an important difference between being an intellectual discipline and being tagged to an intellectual discipline, so we cannot be certain that the conclusion is true. However, the form of the argument is sound and we cannot say that the conclusion is totally unsupported.

Do the reasons support the conclusion?

It is sometimes the case that an author has written a persuasive argument, but the reasons do not support their precise conclusion. If we return to the happiness example, we can see that the author has used a valid argument structure, but she has implied that tagging happiness to intellectual disciplines is the same as making happiness an intellectual discipline. Sceptics may, however, dismiss it as a pseudo-science. So the author has not fully supported her strong conclusion that 'happiness will be taken more seriously'. She has given us reason to consider that 'happiness is likely to be taken more seriously by many people'.

Impact of weakness

We need to question the impact of this slight weakness on the author's main conclusion. In order to consider that 'the state should resume a role in promoting the good life, not just chivvy us along in the global rat race, anxious and insecure', we only need to accept that it is possible to take happiness seriously, not that it will be taken seriously. So the support for the main conclusion is not seriously weakened.

When you are evaluating how well the author's reasons support the intermediate and main conclusions of an argument, you need to identify and comment on key points. Consider whether the reasons do give us grounds to accept the intermediate conclusions, and whether the intermediate conclusions do give us grounds to accept the main conclusion.

At this stage it can be worth returning to the idea of a framework analysis of argument structure. If you pare an argument down to its essence, getting rid of the detail and looking only at the main reasons given to support a conclusion, it is much easier to see whether and to what extent reasons support conclusions.

> **REMEMBER**
>
> A syllogism is a form of deductive argument with two reasons supporting a conclusion.

> **REMEMBER**
>
> In a deductive argument with a valid structure the conclusion must be true if the reasons are true.

WORKED EXAMPLE 7

Let's look at an example of a longer text. This text has been annotated to show *how* the reasoning works. This will help us to decide *how well* the reasons support the conclusion.

In praise of scientific heresy

We have to think the unthinkable to take science forward, even if it annoys the establishment.

When it comes to scientific facts, the identity of our closest living relative is about as certain as they get. Genome sequencing has confirmed to the satisfaction of pretty much everybody that this *context* dubious honour goes to chimpanzees.

Yet this week sees the publication of a paper that seeks to blow that fact out of the water. The authors argue that the DNA evidence is flawed and that, based on traditional taxonomy, orang-utans are clearly closer to us than chimps.

Question at issue It's true that people call orangs the 'people of the forest'. But recall the old saying about extraordinary claims requiring extraordinary evidence. So far, the research appears to be failing that test. All the experts we contacted dismissed the paper's main conclusion, a reaction that seems likely to be repeated when the paper reaches the wider world. *statement of counter opinion*

If its claims are so outlandish, should the research even have been published? Some scientists would clearly have preferred it if the paper had never seen the light of day, and question the judgement of the journal.

IC
↑ That is territory we should tread with care. Ideas that mainstream
R opinion 'knows' to be wrong occasionally turn out to be right. The insights of Galileo, Stan Prusiner – who discovered prions – and many others were once denounced as heresy. And even those that
Ex are wrong can be valuable. *R*

R Science proceeds by questioning its own assumptions and regarding every "fact" as provisional, so alternative hypotheses should be given an airing, if only to reaffirm the strength of the orthodoxy. *Expl. used as R*
R Science that pulls up the drawbridge on new ideas risks becoming sterile. The journal recognised that and should be applauded for its *C* decision to disseminate this challenging paper.

One possible outcome, though, is that creationists will trumpet the paper as evidence that the theory of evolution is crumbling. If the experts themselves cannot get their story straight, they will crow, why should we believe anything they say? *statement of problem that could counter C*

That, of course, is shameless intellectual dishonesty (though what else would you expect from a movement built on intellectual dishonesty?). A paper questioning one aspect of evolution is not evidence that evolution itself is in trouble. Quite the opposite. It is science doing what it is supposed to do. <u>We cannot censor ideas just because we are worried that a small bunch of religious fanatics will twist them for their own ends.</u>

RCA

If the paper achieves nothing else, though, it is a reminder of how uncannily similar humans and red apes are, and what we stand to lose when – for sadly it now appears inevitable – those great apes go extinct in the wild.

R? or Rhetorical persuasion that goes beyond argument?

Source: *New Scientist*, 20 June 2009

The reasoning poses a question, 'If its claims are so outlandish, should the research even have been published?' The main conclusion answers this question (and even goes beyond it) by stating 'The journal should be applauded for its decision to disseminate this challenging paper'.

The framework reasoning is:

R1 That [refusing to publish research we disagree with] is territory we should tread with care. (IC of whole article)

R2 Alternative hypothesis should be given an airing if only to reaffirm the strength of the orthodoxy. (IC of whole article)

R3 We cannot censor ideas just because we are worried that a small bunch of religious fanatics will twist them for their own ends.

R4 This paper reminds us of what we will lose when these great apes (orangutans) go extinct in the world. (Open to interpretation whether this is a reason giving logical support or merely a rhetorical flourish)

C The journal [which published the questionable research] should be applauded for its decision to disseminate this challenging paper.

So – how effectively do these reasons support the conclusion?

The reasons provide reasonable support for the idea that this research should be published, if we accept that 'not publishing' is the same as censoring. The idea that we should be careful about refusing to publish research that is agreed to be wrong (in the light of past mistakes) does strongly support the idea that this research should be published. The second reason works with this to show that publishing ideas does not mean agreeing with them. In a scientific context these two reasons offer strong support to the claim that the research should be published.

EXAM TIP

Looking at how 'reasons' support a conclusion is one part of looking at how 'reasoning' supports a conclusion.

However, there are ways in which the reasons are not sufficient to support the conclusion. First, there is quite a big logical jump from the claim the reasons seem to support, 'This research should have been published' and the conclusion actually stated, 'The journal… should be *applauded* for its decision to disseminate this challenging paper'. Applause, or praise, would require more support.

Second the context of this debate is not only scientific. The context is a world in which publication in a scientific journal *does* confer some form of legitimacy on ideas, in which people may accept and quote these ideas just because they have the authority that comes from being published in a scientific journal. The author's third reason, which is a response to opposing opinion (if not quite counter-argument) tries to deal with this point. However, this reason, that 'we cannot censor ideas just because we are worried that a small bunch of religious fanatics will twist them for their own ends' only deals with part of the problem of the context of this debate. Not censoring ideas because of a minority group is very different to not publishing ideas to avoid misunderstanding on the part of the majority.

Although this third reason tries to fill the logical gap between 'the paper should be published' and 'the journal… should be applauded for its decision to disseminate this challenging paper', it doesn't manage to do this. If valuable scientific ideas really were being *censored*, then we should, perhaps, applaud a decision to publish. But in the context of scientific claims which have not been fully substantiated gaining undue credence in the wider world, it seems just as reasonable not to applaud the journal's decision. So, these reasons do support the idea that, in a scientific context, the work should be published; they do not fully support the claim that 'The journal… should be applauded for its decision to disseminate this challenging paper'.

As ever, it is worth noting that there are different ways to interpret how well reasons support a conclusion in a long, real-life argument. The worked example talks you through one particular interpretation. When you are thinking for yourself whether reasons support a conclusion, you should:

- examine the *logical* link between reasons and (intermediate) conclusions
- consider *to what extent* the conclusion is supported
- ask *to what extent* reasons are focused, relevant and sufficient to support the conclusion
- consider any other issues that might affect the extent to which reasons support conclusions (e.g. it depends whether 'censoring' is the same as 'not publishing')
- be aware of middle ground and possible ambiguity
- justify your interpretation
- choose your language carefully
- use words like 'to some extent'.

When you are considering how well reasons support a claim you should avoid:

- disagreeing with or contradicting the reasons (e.g. censoring ideas is wrong, so the author has supported the conclusion)

- arguing against the reasons or conclusion (e.g. censoring ideas might be the right thing to do sometimes, if they are dangerous ideas, so the author hasn't supported his conclusion)

- using extreme language such as 'always', 'never', 'no support at all' – unless you are sure that there is no room at all for doubt or interpretation.

Assumptions

When you are considering how well reasons support a conclusion, you sometimes have to take into consideration all the things an author has not written down. For example, in the argument about Valentine's Day, (see worked example 6, page 163) the degree of support given to the conclusion depended on whether the argument included the assumption, 'Nothing can outweigh the negative effects of increasing suicide', and on an evaluation of the reasonableness of that claim.

So, it is important to be able to identify and state assumptions precisely and to evaluate the effect they have on the strength of the argument.

It may be that the reasons do not fully support a conclusion because the argument depends on unstated assumptions. In this case, we need to identify the assumptions precisely, and evaluate their impact on the argument. Assumptions may not be problematic. The assumption in the article 'Consumer capitalism is making us ill – we need a therapy state', page 131, paragraph 3, that 'Intellectual disciplines are taken seriously', cannot easily be challenged, and it does form part of a valid argument structure.

However, some arguments rely on assumptions which can be challenged, or which are used in a weak argument structure. For example:

> Dawn is a girl, so she'll be more interested in handbags and shoes than politics.

This argument depends on the assumption that 'Girls are more interested in handbags and shoes than politics.' The structure of the argument is valid:

> **R1** Girls are more interested in shoes and handbags than politics.
> **R2** Dawn is a girl.
> **C** So, Dawn must be more interested in shoes and handbags than politics.

If the reasons are true, the conclusion must be true. However, the assumption here is not just a general statement, but a generalisation. It is too sweeping to say that just because Dawn is a girl she is more interested in handbags and shoes than politics. Because this argument depends on a sweeping generalisation, it does not support its conclusion.

ACTIVITY 12

Look again at B and C arguments in activity 10, page 156. You have already analysed these arguments, so the assumptions in these passages have been identified below to remind you. Now evaluate the impact of these assumptions on the strength of support for the conclusion.

A   The argument assumes that:

    A1 There were no other significant differences in the lifestyles of the twins.

    A2 Signs of ageing do need to be treated.

    A3 These (super-vain) women will not become increasingly anxious about their appearance and have more cosmetic surgery later in their search for perfect youthful looks.

B   The argument assumes that:

    A1 Fines do not inflict lasting suffering on the offender.

    A2 The offender should suffer at least as much/long as the victim.

    A3 If there is no recompense for the victim, or 'pay back' for the criminal, justice has not been done.

ACTIVITY 13

EXAM TIP

There is not always a 'right' answer to an evaluation question. It might be possible to argue that an assumption can be challenged, and therefore weakens the support for a claim. Another candidate might argue that an assumption should be accepted, and therefore does not weaken the support for a claim. Both candidates could get the same mark if they both showed equally strong reasoning and considered the impact of their evaluation on the support for the claim.

How effectively does the reasoning in the following article support the claim that, 'the state sector should be reduced'?

Justify your answer with selective reference to:

■ how well the claim is supported by reasons and intermediate conclusions

■ assumptions and their impact on the strength of the reasoning.

Note that this is an emotive passage. For this exercise, focus *only* on the logical links between reasons and conclusion, and the effect of any assumptions.

This paper acknowledges that there are countless compassionate, conscientious people working selflessly in the public sector. Whether they are teachers, nurses or local authority workers, they are dedicated to producing a better society. We salute them. However, the state sector should be reduced.

The state sector is inefficient, bloated, burdened by layer after layer of pointless bureaucracy and reaching into every nook and cranny of our national life.

> Since 1997, over 600,000 staff have been added to the public payroll, with 6.8 million adults – about one in four of the working population – now employed by the state.
>
> Yet Britain is now no better governed. A Home Office beyond satire … the shambles over tax credits … a multi-billion pound NHS computer that cost three times more than it should … a Defra that can't get payments to farmers … chaos at the Child Support Agency … incompetence is everywhere.
>
> Source: www.dailymail.co.uk

EXAM TIP

When you are asked to 'justify your answer with selective reference to…' you should select key points to discuss. It is better to select three important points to discuss in depth than to mention every issue you notice without developing an interpretation and justification.

Evidence in longer arguments

In this chapter we will build on the concepts from *AS Critical Thinking for OCR*, especially Chapters 3 and 9 and from Chapter 1 of this book. We will concentrate on the use of evidence to support sustained reasoning in a longer passage. The most important point to remember is that evidence should be questioned. Evidence can support an argument by anchoring it firmly in the real world. However, the presence of statistics or evidence in an argument does not automatically make the argument strong. The evidence has to be **relevant**, **adequate**, **reliable** and **representative**. Evidence that does not have most of these characteristics can significantly weaken an argument.

The main question you need to ask about evidence will always be: Is the evidence relevant to the claim it is supporting?

Relevant evidence is precisely focused on the claim it supports, and there is a strong link of inference between the evidence and the conclusions drawn from it.

You will also need to ask:

■ Is the evidence adequate to support this claim?

■ Is the evidence reliable?

■ Is the evidence representative?

Adequate evidence is enough to support a claim. Often we need additional information to be sure that evidence is enough to support a claim, or we find that an alternative explanation of the evidence might weaken the argument. Reliable evidence comes from a source which is reputable, authoritative and without a clear vested interest to mislead. Representative evidence has been collected such that the results can be applied more generally.

There are two approaches to evaluating evidence in a longer passage. You could either start from a general evaluative comment, and give examples to support your evaluation, or you could comment on the strength of individual uses of evidence and build up to an evaluation of the use of evidence in a passage. While you are practising and learning the skills, it may be a good idea to build up a picture slowly by concentrating on each piece of evidence. In an exam, however, you are unlikely to have time to make a comment about each piece of evidence. In these circumstances, you would be better off taking an overview, and picking out key pieces of evidence to support your view. We will concentrate on this second method.

KEY TERMS

Relevance

In Critical Thinking relevance relates to logical reasoning, and in that it refers to a precise link, focusing upon a reason or conclusion. Just being about the same topic does not make information relevant to the conclusion.

Adequate evidence

This is enough to support a claim and does not need additional evidence. It would not be weakened by an alternative explanation.

Reliable evidence

Evidence that comes from a source which is reputable, authorative and without a clear vested interest to mislead.

Representative evidence

Evidence based on a sample which is large enough for the results to be applied more generally and is typical of the group or set from which it is taken.

REMEMBER

!

When we are evaluating the use of evidence, we need to consider:

- Is the evidence relevant? Does it give precise support to the reasons?
- How certain are the links between evidence and reasons?
- Is the evidence reliable and representative?
- Do you need additional evidence to verify a claim?
- Are there alternative explanations which would weaken the argument?

WORKED EXAMPLE 8

Refer to the article, 'Who says nuclear power is clean?', pages 138–40.

How effective is the author's use of evidence? Justify your answer with selective reference to key strengths and weaknesses.

Answer

The author makes precise, relevant and reliable use of evidence to support his claims that nuclear power is not clean, reliable or secure. The sources in paragraph 2 – a chemist and energy specialist and a nuclear physicist – are claimed to be expert and independent, so we expect their evidence to be reliable. It would be even better if we knew their names so that we could check their credentials. If they are found to be reputable, reliable experts, Linklater's use of their evidence will lend considerable weight to his reasoning. If, on the other hand, they were found to be unreliable or at odds with the consensus of scientific opinion, we would treat their claims with more scepticism. Consequently, we would be less inclined to accept Linklater's reasoning, which is heavily based on their claims. The author uses this evidence to show that, although the production of nuclear power may be clean in terms of CO_2 production, the whole process including mining, refining and transportation of ore is increasingly polluting. The evidence he uses precisely undermines the claim that nuclear power is clean. The evidence is also precisely relevant because it shows that nuclear power is unlikely to be more reliable than fossil fuels, because the process of generating nuclear power depends on the use of fossil fuels, 'The so-called "reliability" of nuclear power would therefore rest on the growing use of fossil fuels.' This evidence does rely on some predictions about what 'might' or 'could' happen, so it is not certain. But the suggested course of events seems **plausible** and not improbable.

KEY TERM

Plausible
Could reasonably be the case, not far-fetched.

However, the demonstration that nuclear power is not secure depends on an unsupported leap. The author tells us that Canada will not be the source of future uranium ore, but that we must rely on unstable, undemocratic countries such as Kazakhstan. In order to accept this claim, we would need to know that Canada has very limited supplies; we need to know whether all the countries which might provide ore are unstable or unfriendly; and we must assume that this instability will continue into the future. This link then, although precise, rests on gaps in the evidence and rhetorical moves rather than rational, persuasive use of evidence.

Evidence is used rather more loosely to persuade the reader that the decision to go nuclear will make the case for renewable energy stronger rather than weaker. Each piece of evidence acts as an example rather than to give direct support to claims. The claim that wind turbines, unlike nuclear reactors, can be removed, does make wind turbines seem attractive. It does not necessarily, however, affect the strength of the case for renewable energy , as it gives only one, limited example of how renewable energy is more attractive than nuclear energy. It can't be extended without thought to all renewable energy sources, nor does it show that renewables will be able to provide sufficient energy.

No evidence is given to support the claim that wind turbines are not gravely inefficient in comparison to nuclear power, although this is a claim which clearly could and should be supported by numerical evidence. The example of the Portuguese Government buying wave technology may be good; Portugal, like Britain, has a long stretch of coastline. The fact that a government has bought into technology gives it credibility. On the other hand, even governments can make poor decisions. British decisions should be made on the merits of the technology, rather than based on other governments' decisions.

Overall then, the use of evidence to debunk the claims about nuclear power is fairly strong; the use of evidence to support the claims relating to renewable power is patchy, reliant on examples and stray scraps of evidence.

▪ Wind turbines have been subjected to opposition from the nuclear lobby – but they can be removed, unlike nuclear reactors.

Applying AS evaluation to A2

At AS you learned to evaluate the credibility of a source of evidence by applying credibility criteria as follows:

> 'The author is a journalist on a reputable national paper, so we expect them to use reliable evidence and check their sources. This strengthens the credibility of the document.'

At A2 you need to extend the way you use this sort of evaluation. You need to consider the purpose and limits of an assessment of credibility. Let's take the credibility point that we made in worked example 8, on pages 174–75 'The sources in paragraph 2 … heavily based on their claims'.

Here, the *purpose* of including the assessment of credibility is to help with an evaluation of Linklater's use of evidence in his reasoning. We want to know whether we should accept the evidence he cites – and this depends, in part, on the credibility of his sources.

The *limitations* of this assessment of credibility are:

■ As the experts are anonymous we can only make suppositions about them (note – the author did name them, but these names were edited out of the article for the purposes of this textbook).

■ An assessment of credibility can only guide us as to whether this evidence should be accepted. It cannot provide certain answers, and it might be outweighed by other factors. So your evaluation needs to keep assessment of credibility in its place as one guide amongst many.

Read the text, 'Consumer Capitalism is making us ill – we need a therapy state' in worked example 4, pages 131–32. How effectively does the author's use of evidence support her claims? Justify your answer with selective reference to the use of evidence.

Structural (or logical) flaws

As you learned at AS Level Critical Thinking, there are a number of flaws, or problems, with a pattern of reasoning, which are easily recognisable as weakening the support for a conclusion. In this chapter we will revise flaws which are specifically to do with the structure of the argument and the logical links of inference. We will deal with other flaws in Chapter 10.

REMEMBER

Flaw: a fault in the pattern of reasoning which weakens the support given to the conclusion of an argument.

ACTIVITY

As a reminder, write a short definition of each of the following flaws from your AS Level Critical Thinking course:

Hasty generalisation
Sweeping generalisation
Causal flaw
Inconsistency
False dichotomy (also known as Restricting the Options or the either/or flaw)
Circular argument
Confusing necessary and sufficient conditions
Two wrongs don't make a right
Tu quoque

At AS Level you needed to be able to identify a flaw in the reasoning, to explain what was wrong with it and why this might mean that a particular claim (often an intermediate conclusion) was not supported. At A2 Level you also need to be able to assess how far a flaw weakens an argument overall. We will not deal with all of these flaws in detail but will concentrate on evaluating the extent of the weakness. First of all, you should practise identifying flaws in reasoning to revise your AS skills. We will return to activity 16 later to work through an evaluation of the effect of the flaw on the strength of the overall argument.

ACTIVITY 16

Name and explain the flaws in the following texts:

A The Tibetan antelope and the guanaco, a wild relative of the camel, have resisted domestication and have both been hunted almost to extinction by people wanting their soft underfur for wool. The musk ox, vicuna, alpaca and other domestic wool-producing animals, such as the cashmere-producing goat and angora-producing rabbit, are plentiful. This contrast shows that domestication ensures the survival of a species, whereas remaining wild is a one-way ticket to extinction.

Source: OCR Unit 4, June 2007

B For years we have been fascinated by accounts of gladiatorial brutality in the Roman arena. Modern representations have shown either a bloody free-for-all, or a demonstration of prowess in which death was rare. Forensic evidence from the remains of gladiators in the cemetery at Ephesus indicates that neither representation is accurate. It seems that gladiators fought according to strict rules. Injuries suggested that gladiators used one type of weapon per fight. Ten of the sixty-seven gladiators examined died from squarish blows to the back of the head which may have been inflicted after the fight by a backstage executioner.

Source: OCR Unit 4, January 2007

C The choices and technicalities involved in buying and using digital gadgets are confusing. It can be frustrating trying to make your new gadget work. If you want an MP3 player, for example, you need to choose a manufacturer, choose the right Microsoft software, and surf a multiplicity of Microsoft compatible online music stores. Microsoft claims that this gives the consumer choice. However, many consumers are choosing to buy the iPod which is tied to iTunes software and the iTunes online music store, instead of assembling a package from different manufacturers. Furthermore, consumers buy products, but often don't buy the content and accessories they need to fully use their new gadgets. For example, half the US consumers with high-definition TV sets don't subscribe to HDTV programming. It is clear that digital industries need to sell fully integrated end-to-end experiences such as the iPod rather than standalone devices. Consumers should welcome Microsoft's development of the Zune as a full digital experience to rival the iPod.

Source: OCR Unit 4, June 2007

D Farmers are increasingly deciding to grow biofuels on their land. There was a particularly noticeable trend in this direction between 2005 and 2008. One reason for this is that it pays better than food production. Another is that Western governments have introduced targets for up to 10 per cent of transport fuels to come from biofuels. Food prices have risen significantly. Between April 2007 and April 2008 the price of rice almost tripled, for example. Even in the UK shopping bills have risen uncomfortably, and in the poorest countries millions of people face starvation. It is clear that biofuels are to blame for this famine. The grain that fills the tank of a single SUV would fill a person's belly for a whole year. Governments must withdraw legislation relating to biofuel targets.

- Biofuels – the way forward?

ACTIVITY

Re-read the argument about family holidays in activity 6, page 134. Name and explain any flaws you find.

REMEMBER

These passages may have other sorts of flaw and weakness, such as rhetorical moves, including straw person. These weaknesses are dealt with in Chapter 10. For now, you just need to look for the flaws listed at the beginning of this chapter.

Evaluating the effect of a flaw on the strength of reasoning

When you are evaluating the effect of a flaw in reasoning on the overall strength of that reasoning, you need to take into consideration the types of reasoning being used. In a short argument, a flaw can mean that there is no effective support for the conclusion.

Let's look at an example:

> Eating apples keeps you healthy. Jenna's Granddad used to eat an apple a day and he lived to 99.

This argument does not support its conclusion that, 'Eating apples keeps you healthy'. It generalises from just one example; one example is insufficient to support a general claim. This reasoning also assumes that Jenna's Granddad lived to such an old age because he ate an apple a day. That is, it also contains a causal flaw. We would need to investigate why he lived for so long and not just accept that his apple eating caused his long life. If we are not sure that the apples caused the long life, we can't be sure that apples keep you healthy, so the conclusion is not supported. As there is no other reason to support the conclusion, we cannot accept the conclusion on the basis of this reasoning.

In a longer piece of reasoning with more than one strand of reasoning, there is a much greater chance that a flaw will have a small impact.

WORKED EXAMPLE 9

Re-read the article, 'New technology may be changing the human brain', pages 121–22.

As we saw in chapter six, this passage is not really an argument, although it contains both reasoning and argument. It has two main strands of reasoning, one of which has a train of thought but no argument; the other does contain an argument, which concludes 'Politicians should take a valuable ten minutes to read and reflect on Baroness Greenfield's fine speech'.

In paragraph 3 the author makes a sweeping generalisation, talking about 'text and computer messaging, using the post-grammar, post-spelling shorthand that everyone under 30 finds normal and everyone over 40 finds menacing'.

This could be stated as; John is under 30 and loves texting and computer messaging. His father, aged 50, finds it menacing.

So, how do we evaluate the impact of this flaw on the strength of the reasoning?

Answer

The author makes a sweeping generalisation saying that everyone under 30 finds post-grammar, post-spelling shorthand normal and everyone over 40 finds it menacing. But lots of 18-year-olds use proper English, especially in essays, and there are older people who use text language. Because one counter example causes serious problems for a general rule, this sweeping generalisation seriously weakens her argument.

Comment

Is the author's claim that 'In just a couple of decades, we have slipped away from a culture based essentially on words to one based essentially on images, or pictures' seriously weakened? We've identified a sweeping generalisation and we can show that not *everybody* feels the way that the author says they do. But it is still possible that most people feel this way and our experience would indicate that a significant majority of young people are comfortable with textspeak (often as well as formal English), whereas a significant number (if not necessarily a majority) of older people find textspeak intensely irritating and even threatening. And if most people feel this way, it would still be possible to talk of a general cultural change during the past couple of decades. So the sweeping generalisation only weakens the support for the claim very slightly.

It is more significant that the author argues from a change in the use of language to a slip from a culture based on words to a culture based on pictures. Text language is language not pictures, so it does not support the claim that 'we have slipped from a culture based essentially on words to one based essentially on pictures' at all.

The main conclusion of the argument is that 'Politicians should take a valuable ten minutes to read and reflect on Baroness Greenfield's fine speech'. In order to support this weak conclusion, the author needs only to show that Greenfield's speech contains some important ideas that might be relevant to politicians. Because Greenfield gives us some reason to suppose that new technology might change the way we learn and because learning is something the government has responsibility for in the UK, the author has provided enough support for the conclusion that at least some 'Politicians should take a valuable ten minutes to read and reflect on Baroness Greenfield's fine speech'. Even the weak support for the claim that our culture has slipped to one based essentially on pictures does not mean that the main conclusion is unsupported, because it is supported by this different strand of reasoning.

So we can see that it is important to really think about how a piece of reasoning works, and the extent to which a flaw weakens it. Someone who wrote that the sweeping generalisation seriously weakened the argument would show that they had misunderstood the way the argument worked.

We will return to this argument in later chapters to consider some of the other strengths and weaknesses in the reasoning.

It is important, however, to note that one flaw can be enough to significantly weaken the reasoning in a longer passage of reasoning if it is central to the argument.

As ever, it is normally possible to interpret the strength of reasoning in different ways. When you are thinking for yourself how strong a piece of reasoning is, you should:

■ select key points to refer to

■ keep your focus on the claims the author is supporting

■ consider the strength of the claims the author is supporting; are they strong claims that need a great deal of support or weak claims that require very little support?

■ consider where a flaw is in the reasoning – is it central to the framework reasoning, part or just one strand, or even in a part of the passage that isn't argument?

■ consider the *extent* to which a flaw weakens the support for a claim

■ justify your interpretation, relating your comments to the reasoning in the passage.

So how will these skills be tested in the exam?

One common way of testing these skills is to ask: 'Evaluate the support given by the reasoning to the claim, "…" Support your evaluation by selectively referring to key strengths and weaknesses in the argument and their effect on the overall strength of the reasoning.'

Be aware, though, that the skills we have discussed in this chapter are normally tested together with the skills discussed in Chapter 10. There is also a much more detailed look at how your evaluative skills will be tested in Chapter 10.'

You will now put these skills into practice on medium length passages. You will have the opportunity to practise on longer texts in Chapter 10.

ACTIVITY

Return to activity 16 on page 176. You have already identified the flaws in these arguments. Now evaluate the impact of these flaws on the strength of support for the conclusions of the arguments.

ACTIVITY 19

Evaluate the support given by the reasoning in the following passages to the main conclusion. Support your evaluation by referring to key flaws in the reasoning and their impact on the strength of the reasoning.

A The Divorce Reform Act, which made it easier for couples to obtain a divorce, came into effect in 1971. The annual rate of divorce has risen steadily since 1971. This law has led directly to family breakdown.

B Fairness appears to be an instinctive trait common to primates. Researchers taught capuchin monkeys to trade small rocks for food rewards, serving two monkeys side by side so that each could see the trades offered the other. At first, the experimenters always gave the monkeys cucumber for their rocks. Then they began giving one monkey a grape, which capuchins prefer to cucumber. The other monkeys then often refused to trade. In another experiment, monkeys cooperated to pull a heavy bar to reveal food. A monkey who had eaten her portion of the food would return to help a second monkey get hers.

C Global warming is a scam with no foundation in fact, perpetrated by dishonest, incompetent scientists with vested interests and no understanding of logic. The only evidence that human activity causes climate change is that temperature has increased since western industrialisation. There is a closer correlation between this latest warming and everyone getting the vote. In science, the fact that events coincide does not mean that there is a causal link between them.

D Our house went on the market on Wednesday 1 March. The estate agents didn't put a for sale sign up until Wednesday 8 March. It also took a week to get the house advertised on www.rightmove.co.uk. When I phoned the estate agents, they said it was a problem with the website, but they had sent all the details on Friday 3 March. When the details came up on the website, there was a for sale sign in the picture of the house. The estate agent was not telling the truth.

EXAM TIP

In the Unit 4 exam, you will be asked to evaluate the support given by the reasoning to a particular claim. You should select key strengths and weaknesses to discuss. There is no need to mention absolutely everything.

ACTIVITY 20

Evaluate the support given by the reasoning in the following passages to the main conclusion. Support your evaluation by making reference to:

■ flaws in the reasoning and their effect on the strength of the reasoning

■ assumptions which must be made and their effect on the reasoning

■ how well the claim is supported by reasons and intermediate conclusions.

A A woman who conceives as a result of contraceptive failure has not voluntarily undertaken a duty towards the foetus. So she cannot be held to have a duty towards the foetus, since she did all she could to avoid becoming pregnant. It would be quite unreasonable to tell women that they must live like nuns unless they are willing to run the risk of carrying a pregnancy to term, giving birth and then either caring for an uninvited member of the family for the next 18 years or suffering the mental anguish of giving a child up for adoption.

B We should take no notice of those extreme liberals who want to ensure that terrorists receive a fair trial. What about the rights of those who are killed or maimed while going about their lawful business? Terrorists do not care about the rights of their victims. So we should not care about their right to a fair trial.

ACTIVITY 21

Re-read the argument about family holidays in activity 6, page 134. How effectively does the reasoning support the claim that, 'family holidays are best avoided?' Justify your answer by selecting key strengths and weaknesses to evaluate.

Summary

You should now be able to:

■ evaluate the structure of reasoning to see whether a claim is well supported by considering:

- how effectively reasons support a conclusion

- how effectively evidence is used to support a conclusion

- to what extent flaws weaken the reasoning?

10 Evaluating reasoning: other strength and weakness in real-life reasoning

Learning objectives

Evaluate the effect of other reasoning devices on the strength of an argument including:

- appeals
- rhetorical persuasion
- counter-argument
- hypothetical reasoning
- analogy.

Evaluating other reasoning devices

In Chapter 9 we looked at strength and weakness in the structural support in reasoning. In this chapter we will be looking at a number of devices that can be used in reasoning, which may be weak or strong. These will include appeals, some flaws, rhetorical persuasion, counter-argument, hypothetical reasoning and analogy.

ACTIVITY

Revise your AS understanding. Define the following terms:

appeal to authority	attacking the arguer
appeal to tradition	straw person
appeal to history	slippery slope
appeal to popularity	conflation
appeal to emotion	equivocation

Interpretation

Interpretation and justification are even more important with the reasoning devices we are considering in this chapter than in previous chapters.

Appeals

You are familiar with appeals to popularity, tradition, history and authority. Appeals to emotion can be categorised according to the emotions they arouse, for example, appeals to fear, vanity, self-interest and novelty. They tend to play on our feelings, such as our fear of change or desire to do what is best for ourselves.

An appeal to fear or an appeal to your self-interest or vanity might persuade you to agree to something. However, if you look more closely, you might see that there is no good reason given to support the conclusion. For example:

> Any intelligent person can see that murderers should never be released from prison.

Here, the writer is appealing to vanity, trying to persuade readers to accept their opinion by playing on their desire not to look stupid. The writer has not addressed any reasons why murderers should, or should not, be kept in prison for their natural lives.

• Should murderers be kept in prison until they die?

Are appeals always weaknesses?

Appeals are not necessarily flaws which weaken the support for a conclusion. This is partly because they are not trying to strengthen the rational support for a conclusion. A strong argument which gives good reasons to keep murderers in prison would not become weaker because it also included an appeal to popularity, for example. On its own, however, an appeal does not usually give us a reason to accept a conclusion. Let's look at an example:

> We have always smoked in the office. We should be able to carry on smoking in the office.

Just because we have always smoked in the office does not mean that it is the right thing to do. There are good reasons not to smoke in offices – it is bad for everyone's health, smelly and unappealing. So the appeal to tradition does not support the conclusion. As it is the only reason given to support the conclusion, the conclusion is unsupported.

However, we might want to take tradition into account in an argument. There may be good reasons to prefer something which has stood the test of time to something new and untried. Furthermore, people often have emotional attachments to old, familiar things. This sort of emotional, subjective reason can be taken into consideration. It does not necessarily outweigh other considerations, but an appeal to tradition is not necessarily a weakness.

> **REMEMBER**
>
> You may find it useful to refer back to Chapter 10 of the AS book to revise your AS understanding of appeals.

EXAM TIP

At A2 Level Critical Thinking, if you choose to comment on an appeal as part of your evaluation of an argument, you should consider how reasonable the appeal is, and whether it forms part of a strong argument, or is the only attempt to support a claim.

Let's look at another example:

> Most experts agree that the MMR vaccine is not dangerous. The one expert who disagrees has been found to have a vested interest, and has been discredited. Your child is considerably more likely to get a serious illness such as measles without the jab, even if single jabs are used instead of the combined MMR vaccine. So we should probably allow our children to be vaccinated with the MMR vaccine.

In this case, the appeal to authority is reasonable. Although we could not conclude that we should definitely allow our children to be vaccinated on the basis of this appeal to authority, we would need a very good reason to reject the authority of many experts. Furthermore, there are additional reasons given to support the conclusion that we should probably allow our children to be vaccinated with the MMR vaccine. A fear that a vaccination might be dangerous should not outweigh expert opinion that lack of vaccination is more dangerous. So this appeal is not a weakness and the conclusion is supported.

ACTIVITY 23

Evaluate the use of the appeal to tradition in the following argument.

> Tony Blair was wrong to abolish the office of Lord Chancellor in 2003. Britain has had Lord Chancellors for hundreds of years, and the position has helped to ensure the stability and fairness of our judicial system during that time. There are those who argue that it has been inefficient to have one minister combining the roles of Speaker of the House of Lords, Minister for Constitutional Affairs and Head of the Judiciary (appointing judges and overseeing their work). They have also suggested that this position of Lord Chancellor has contravened the principle of separation of political and legal powers. However, such a radical break with tradition should not have been announced suddenly without wide consultation and debate.

ACTIVITY 24

Evaluate the use of appeals in the article, 'Who says nuclear power is clean?, pages 138–40.

Slippery slopes

At AS Level Critical Thinking we defined a **slippery slope** flaw as reasoning which moves from one minor event through a series of unconnected events to an extreme consequence. There are many examples of such extreme slippery slopes to be found. However, there are also more subtle versions, where the events are connected, and the extreme consequence does not seem so unlikely. For example:

> Once a man is permitted on his own authority to kill an innocent person directly, there … are no longer any rational grounds for saying that [killing others] can advance so far and no further. Once the exception has been made it is too late. Euthanasia under any circumstances must be condemned.
>
> Once the respect for human life is so low that an innocent person may be killed directly at his own request, compulsory euthanasia will necessarily be very near. This could lead easily to killing all incurable cancer patients, the aged who are in public care, wounded soldiers, all deformed children, the mentally afflicted, and so on. Before long the danger would be at the door of every citizen.
>
> Source: Bishop Joseph Sullivan, 'The immorality of euthanasia', in *The Morality of Mercy Killing*, Westminster MD: Newman Press, 1950

In this case, it is not clear that Bishop Joseph Sullivan's slippery slope is a weakness.

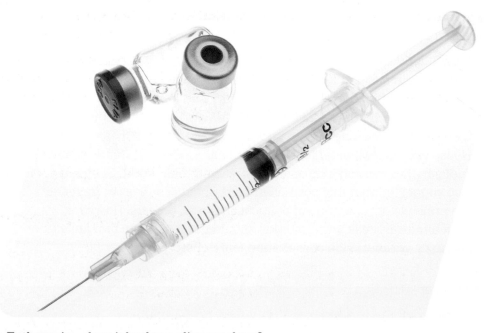

■ Euthanasia – does it lead to a slippery slope?

It does seem that there is a psychological barrier to killing innocent people. Once we have broken down that barrier, it is hard to know how we would prevent the category of people who can be killed from being extended to those who have not given their consent. It is easy to imagine a government which refuses health treatment to the obese, to smokers or to drinkers because they have not looked after themselves, deciding that those with specific illnesses cost the state too much money, and should be assisted in an early, painless and non-voluntary death. It is easy to imagine relatives who are happy to ease Granny out of her misery when she is not able to speak for herself, especially if Granny is both rich and irritating. This is a good reason for keeping that psychological barrier intact.

On the other hand, there may be ways of exploring logical differences between exceptions to the principle that we should not kill innocent people. It may not be a necessary consequence of allowing voluntary euthanasia. There is also a big step between compulsory euthanasia of the old, ill and deformed and the danger being at the door of every citizen. It is not an impossible step, especially in a society as obsessed with physical beauty and body image as ours. But it is still a big step. So, although there is some strength in this particular piece of slippery slope reasoning, there are also logical weaknesses.

ACTIVITY 25

Some European countries allow limited euthanasia for the terminally ill. Others ban euthanasia altogether. Research the arguments that are used for and against euthanasia. Have any of them successfully answered the concern that allowing voluntary euthanasia may be the first step on a slippery slope?

Rhetorical persuasion

Rhetorical persuasion is the use of linguistic and emotional devices in persuasive argument. Although these devices rarely strengthen an argument rationally, they are not always serious weaknesses. You will need to evaluate the use of rhetorical persuasion in reasoning, judging whether each instance is reasonable or not. It is important to remember that, in Critical Thinking, we are primarily concerned with the strength of reasoning rather than the effectiveness of the language itself.

It can be reasonable to use rhetorical persuasion in real-life reasoning. Real-life reasoning is not formal logic; it aims to entertain and persuade real people, who are not always rational. At its best rhetorical persuasion can be a way of organising and expressing a rational argument. It can be a way of linking our rational and emotional understandings of an issue, and of taking into consideration an audience's existing emotions and attitudes.

At its worst, rhetorical persuasion is emotive, manipulative and intellectually empty, used to inflame passions and incite people to act without thinking.

When you are evaluating the role of rhetorical persuasion in a passage you should:

■ consider the purpose of the reasoning

■ consider the relationship between the rhetorical and rational persuasion

■ consider the extent of the rhetorical persuasion (is it exaggerating slightly or inflaming strong emotions?)

■ refer specifically to the reasoning in the passage

■ justify your interpretation.

You do *not* need to know formal or technical terminology to talk about rhetorical persuasion. You will find it useful to use, everyday terms such as, 'exaggeration', 'emotional language', and 'suggestion', or 'implication'.

> **REMEMBER** ①
>
> Although there are many different definitions of rhetoric, we defined rhetorical persuasion in Chapter 6 as: the use of linguistic and emotional devices in persuasive argument.

Emotional language

Language which makes us emotional is often used instead of clear, precise language which expresses reasons to support conclusions. Let's look at two ways of putting the same point:

> **A** It's time our fine, hardworking nurses got the recognition they deserve. These saints of our society slave away night and day, toiling for the benefit of us all.
>
> **B** Nurses are hard working, dedicated professionals who provide care to those in need. We should recognise this and reward them appropriately. Nurses' pay should be increased to take into account the professional training, the long, hard hours, the disruption of shift work and the importance of the services they provide.

Passage A uses emotional language to persuade us. Nurses are described in glowing terms, making us feel that they deserve more. However, it is barely an argument, so there is almost no rational support for the claim that it is time our fine, hardworking nurses got the recognition they deserve.

Passage B is more factual, and clearly gives reasons to support the conclusion in the last sentence. It requires the reader to work a little harder – and it is harder to use your reason than it is to respond emotionally. It is, however, worth it in the long run if it helps you to make better decisions. For example, we would certainly want to make decisions about issues such as people's pay, or who to vote for, on the basis of reason rather than fear or vanity.

When you are evaluating the effect of the use of emotive language on the strength of reasoning, you need to consider the author's purpose, and the extent of the emotion argued. It is probably reasonable for an author to take into consideration their audience's existing emotions or attitudes. It is less reasonable to inflame hatred and suspicion against a particular group of people using very strongly emotive language.

Conflation and equivocation

As you learned at AS Level Critical Thinking, **conflation** is bringing two or more different concepts together and treating them as the same. For example, in the article in worked example 4, page 131, the author treats unhappiness and mental ill health as the same.

KEY TERM

● **Conflation**
Bringing different concepts together and treating them as if they were the same.

But there is an even more pressing reason to take happiness seriously – unhappiness is an expensive business. Mental ill health is the biggest single cause of incapacity and costs the country an estimated £9 billion in lost productivity and benefits. The weight on the NHS is enormous.

This weakens her argument because there are clear differences.

Equivocation is the use of a single word with different meanings in the same argument. For example:

It is generally recognised that being able to choose whether or not to have a child is a universal right. This is why many countries have criticised the Chinese government's policy of only allowing couples to have one child. Couples in the UK who are unable to have children naturally are being deprived of this universal right of procreative choice unless they can afford expensive medical procedures. So the British government's failure to allow these procedures on the NHS is a breach of this universal right.

In this case, there is an equivocation, with the first 'universal right' meaning a freedom to do something and the other two references to 'universal right' meaning a right to receive something. There is also a conflation between choosing how to use your natural abilities, and a right to treatment to overcome natural problems with reproduction.

KEY TERM

Equivocation ●

Changes in meaning from one use of a word to another within an argument.

ACTIVITY 26

Re-read passage A: Packed lunches in activity 3, page 122. Evaluate any rhetorical attempts to persuade and their impact on the overall reasoning.

WORKED EXAMPLE 10

Let's consider the role of emotion and language in the passage about family holidays in activity 6, page 134.

How reasonable is the author's use of rhetorical persuasion in this passage?

Answer A
The author's purpose here is to make us laugh at ourselves about the ways in which we behave on holiday. Although it is an argument to support the conclusion 'family holidays are best avoided', it also works on another level. The author probably doesn't really want to persuade us to accept the stated conclusion, but is using rhetorical persuasion including emotive language and humour to make us

question our behaviour and expectations. (We do not live in a world of pure logic – we are people with emotions as well as reason, and authors need to take this into account.) A serious, rational argument telling us that we are ridiculous and should change our behaviour would probably offend people and have no effect. So in this instance, it probably is reasonable to use exaggeration and emotional persuasion.

Answer B

The argument is very rhetorical and emotive which weakens it.

Answer C

The argument is very rhetorical. It uses exaggeration, juxtaposition of ideas and emotive language, which mean that the rational support for the conclusion is weakened. For example, 'and neither [parents nor children have] anything to say that the other would find interesting', clearly overstates the problem. Combined with the exaggeration of what parents and children want to do on holiday, this means there is little support for the (exaggerated claim that 'we spend the whole holiday squabbling' and if we don't spend the whole holiday squabbling, there is less reason to think that 'family holidays are best avoided'. However, the exaggeration is very funny. If the author's purpose is to entertain us rather than persuade us to accept a conclusion with good reasons, then the rhetorical language works. We can imagine variants of the scene pictured, and we have probably experienced family arguments (on holiday) about similar things.

So, even though it is not strong argument, it is a reasonable way of making us think about holidays. It's not as if it's a racist rant.

Comment

Answer A considers the author's purpose and makes a strong evaluation of the use of rhetorical persuasion and emotional language as a way of achieving the author's aim. It shows a clear awareness of the difference between the stated conclusion of the argument and the probable purpose of the reasoning. The candidate has interpreted the role of reasoning and justified this interpretation. However, the consideration of the extent of the emotion is implicit. The answer could be improved by some consideration of how emotive the language is and how the rhetorical persuasion is used in the passage, with clear reference to this argument. The current answer is limited to a justification for the reasonableness of using rhetorical persuasion at all.

Answer B is a typical stock answer which does not address the reasoning at all. The candidate could improve this answer by giving an example of the rhetorical persuasion used and showing how/how much it weakens the argument. It would be even further improved if they could then make a link if, or to what extent, this use of rhetorical persuasion is reasonable.

Answer C shows a fairly strong appreciation of both the strength and weakness of using this kind of rhetorical persuasion. It is perhaps not as sophisticated as answer A, but it does consider the reasonableness of using rhetorical persuasion in terms of the reasoning and the purpose of the passage. It attempts to consider the extent of the emotional language used, 'it's not as if it's a racist rant', but this carries across as an after-thought, an attempt to tick a box rather than a real evaluation. The candidate might have been better to say, 'The language uses emotion, suggestion and exaggeration, alongside a structure of reasoning, but it is not very emotive. It does not rouse us to passionate feelings as a racist rant would. So to this extent the rhetorical persuasion is reasonable rather than extreme'.

ACTIVITY

Evaluate the use of rhetorical persuasion in the article, 'New technology may be changing the human brain' in worked example 2 on pages 121–22. (Remember to consider the impact of any strength or weakness on the strength of support for the conclusion.)

ACTIVITY

Re-read passage B: Selfish, smug, self-righteous, unbearable two-wheeled idiots in activity 3, page 123. Evaluate the reasoning in the passage. Support your evaluation with reference to:

- **any flaws in the reasoning and their impact on the overall reasoning**

- **any rhetorical attempts to persuade and their impact on the overall reasoning.**

REMEMBER

You will gain credit for identifying strength as well as weakness.

Evaluating the use of counter argument

As we discussed in Chapter 8, page 148, counter-argument means 'opposing' argument. This might be seen in two arguments, one countering the other. It is also commonly seen within one argument; when an author includes all, or part, of an argument that opposes their own (that is a counter-argument) in their own argument. They often also respond to this counter-argument.

KEY TERMS

● **Attacking the arguer** (*ad hominem* flaw)

A form of reasoning that dismisses an opposing view by attacking the person putting forward that view rather than addressing their reasoning.

● **Straw person**

This flaw misrepresents or distorts an opposing view in order to dismiss it.

Attacking and misrepresenting the opposition

Attacking the arguer rather than the argument, and misrepresenting the opposition's arguments (the **straw person** flaw) are weaknesses specifically related to the use of and response to opposing arguments (counter-argument). Sometimes these patterns of reasoning may seem to make your own argument more persuasive. If you make an arguer who is countering your views look idiotic, your arguments may initially seem more appealing. However, the argument will not become rationally stronger, and in Critical Thinking we are primarily concerned with arguments that persuade us with good, strong reasons.

In the OCR Unit 4 exam you might have to evaluate the effectiveness of counter-argument in either of these forms. There might be a passage in which an author responds to a series of counter-arguments. In this case you might be asked:

> How effectively does the author respond to counter argument?

Alternatively there might be two passages, one of which counters the other. In this case you might be asked:

> How effectively does document 2 respond to the reasoning/claims in document 1?

or

> To what extent does document 2 counter the reasoning/claim in document 1?

Evaluating the use of counter-argument

When you are evaluating an author's use of and response to a counter-argument within their own argument you should:

■ consider whether the author has chosen key counter-arguments to include in their argument

■ consider whether the author has properly answered (refuted) the counter-argument

■ consider whether the author has strengthened their own reasoning by including and responding to this counter-argument

■ focus on precise claims

■ consider whether there are any attacking the arguer or straw person flaws

■ justify your interpretations.

REMEMBER ❗

It is possible to interpret the author's use of and response to counter-argument in different ways. It is important to justify your interpretation with specific reference to the reasoning.

WORKED EXAMPLE 11

How effectively does the author use and respond to counter-argument in the following passage? Justify your answer.

The author of this passage writes, 'One possible outcome, though, is that creationists will trumpet the paper as evidence that the theory of evolution is crumbling. If the experts themselves cannot get their story straight, they will crow, why should we believe anything they say?

That, of course, is shameless intellectual dishonesty (though what else would you expect from a movement built on intellectual dishonesty?). A paper questioning one aspect of evolution is not evidence that evolution itself is in trouble. Quite the opposite. It is science doing what it is supposed to do. We cannot censor ideas just because we are worried that a small bunch of religious fanatics will twist them for their own ends.'

Source: *New Scientist*, 20 June 2009.

Answer A
The author uses *ad hominem*, attacking the arguer. This weakens the conclusion. The author uses straw man, being rude about other people. This weakens.

Answer B
The author treats creationists as if their reactions were the only reason not to publish this article. By doing this he distorts the real counter to his argument, which is based in the misunderstandings of the majority. This means that his answer misses the real point as well. So his claim that 'we cannot censor ideas because' of a small minority is a straw person and if censoring ideas isn't the issue, we don't need to applaud the journal for its decision to publish this paper.

Answer C
The author attacks creationists instead of their argument, calling them 'intellectually dishonest', a 'small bunch of religious fanatics' and accusing them of 'twisting' ideas. This is unfair to the creationists and the author should answer their argument instead.

EXAM TIP

Finding flaws such as attacking the arguer or straw person flaws is only one part of evaluating an author's use of and response to counter argument.

Comment
Answer A merely names weaknesses without showing where they occur in the passage or properly evaluating the extent to which they affect the strength of the reasoning. 'This weakens' is a rather unenlightening, stock phase, which does not communicate to the examiner what (if anything) the candidate has understood.

Answer B is a fairly strong answer, which focuses on the straw person flaw, explaining it with reference to this specific reasoning, and considering how this affects the strength of support for the conclusion. It is probably a reasonable decision to focus on the straw person rather than the *ad hominem* flaw (attacking the arguer) as it weakens the support for the conclusion more significantly.

Answer C has identified a weakness in the reasoning with reference to the text. However, it has not really evaluated the significance of this weakness or told us to what extent it weakens the support for the conclusion.

ACTIVITY 29

Read the article, 'Consumer capitalism is making us ill – we need a therapy state', pages 131–32.

a) Evaluate the use and rejection of the counter-claim 'The emotional life of citizens in no business of the state…'

b) Evaluate the use and dismissal of the counter-claim 'To some, these kinds of interventions represent a nightmare scenario of a nanny state, an unacceptable interference in personal freedom. If people want to pursue their own unhappiness, then the state has no right to stop them.'

Evaluating argument and counter-argument

If you are evaluating two different arguments when one counters or responds to the other, you can use similar thought processes. You should:

■ consider whether the second argument/passage really refutes, responds to or answers the first

■ focus on precise claims

■ justify your interpretation.

WORKED EXAMPLE 12

Read Documents 1 and 2 and then answer the question that follows.

Document 1

I was sent the now notorious 'police spotter card' through the post. It's an official laminated card for 'police eyes only' and labelled as coming from 'CO11 Public Order Intelligence Unit'. The card contained the photographs of 24 anti-arms trade protesters, unnamed but lettered A to X. My picture appeared as photo H. You can imagine my reaction at finding I was the subject of a secret police surveillance process … I was delighted. I phoned my agent and told him I was suspect H. He replied: 'Next year we'll get you top billing … suspect A.'

The Metropolitan police circulated the card specifically for the Docklands biannual arms fair in London to help its officers identify 'people at specific events who may instigate offences or disorder'. Which is such a flattering quote I am thinking of having it on my next tour poster. While being wanted outside the arms fair, I was legitimately inside researching a book on the subject, and uncovered four companies illegally promoting 'banned' torture equipment. Questions were later asked in the Commons as to why HM Revenue & Customs and the police didn't spot it. Though, in fairness, none of the torture traders featured on the spotter card.

What exactly was I doing that was so awfully wrong as to merit this attention? Today's *Guardian* revelations of three secret police units goes some way to explain the targeting of protesters and raises worrying questions. The job of these units is to spy on protesters, and collate and circulate information about them. Protesters – or, as the police call them, 'domestic extremists' – are the new 'reds under the bed'.

Many of those targeted by the police have committed no crime and are guilty only of non-violent direct action. So it is worth reminding ourselves that protest is legal. Sorry if this sounds obvious, but you might have gained the impression that if three police units are spying on and targeting thousands, then those people must be up to something illegal.

The very phrase 'domestic extremist' defines protesters in the eyes of the police as the problem, the enemy. Spying on entire groups and organisations, and targeting the innocent, undermines not only our rights but the law – frightfully silly of me to drag this into an argument about policing, I know.

Protest is part of the democratic process. It wasn't the goodwill of politicians that led them to cancel developing countries' debt, but the protests and campaigning of millions of ordinary people around the world. The political leaders were merely the rubber stamp in the democratic process. Thus any targeting and treatment of demonstrators (at the G20 for example) that creates a 'chilling effect' – deterring those who may wish to exercise their right to protest – is profoundly undemocratic.

No police, secret or otherwise, should operate without proper accountability. So how are these three units accountable? Who has access to the databases? How long does information remain in the system? What effect could it have on travel and future employment of those targeted? How closely do these units work with corporate private investigators, and does the flow of information go both ways? Do the police target strikers?

A police spokesman has said that anyone who finds themselves on a database 'should not worry at all'. When a spokesman for the three secret units will not disclose a breakdown of their budgets, and two of the three will not even name who heads their operations (even MI6 gave us an initial, for God's sake), then the words 'should not worry at all' are meaningless. Indeed, when the police admit that someone could end up on a secret police database merely for attending a demonstration, it is exactly the time to worry.

Source: Mark Thomas, 'Doth I protest too much?', guardian.co.uk, 25 October 2009.

Document 2

It's no big deal that the police are looking for trouble-makers at protests. Just because Mark Thomas doesn't like the police looking out for him doesn't mean that the rest of us shouldn't be safe from him and people like him. It's not as if it's a new thing for the police to keep files on subversive protesters – they used to keep files on CND [Campaign for Nuclear Disarmament} protestors in the 1980s, and that has hardly led to Britain being a repressive police state.

Also, we have to accept that it's the police's job to allow legal business events to take place safely. So they keep a list of people who might make it unsafe. It's not so different from keeping a list of football hooligans to prevent match violence. Or from the shop keeper who has a list of local trouble makers so that he can stop them stealing his goods.

How effectively does Document 2 respond to the reasoning in Document 1? Justify your answer by selecting key strengths and weaknesses to evaluate.

Answer A

Document 2 responds quite well to the reasoning in Document 1. First because it shows that people aren't ending up on a database 'merely' for attending a demonstration – they are on a database because they are threatening legal business. He only says that 'many of these targeted by the police are guilty of no crime'. This implies that many more are guilty of some crime, not just legal protest. It is not clear whether Mark Thomas is, or ever has been, violent, and the author of Document 2 uses rhetorical persuasion to imply that he has been, or is, a threat ('Safe from him and people like him'). This is weaker than giving us evidence and may just be attacking the arguer but this weakness is minor – the question left open is whether Mark Thomas should be on the list, not whether there should be a list at all.

The response is strengthened by the idea that the policy used to keep files on CND protestors. Although two wrongs don't make a right, the author here is showing that Mark Thomas, the author of Document 1, is using slippery slope reasoning, implying dramatic consequences of the police keeping a simple list. By showing that these dramatic consequences didn't happen before, the author is calming fears roused by Thomas. So in a way, rhetorical reasoning is answering rhetorical reasoning.

Answer B

Document 2 does not respond very well to the reasoning in Document 1. The main lines of reasoning in Document 1 are that non-violent protest is legal, so the police should not be targeting non-violent protestors; protest is an effective part of democracy; and the police should be accountable so shouldn't be operating in secret.

Document 2 focuses only on the idea of the police keeping lists, and not on the ideas of innocent people being on the lists, on the idea of the role of protest in democracy or, most importantly, on the idea that these lists are secret and unaccountable. Thomas is not suggesting that the police should not keep lists of potential trouble makers – he is arguing that these lists should not be secret and should not relate to legal activities. Keeping open lists of football hooligans who break the law (by assaulting others) is very different from keeping secret lists of people who are doing nothing illegal (but who do oppose Government policy and big business interest re the arms trade). So Document 2 provides a very poor response to the reasoning in Document 1.

Answer C

Neither of these documents provides clear, cogent reasoning. Both are very emotive, using rhetorical persuasion instead of giving reasons. Both of them are bound up in giving their own opinion rather than answering each other. Document 2 seems so determined to support the police that it seems even to have some kind of vested interest – perhaps the author is a policeman who can't accept the police are doing wrong?

Document 2 ignores the emphasis in Document 1 on protesting being legal. We don't need to be kept safe from people doing legal things. The problem is with illegal arms traders not legal protestors.

The author of Document 2 cannot see that the actions of the police in the 1980s have led to us being more repressed by the police than we were then. We should fight the police at every opportunity to keep our democracy safe.

Comment

Answer A is quite strong. It considers whether the second document really responds to the reasoning in the first. It selects points to evaluate, focuses on precise claims, and justifies the interpretation with an awareness of the extent to which Document 2 assumes the reasoning in Document 1. This answer focuses on the rhetorical tactics used by both authors, and how Document 2's use of rhetorical persuasion is both a strength and weakness in its answer to Document 1. There is perhaps too much use of weakness in Document 1 attributed to strength in Document 2 – to a certain extent the candidate has picked up on a rhetorical line of reasoning in Document 2 and provided the strong reasoning themselves, rather than evaluating the actual strength of Document 2's response. To improve, the candidate could also have considered the important issue of 'secret' lists.

Answer B is also strong. It is exceptionally well focused on the extent to which Document 2 answers the reasoning in Document 1. Because the candidate has a very strong grasp of how the reasoning in Document 1 works, they are well able to evaluate the response. The candidate has selected what is probably the most important weakness in Document 2's response to evaluate.

Answer C is much less focused than answers A and B. It makes some relevant evaluative points but does not link them properly to the issue of how well Document 2 responds to Document 1. The point about the author of Document 2 having a vested interest to support the police could be made relevant; the candidate could focus on the defence of the police rather than answering the specific charges made by Mark Thomas, the author of Document 1. However, the candidate speculates about the author and forgets to use the point to answer the question.

The next two points the candidate makes also could be made relevant, but the candidate states their own opinion rather than evaluating how effectively the author has responded to the reasoning in Document 2. The candidate might consider also their use of language. They probably do not mean that 'we should fight the police'. They probably mean that we should 'fight police repression'. It would be even better to say 'Thomas has raised an important point about secret police activity which is not answered by the CND example: Thomas's implications, that we should oppose repressive policing stands'.

Evaluating hypothetical reasoning in real-life reasoning

Hypothetical reasoning looks at the consequences which might come about if something happens. As you learned at AS level, hypothetical reasoning commonly occurs in the form 'if…then'. However, hypothetical reasoning can occur in other forms. For example, in the article 'Consumer capitalism is making us ill – we need a therapy state' (worked example 4, pages 131–32) the author considered what might happen if the state took a role in our happiness:

This raises the prospect of a future politics where emotional well-being could be as important a remit of state public health policy as our physical well-being. In 10 years' time, alongside 'five fruit and veg a day', our kids could be chanting comparable mantras for daily emotional wellbeing: do some exercise, do someone a good turn, count your blessings, laugh, savour beauty.

We might also be discussing emotional pollution in much the way we now discuss environmental pollution. Top of the list would be advertising … There would also be a strong rationale to increase subsidies for festivals, parks, theatres, community groups, amateur dramatics, choirs and sports clubs.

This form of hypothetical reasoning does not take the common 'if … then' pattern. However, it is hypothetical in that it looks at the consequences which might occur if we accepted that the state had a role in our happiness. When you evaluate the use of hypothetical reasoning in a longer, real-life text you should:

■ consider how likely the consequences are

■ consider how the hypothetical reasoning is being used and whether/to what extent it achieves its purpose

■ refer specifically to the reasoning

■ justify your interpretation.

The role of this passage in the argument is to illustrate how a political concern with our emotional well being might develop (in a non-threatening way) *if* we allowed it to.

How likely are the hypothetical consequences of allowing the state a role in our emotional well being, and how well does this reasoning support the author's conclusion that 'the state should resume a role in promoting the good life, not just chivvy us along in the global rat race, anxious and insecure'?

None of the possible consequences examined are unlikely. Chanting mantras, discussing emotional pollutants such as advertising, and increasing funding for leisure pursuits such as festivals are all probable. However, they are not necessarily all positive. Children chanting mantras for well being smacks of brainwashing, for example. The author has also omitted negative consequences that might occur, and part of our evaluation can be to consider probable consequences which the author has neglected. People are currently demonised for choosing unhealthy lifestyles. The prospect of a similar witch hunt against people who make emotionally unhealthy choices is terrifying. Might our reliance on the government to sort out our emotional lives lead to greater dependency and unhappiness?

So, this scenario provides support for the conclusion to the extent that it sketches realistic possibilities. However, this support is limited.

Analogies

Analogy is a pattern of reasoning which claims that two situations are so similar that if we accept a claim or conclusion about one situation, we should also accept it about the other. Analogy is used to make it easier to follow a pattern of thought, to create a clear image to help us understand abstract reasoning or to highlight a pattern shared by two situations or arguments.

REMEMBER

Analogy is a form of argument which uses parallel situations to encourage the audience to accept a conclusion.

▪ More funding for leisure pursuits – a possible consequence?

Evaluating analogies

In Critical Thinking for OCR Unit 2 we looked at six steps of evaluating an analogy:

1 Identify precisely the situations being compared.
2 Identify the conclusion being supported by the analogy.
3 Consider significant similarities between the situations.
4 Consider significant differences between the situations.
5 Evaluate whether the differences outweigh the similarities.
6 Decide whether the analogy helps support the conclusion.

In Unit 4 you will not need to work through these six steps in the precise, detailed way you did at AS. If there is an analogy in the article you have been asked to evaluate, you could include your evaluation of how strong the analogy is and the effect this has on the strength of the reasoning with your general evaluation of the strength of the reasoning. You should quickly go through the six steps of evaluating an analogy in your mind, and write down the most important conclusions you come to, using these to comment on how strong the author's argument is. At AS you needed to demonstrate that you had some very specific skills, one at a time. At A2 the emphasis is on selecting the right skills to use and applying them to a wider task.

Let's take an example:

Last week the Professional Association of Teachers called for websites such as YouTube to be banned, to prevent bullying of children and teachers. Kirsti Paterson, who proposed the motion, said that one teacher had been the subject of a death threat – a pupil had posted a doctored picture online, rendering the teacher headless and added the caption, 'You are dead.'

Now, I would suggest that bullying is in the eye of the beholder – one man's victim of bullying is another's opportunity to educate, perhaps by posting a comment, pointing out that the correct tense to have employed would have been the future indicative, 'You will be dead', or perhaps a nice subjunctive, 'You would be dead, were I to be an all-powerful despot and not some manky, acne-riddled teen'.

We mustn't be bullied into closing YouTube*. I think it's safe to assume that most people don't support the idea of closing down websites they don't like – the magnificent Emma-Jane Cross, the chief executive of the charity BeatBullying, responded to last week's suggestion by declaring, 'Calls for social sites like YouTube to be closed because of cyberbullying are as intelligent as calls for schools to be closed because of bullying'.

* This sentence added to make conclusion clear out of context of whole article.

Source: Natalie Haynes, *The Times*, 6 August 2007

In the last line of this extract from a longer article there is an analogy: 'Calls for social sites like YouTube to be closed because of cyberbullying are as intelligent as calls for schools to be closed because of bullying.' Let's evaluate the strength of this analogy and its effect on the strength of support for the conclusion that 'we mustn't be bullied into closing YouTube.'

The analogy in the last line is effectively an appeal to vanity, manipulating our emotions and our pride and using mild humour to persuade us that closing sites like YouTube because of cyberbullying would be unintelligent. This appeal in itself is quite weak, as it plays on our emotional resistance to bullying, so it doesn't give strong rational support to the conclusion.

Bringing your skills together in the exam

In the Unit 4 exam you are likely to be asked one or two evaluative questions which refer to one, two or three documents. As we have seen, having a clear understanding of how the reasoning works and what sorts of reasoning are being used will help you to evaluate the reasoning.

The evaluative questions you are asked are likely to be quite broad, and you will need to select key strengths and weaknesses to evaluate in your answer. You might use any of the skills you have developed in the last two chapters. Depending on the nature of the documents and the nature of the question, you may need to use some of these skills more than others. For example, the passage you were asked about may contain several structural flaws, but very little rhetorical persuasion, so you would need to discuss the structural flaws in your answer but would not need to say much about rhetorical persuasion. Alternatively, the documents may be an argument and counter-argument, in which case it is likely that you would need to focus your answer on the extent to which one document answers the other. Let's consider several possible questions that could be asked.

WORKED EXAMPLE 13

Re-read the article 'In praise of scientific heresy' in worked example 7, pages 166–67, which we will now refer to as Document 1, and Document 2 below. Then consider the following questions.

Document 2: I am the middleman, but you really wouldn't want to cut me out.

Nothing turns the heads of normally sane news reporters to insensate goo so much as a juicy story about… what? Sex? Celebs? Celebs having sex? Financial scandal?

No, none of these. I'm thinking about human evolution. Or more specifically, the search for the 'missing link' – that evolutionary stepping-stone between Man and the Apes. Remember *Darwinius* (aka Ida), a tiny fossil monkey-like creature, subject of TV documentaries and a book deal, all sewn up before the little chap had even been properly described scientifically? The poor thing was hyped to the public as the biggest discovery ever made – key to our evolution.

The scientific paper, when it came, was perfectly respectable. It made no such claims, but would have been seen by far fewer people than the TV shows – even though it was, and is, freely available.

In my job as a scientific editor for *Nature*, I get to hear about important scientific discoveries months – sometimes years – before you do. Now, some may say science should be completely open, broadcast in real-time, without people like me acting as unelected arbiters of what you should see and hear.

What these voices never say is that the volume of science generated is huge. Trying to choose the science you want from the deluge is like trying to collect a thimbleful of water from a fire hose. And that's even before rating it for quality.

So, even if you had the stomach to be presented with science in the raw – all of it – how could you be sure that what you select has been properly validated, isn't half-cooked, or even flat-out wrong?

You wouldn't lack for guidance for long, though, because any number of special-interest groups, from PR agencies to drug companies, will line up to promote the science that best suits their bottom line. That's where we insiders step in. When journal editors receive scientific papers describing major new finds, our first call isn't to a PR company or TV station, but to a selection of experts in the field. Their job is to evaluate the new claim, pick holes in it and make suggestions for improvement. Quite often these experts will disagree with the authors of the paper and with each other. I'll act as a chairman – or ringmaster – working to achieve consensus, so that what eventually gets into the public eye is as good as it can be.

This process can be long, complex and subtle – and best conducted away from the media glare. We'll only let a finding take its turn on stage when all agree that it's good and ready. That way, you – the public – will have some assurance that the science you see is good, and not self-serving spin. Lurking in the shadows, we editors are guardians of reality against the superficial glitter of the matrix. You don't even have to decide which pill you're going to take – the red one, or the blue – because we have done it for you.

Source: Henry Gee, 'The Insider', *BBC Focus Magazine*.

1 **How effectively does the reasoning of Document 1 support the claim, 'The journal should be applauded for its decision to disseminate this challenging paper?' Justify your answer by selecting key strengths and weaknesses to evaluate.**

2 **To what extent does the heading of Document 2, 'I am the middleman, but you wouldn't want to cut me out', follow from the reasoning in the article?**

EXAM TIP

The key strengths and weaknesses you select will be different for different kinds of questions.

3   **To what extent does the reasoning in Document 2 counter the reasoning in Document 1? Justify your answer by selecting key strengths and weaknesses to evaluate.**

4   **Is the reasoning stronger in Document 1 or Document 2? Justify your answer by selecting key strengths and weaknesses to evaluate.**

Let's consider how the answers to questions 2 and 3 might be different.

Answer to question 2

Notes – not arg, no C.

Report, C ASS "Science … open… without people like me acting as undetected abilities of what you should see and hear".

Purpose – counter this claim by supporting unstated C??

R – science huge → IC (rhet q) → validated?
R – interest groups promote their line
R – science editors help avoid this – chairman – IC public assurance that sci good
Rh claims – "we are guardian of reality"
R "You don't have to decide… we have done it for you"
∴ you wouldn't want to cut me out
∴ science shouldn't be completely open

But: example of hype re Ida shows system re middleman didn't work.

But: what if we don't want someone to do the thinking for us? Scary

Strong: science huge – good point
(Quality – good point – CT Skills?) ⟶   analogy?
*   → no. just image.*

But: are science journalists very different from PR people? – He says so.

The headline follows from the reasoning of Document 2 to a certain extent. The author doesn't state this conclusion, but clearly intends to show that his job is important as part of a response to the counter-argument that, 'Now, some may say science should be completely open…. without people like me acting as unelected arbiters of what you should see and hear'.

The reason that science is huge does make a strong case for keeping the middleman, or at least someone to select key aspects for us to attend to. The question about validation seems strong but isn't as strong – although each of us probably can't read all the science there is, we could apply our own thinking skills to what we do read. However, there probably is a role for quality control, so this reason still gives some support to the headline that we don't want to cut the middleman out.

The idea that science editors are reputable people who check with experts rather than just hyping whatever suits them does seem to support the claim that we want science editors as middlemen. Better to have impartial, knowledgeable people in the middle – if we accept his claims. He might have a vested interest or portray himself as impartial and objective when actually he just wants to keep his job. So we read to be skeptical about the value of middlemen. This is increased by the fact that the media hype about Ida, which presumably did include scientific editors, shows that we still don't get good quality science. So perhaps the middlemen are not as valuable as Gee claims.

The last paragraph is rhetorical persuasion/reason to show that science editors guard us. But it actually undermines its purpose if the reader values thinking for themselves because it shows science editors as rather frightening manipulators deciding what reality is and doing our thinking for us. Those who value free thought might see this as a strong reason against the headline that 'you really wouldn't want to cut me out'.

So there is some support for this claim, but there are some weaknesses that mean it doesn't fully follow from the reasoning.

Answer to question 3

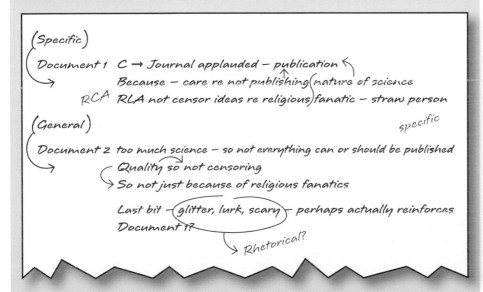

(Specific)
Document 1   C → Journal applauded – publication
                    Because – care re not publishing (nature of science)
              RCA   RLA not censor ideas re religious) fanatic – straw person

(General)   specific
Document 2   too much science – so not everything can or should be published
                    Quality so not censoring
                    So not just because of religious fanatics
              Last bit – (glitter, lurk, scary) – perhaps actually reinforces
              Document 1?
                          → Rhetorical?

Document 2 wasn't written specifically to counter Document 1, but, 2 does contain some ideas which might be used to counter the reasoning in Document 1. Document 1 is making a case about whether a specific article should have been published, whereas Document 2 is making a general case about whether someone should select the science the public gets to see. It is possible that we could accept Document 2's claims that someone should select and also accept Document 1's claims that the paper about orangutans should have been published. However, the reassurance in Document 2 might give us some reasons why that paper should not have been published: the idea that there is too much science shows that not everything can be published, which means that 'not publishing' is not the same as 'censoring', as Document 1 implies, thus weakening this part of Document 1's reasoning. Document 2 raises the issue of quality – which is also mentioned in Document 1 and gives use more reasons to think that low quality science should not be published. So, if this paper on orangutan is 'failing the test' of 'extraordinary claims requiring extraordinary evidence' (Document 1) and special interest groups will promote it regardless of quality (Document 2), then perhaps it would make sense for the scientific editors to withhold publication until the quality is more certain. It depends whether this is publication for debate in the scientific community or publication for the general public.

So, the reasoning in Document 2 does give us some grounds to oppose the conclusion of Document 1. However, at the end of it might also support the reasoning in Document 1. It is much less frightening to think that there is some bad research in publication than to think of science editors doing our thinking for us. To keep debate alive, to stop science 'becoming sterile' (Document 1) and to keep the emphasis on free thinking, perhaps we really should applaud the journal's decision to publish the paper.

So, overall, although Document 2 gives some reasons which might weaken the reasoning in Document 1, it ends up strengthening it by making the censorship argument seem less like a straw person.

Comment

What are the similarities and differences?

■ Both answers are quite short and focused on answering the question. Both answers leave out a lot of points that could have been made and develop a few points in detail.

■ Both answers consider strengths and weaknesses and come to an overall judgment.

■ Both answers justify an interpretation.

■ Both answers show a clear understanding of the structure of the reasoning as part of the evaluation.

But:

■ The answer to the first question focuses on how well the reasons support a particular claim.

■ The answer to the second question focuses on the extent to which the claims in Document 2 counter, weaken or even strengthen the claims in Document 1.

■ So we can see that different evaluative skills have been used. Different key points are appropriate for answering different questions.

Summary

You should now be able to:

■ evaluate reasoning drawing on a number of different skills to answer different specific questions.

Learning objectives

Write your own arguments with:

- a clear structure of reasoning with reasons which support intermediate and main conclusions as well as strands of reasoning
- identifying possible counter-arguments and responding to them
- clarification of key terms.

Communicating your own ideas in a clear, precise and reasoned way is an important skill, both in Critical Thinking and in life. We all need to be able to support our own opinions or suggested courses of action and deal with opposition to them. Improving your skills in developing your own arguments is the focus of this chapter.

At AS Level Critical Thinking you learned to support a clearly stated conclusion with reasons, evidence and examples in a structured argument. You may have included a short counter-argument in your reasoning.

Many of the principles for writing a strong argument at A2 Level Critical Thinking remain the same. You must:

- have a clearly stated conclusion
- consider whether the reasons you give provide strong support for the conclusion you have stated
- structure your argument carefully.

We will revise all these skills and, in particular, we will extend your ability to structure your argument using:

- strands of reasoning
- response to counter-argument
- clarification of key terms.

Stating your conclusion clearly

There are two elements to remember when stating your conclusion. These are:

- you must write down your conclusion
- you must be clear and precise about what your conclusion is.

Writing down your conclusion

In everyday life you will be asked to give or write down your (considered) opinion, answer questions or put forward proposals for action. It is important in these cases that your reasoning does include a statement of your conclusion. People often give reasons, but leave their audience to draw the conclusion for themselves, on the basis that it is obvious. There are three problems with this approach:

1 If you have not stated your conclusion, you will not have provided an argument but simply some ideas on a theme.
2 What is obvious to you may not be obvious to others.
3 Even if it is obvious that you agree or disagree with a general idea, your precise conclusion may be less clear.

Let's take an example:

> School uniform reduces the bullying that occurs because of individuals' choice of clothing and the amount of money they are able to spend on clothes. It makes getting up in the morning simpler as you do not have to choose what to wear, or look for matching clothes. It acts as a badge of identity, drawing pupils closer together into a community.

In this case, it is clear that the speaker is broadly in favour of school uniform. It is not clear whether the speaker would support any or all of the following claims:

■ Schools should consider adopting a school uniform.

■ Schools with social problems such as bullying should adopt a school uniform.

■ School uniform should be compulsory in the sixth form.

These claims are very different, and require different reasoning to support them. So it is important to write down your conclusion. This allows you to check whether you have supported your precise conclusion, and have not just given general support to a vague idea.

> ## REMEMBER
>
> Write down your conclusion, even if you have been told what it is. You will gain higher marks if you do.

Stating your conclusion precisely

In the A2 Critical Thinking exam you will be given a claim to support or challenge. For example, you could be asked to support or challenge the claim that 'School uniform should be compulsory.' You have a number of options.

1   You can write an argument which supports or challenges the conclusion as it is, for example:

> School uniform should be compulsory.
> School uniform should not be compulsory.

However, these are both very strong conclusions. As we discussed in Chapter 9, a strong conclusion can be weakened by a single example. To make your argument stronger, you may need to make the conclusion weaker. You can remind yourself how to do this by looking at Critical Thinking for OCR Unit 2, Chapter 14, pages 226–43.

Either of these strong conclusions may feel too limiting. You may wish to say that neither 4-year-olds nor 18-year-olds should be compelled to wear a uniform, but that 14-year-olds should have to. This leads us onto the second option:

2   You could qualify the conclusion so that you are supporting or challenging it to a certain extent, for example:

> School uniform should be compulsory, but only in secondary schools.
> School uniform should not be compulsory except where a school council has voted it in.

A further difficulty might be that there are words in the claim you have been given to support or challenge which are vague or ambiguous. So, you now have a third option:

3   You may need or wish to specify or limit the meanings of words and reflect this in your conclusion.

- When we say 'uniform', what do we mean?

'Compulsory' might mean any of the following:

- Every schoolchild in the country has to wear a uniform.
- Schools must enforce a uniform on their pupils.
- If a school chooses to have a uniform, pupils must wear it.

'Uniform' might mean:

- Clothes in the same colour scheme such as a striped blazer and boater with badge or khakis and beret.
- Girls must wear skirts which end at the knee. Boys must wear trousers which fasten at the waist (not the hips) and end at their ankles.

So, your conclusion might be:

It should be compulsory for schools to require pupils to wear decent clothing in the same colour scheme at secondary school.

or

School uniform should be a matter of choice for the school, but where a school imposes a uniform, students should have no leeway at all in modifying it.

or

Most schools should have uniforms and require their students to wear them, but it should remain a matter of choice for the school and not be enforced by the government.

We will show how to clarify key or ambiguous terms in your argument later in the chapter.

ACTIVITY 30

Consider how you might qualify the following claims if you were asked to support or challenge them. Make sure you are not completely changing the claim.

a) Sixteen-year-olds should be given state-funded accommodation.
b) It is wrong to be frivolous.
c) Local transport networks should be state run.
d) Happiness should be studied in schools.
e) Investing in further nuclear reactors would be a disaster.
f) People should not wear pink.
g) War is wrong.

REMEMBER

Consider how strong a claim is. Strong claims need much more support than weak claims.

Challenging or countering a conclusion

You may be asked to support or challenge/counter a claim that is given to you, as follows:

'People should never wear pink.' Write your own argument to support or challenge this claim.

It is worth considering what it means to challenge – or counter – a claim. It is tempting to take a strong negative claim, such as 'People should never wear pink' and turn it into an extreme positive claim, such as, 'People should always wear pink'. However, in the world that we live in it would be very difficult to justify this view, so you would have difficulty finding reasons strong enough to support your claim. You would need to challenge some fairly strongly held principles, such as 'We should have freedom of choice'. It would be better, then, to find a more moderate way of phrasing your challenge to the conclusion or to qualify your challenge so that you can support it. Other possibilities might be:

■ People should sometimes wear pink.

■ Some people should avoid wearing pink.

■ People should wear pink if they want to.

Whether or not to wear pink is, of course, a relatively frivolous consideration, unless you work in the fashion industry. But there are choices and concepts where the strength of your opposition could make a real difference. Let's consider the claim given in the June 2009 Unit 4 exam.

'Freedom of choice should always be limited.' Write your own argument to support or challenge this claim.

In our society, we put a great deal of emphasis on freedom of choice, so many candidates are likely to want to challenge a claim like this. How can it be challenged? Let's consider some possibilities.

■ Freedom of choice should never be limited.

Unlimited freedom of choice seems impractical, undesirable and hard to support. This is an extreme claim at the other end of the spectrum from the original claim.

■ Freedom of choice should sometimes be limited.

■ Freedom of choice should always be limited in some circumstances, but never in other circumstances.

■ Freedom of choice should not always be limited.

Any of these last three claims could be supported with reference to specific circumstances in which freedom of choice should or should not be limited.

How you challenge and qualify this conclusion depends on how you are defining the key terms. We have considered how different understandings of 'uniform' and 'compulsory' affected the precise conclusions we drew. When we are dealing with a claim like 'freedom of choice should always be limited', the effects of different definitions are much more profound. Here are some questions to help you think about what these terms mean.

■ What is freedom of choice? How is it related to freedom more generally? How is it related to specific choices? Is choosing to act (e.g. in a criminal way) the freedom of action or the freedom of choice? Should I be able to choose to give birth to a specific sort of baby? What if my choices limit someone else's choices – whose freedom of choice?

■ What is limited? Does this relate to practical possibility (e.g. my choice to dance on the sun is limited by the physical impossibility)? Does this mean completely taken away, so I don't have any choices (and therefore no freedom to choose)? Does it mean that I am free to make a choice, but some specific choices are not allowed/avoidable (e.g. I am free to choose what to have for dinner, but I can only order what is on the menu; or I am free to choose to have a baby, but I can only have a baby by natural means or adoption)? How is my freedom of choice limited? Who is limiting it? The government, the fertility clinic, the restaurant owner, society more generally? Does conforming to social norms count as limiting freedom of choice? Do laws and punishment (e.g. prison) limit my choices, or do I have the freedom of choice to do the illegal act and take the consequences?

These are just some of the things you might think about. Let's look at how these definitions might affect the conclusion. For example, if you think that a government should not generally stop people making choices for themselves, but that some choices should not be available, you might conclude 'Freedom of choice should not be limited but some choices should be restricted'.

If you think that taking some choices away is limiting your freedom of choice, then you might conclude, 'Freedom of choice must always be limited, but not totally taken away'.

Which comes first, conclusion or reasoning?

We are focusing very strongly on deciding on a conclusion as the first step in the process of writing an argument. But we are also talking about quite a lot of thinking about defining terms and qualifying the conclusion. Can we really know what the conclusion is before we have done the reasoning?

Deciding on your conclusion does involve some processes of reasoning, but these processes should be part of your thinking and planning time. You should start to write your argument only when you have done most of your thinking and have a very clear idea of your framework reasoning.

Supporting your conclusion with reasons

As we discussed at AS Level Critical Thinking and considered in Chapter 6 of this book, reasons must be precisely focused on a conclusion. A reason should give us grounds to accept a conclusion, and should not ramble on about the same topic. Reasons should give strong support to the conclusion. There are two issues here:

- strength of conclusion
- focus of reasons.

Strength of conclusion

Strong conclusions require very strong support. For example:

> All rap artists promote aggressive behaviour.

We only need one example of a rap artist who does not promote aggressive behaviour to undermine this claim. It would be very hard to provide support for a claim which did not allow for a single counter example. We would have to demonstrate that every single rap artist promoted aggressive behaviour and, even then, we could not allow for new rap artists who were different.

We could make the claim a bit weaker, to make it easier to support:

> A significant number of rap artists promote aggressive behaviour.

What if we weakened the claim further?

> A few rap artists might promote aggressive behaviour.

Now we are not saying anything much at all. Almost anything might be the case. This claim has become so weak it is almost pointless. Little support is required for such weak conclusions – but neither do we learn anything of significance.

Focus of reasons

Evidence must precisely support a reason without leaving gaps in your knowledge, and reason must be focused on a precise conclusion, not just on the same topic. For example:

> **R** John is concerned about the environment.
> **C** John should buy an electric car.

The reason is very general, and does not give a strong reason why John should buy an electric car. If John walks everywhere, buying an electric car would make his lifestyle worse for the environment. If he flies a great deal, buying an electric car would not help him conserve the environment.

Using your evaluative skills to ensure your reasons to support your conclusion

At A2 Level Critical Thinking we have extended this idea: looking at an author's work, we may decide that they have provided good support for their intermediate conclusion but have not gone on to provide sufficient support for the move to their main conclusion. For example, in the article, 'Who says nuclear power is clean?' in activity 7, pages 138–40, the author provided good support for the intermediate conclusion that 'The truth is that this form of energy is, in the end, no more safe, reliable or clean than the others.' However, this does not in itself mean that the UK should invest in renewable energy. More work was needed to support the main conclusion.

You can apply the same thinking to your own arguments when you are trying to ensure that you provide good support for your main conclusion. Ask yourself:

> 'Does this reason really mean that I have to accept the main conclusion of my argument?'

For example:

> 'How well does the fact that school uniforms can help to create a sense of community support the claim that uniforms should be compulsory?'

ACTIVITY 31

Look again at two claims we considered earlier:

- **Schools with social problems, like bullying, should adopt a school uniform.**
- **School uniform should be compulsory in the sixth form.**

a) **Form and draft out all your ideas.**
b) **Write lists of reasons which support and oppose each claim.**
c) **Consider how the support and opposition for the two claims are different.**
d) **Select key points and write a short argument (about 150 words) to support or challenge each of these claims.**

Assessing your own arguments

You will need to develop the ability to assess your own arguments. There are no suggested answers for the activities in this chapter, which ask you to write arguments because there are so many different ways of being right. Each activity is followed by a worked example showing you some ways in which arguments can be weak or strong, and helping you to focus on assessing and improving the quality of your own reasoning. You should also use the mark schemes for F504. Full versions are printed on the CD-ROM that accompanies this book in the Exam Café section, and you can find the most recent versions on the OCR website.

WORKED EXAMPLE 14

'**School uniform should be compulsory in the sixth form.**' Write a short argument (150 words) to support or challenge this claim. When you are assessing your work in this activity, you should focus on:

■ **How well the reasons (and intermediate conclusions) support the main conclusion.**

Answer A

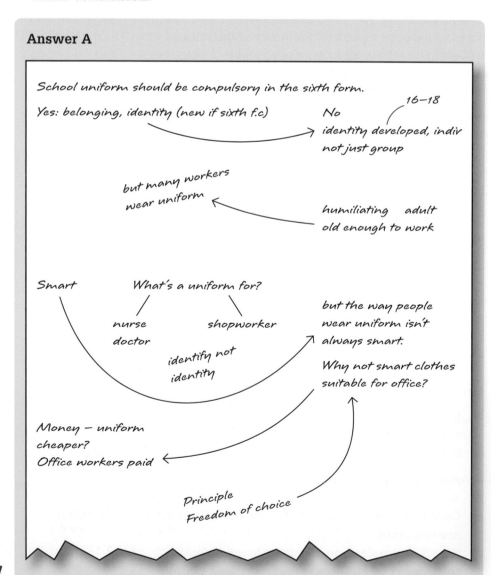

Although there is a case for making school uniform compulsory in the sixth form, (IC) on balance it is better to allow 16–18-year-olds to wear their own choice of clothes. The reason often given in support of school uniform, that it helps young people to (CA) develop a sense of belonging and group identity, is inappropriate (IC) in the sixth form because sixth (R) formers are young adults. This means (Expl) that they have left insecure adolescence and are developing their person identity (79).

Many young adults find it (IC) humiliating to have to wear a uniform that marks them as children, especially if (R) they have friends who are already working. They feel they are (R) being branded. It's also an important part of (R) growing up that young people should develop the skill and responsibility to dress well. So, in a society that values (P) freedom of choice, school (C) uniform should not be compulsory in the sixth form. (150 words)

Comment

This student has planned effectively, considering lots of ideas and how they relate to each other. They have seen that the second title needs specific evidence from research, whereas the first can be done from general knowledge.

The argument has been carefully structured, and the reasons do give some support to the intermediate and main conclusions. It's not conclusive proof, but the question is not asking for conclusive proof, just a reasonably strong line of reasoning (in the form of an argument).

The principle has been tacked on at the end rather than integrated into the argument, but this student is ready to move on and include complexity in their argument. Note that they have annotated their work, considering the argument elements they are using, and counting words. This is not necessary in the exam (and may even distract the examiner), but it is certainly useful to analyse your arguments when you are practising.

Answer B

School uniform should be compulsory in the sixth form because everyone should be treated the same. It's not fair if sixth formers get to wear nice clothes while everyone else is wearing uniform.

Wearing school uniform can reduce bullying. Lots of bullying happens when some children pick on others for being poor or having poor fashion taste. Children shouldn't be allowed to bully each other because it can have a long lasting psychological effect and it's not very nice.

Wearing school uniform can help make everybody feel like they belong to a school. It's part of group identity building. Group identity is important according to Professor Black who did a study into group identity.

It's easier to wear school uniform because you don't have to worry about what you are going to wear in the morning. Your uniform is just there. It doesn't matter what you want or what you like, it's just easy and anyway, no one likes going to school. Uniform is just another one of these things to hate about school. So it should be compulsory.

Comment

This student has shown no evidence of planning, and the argument is just about basic. There is some reasoning present, and the reasons in the first paragraph are related to school uniform being compulsory in the sixth form. It's not especially strong reasoning, however.

The rest of the passage seems to be ideas that the student has remembered from other activities they have done and have written down, without thinking whether they relate to school uniform being compulsory in the sixth form. They have recognised the need to show why group identity building is important, but the vague reference to Professor Black without citing evidence is very weak.

By the end of this answer the student is rambling, writing down anything they can think of on the subject of school uniform. The very last part is incoherent. It doesn't make sense to say, 'Uniform is just another one of those things to hate about school so it should be compulsory'.

This student needs to concentrate on writing simple arguments with reasons which are fully relevant to the conclusion.

ACTIVITY 32

Choose one of the claims from activity 30, which you have qualified.

Write a short argument to support or challenge it. Concentrate on making sure that your reasons support your intermediate and main conclusions really strongly. You may like to work with a partner to discuss how well the links of support in your arguments work.

WORKED EXAMPLE 15

'People should not wear pink.' Write a short argument to support or challenge this claim.

Answer A

> People should not wear pink
>
> Why not wear pink?
> men–social stereotype
> baby girls — social moulding
> hideous colour (personal opinion?)
> Unfashionable?
>
> People should wear pink if they want to
>
> Free choice
> beauty in the eye of the beholder
> Who cares?
> resist social pressure
> Reclaim pink?

Some people say we shouldn't wear pink. They say men shouldn't wear pink because of social stereotypes. They say it is wrong to mould baby girls by making them wear pink. They give their opinion that pink is a hideous colour. They say that pink isn't fashionable.

Other people say that people should wear pink if they want to. They say it's a free country and we can choose what to wear. They say that beauty is in the eye of the beholder and we can wear what we want. They say we should resist social pressure and reclaim pink as a colour for tomboys.

So people should wear pink if they want to.

Comment

This student has not written an argument. The answer reports two different opinions, listing things that people with those opinions say. There is a personal opinion at the end, but we are given no reason to accept it. They need to choose one side of this debate and write reasons to support a conclusion.

Answer B

We live in a society where we believe in freedom of choice. This means that decisions about what colour to wear should be made freely too. So people should wear pink if they want to.

Arguments about gender stereotyping or social moulding might affect whether you want to wear pink. For example, women who want to avoid being seen as girlish and weak might choose not to wear baby pink. However, this does not mean that they should not wear pink.

Fashionistas might tell us that we should or should not wear pink, black, tassels or frills. But clothes are not about other people telling us what we should or shouldn't do. Clothes are for comfort and practicality.

Comment

This short argument begins very well. The student has applied a general principle to a specific situation, and providing we accept the principle, this reasoning strongly supports the conclusion. The second paragraph begins to look at what wanting and choosing might mean and is fairly effective. The third paragraph, however, begins to wander and is not fully related to the conclusion.

Argument structure

As you learned at AS Level Critical Thinking, it is important to structure your argument and have some logical progression of ideas, rather than just writing down your ideas as they occur to you. At AS Level Critical Thinking you considered:

■ placing your main conclusion at the beginning or end of an argument

■ including an intermediate conclusion

■ using two to four different reasons

■ using evidence or examples to support each reason.

At A2 Level Critical Thinking this still provides the basis of a sound argument structure, but we will look at how to extend it to allow for greater complexity of thought.

Strands of reasoning

REMEMBER

A strand of reasoning is a line of thought which has been developed. For example, a reason may be supported with a short argument consisting of reasons, evidence and examples; this would turn it into a strand of reasoning supporting an intermediate conclusion.

One way to extend the AS Level Critical Thinking structure to A2 Level is to use strands of reasoning. In Chapter 6 we looked at identifying strands of reasoning in an author's work.

For example, in the article 'Consumer capitalism is making us ill – we need a therapy state', pages 131–32, Bunting uses three main strands of reasoning:

1 She establishes happiness as something which can be taken seriously.
2 She shows how the state could be involved in happiness in a (fairly) acceptable way.
3 She shows that the state contributes to our unhappiness.

She draws the conclusion that 'The state should resume a role in promoting the good life, not just chivvy us along in the global rat race, anxious and insecure.'

The author of the article 'Who says nuclear power is clean?', pages 138–40 had two main strands of reasoning, one of which was broken down into three sub-strands:

1 The claims that nuclear power is clean, reliable and secure are wrong.
2 Renewable energy seems attractive in comparison with nuclear power.

He concludes that 'The British government must not exclude options other than nuclear power.'

Developing your own strands of reasoning

So, how can you create strands of reasoning to structure your argument?

Let's look at the basic model you used for developing your own arguments at AS Level Critical Thinking:

> 'Universities are only able to expand because they are lowering entrance standards.' Counter this claim.
>
> Adapted from OCR AS Critical Thinking Paper, January 2006

A good AS Level answer might have the following structure:

R1	Wider access from different social groups
Examples	Working people, ethnic minorities
R2	Students more motivated
IC1	Students achieve higher grades
Evidence	Student survey, grades
R3	Teaching improved
IC2	More students achieve highly
Evidence	Grades
IC3	So there are a number of reasons why universities are able to expand which do not depend on granting admission to less able students.
C	So universities are not able to expand only because of lower entrance standards.

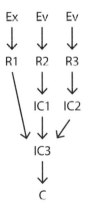

We can see three strands of reasoning beginning to emerge, relating to wider access, higher motivation among students and better teaching. Each strand of reasoning could be developed further:

1 Show how wider social access allows universities choice of more able students.
2 Support the idea that students are more motivated – why, what evidence?
3 Support the idea that higher motivation leads to higher grades – how?
4 Support the idea that teaching has improved – how?
5 Support the idea that changes in teaching have led to higher grades.
6 Deal with the inevitable counter-argument that higher AS and A2 Level grades merely

mean a lowering of standards further down the education system (we will look at dealing with counter-arguments in more depth later in this chapter).

It is important to remember that each of these points can be developed with a few well chosen words. It is not necessary to write more, but try to make better use of the words you do use.

Contrast the following two answers:

Answer A

Lots of young people who are studying for A Levels today are more motivated than they used to be which makes them get higher grades than people used to in our parents' generation. So universities can let in a lot of people with high grades and this does not need to be because they are lowering standards. (57 words)

Answer B

Young people increasingly understand the social, financial and emotional benefits of studying for a degree, such as meeting friends with similar interests. They are, therefore, increasingly motivated to work hard to master their subjects and so achieve high grades. Students are using their abilities and showing universities they deserve a place. This allows universities a wider choice of able candidates. (60 words)

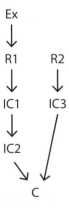

Answer B uses only three more words than *Answer A*. Yet it is much richer in terms of ideas and structure, as the diagrams show.

Categorising reasons to support ICs

Once we have brainstormed an idea, it is sometimes possible to see that our reasons fall into several different categories. For example:

> The government should increase funding to improve mental health in the country.

Reasons to support this claim might fall into the following categories:

- economic (what it would cost, how much money is available, how much money would be saved, etc.)
- political (whether it would win or lose votes, what else it might lead to)
- moral (is this the right thing to do?).

Each category could form a strand of reasoning with several reasons, examples and evidence to support an intermediate conclusion. The framework structure of your argument might be:

> **CA** (C) Focusing on mental health might be politically damaging.
> **IC1** (RCA) Not focusing on mental health might be more politically damaging.
> **IC2** In economic terms, it would be beneficial to improve mental health.
> **IC3** Improving mental health would be the right thing to do.
> **IC4** There are more advantages to improving mental health in the country than to not improving it.
> **C** The government should increase funding to improve mental health in the country.

You can see that your first strand of reasoning would be a response to the counter-argument. IC4 would be an intermediate conclusion supported by all of the first three intermediate conclusions.

ACTIVITY

'The government should increase funding to improve mental health in the country.'

a) Write lists of reasons and evidence to support or challenge this claim in the three categories of economic, political and moral.
b) Write a short argument with three clear strands of reasoning to support or challenge this claim.
c) Work in groups to edit the arguments. Look for unnecessary words, repetition or vagueness. Help each other to improve the clarity of your arguments.

WORKED EXAMPLE 16

> **Answer A**
>
> It is expensive if people have mental ill health. People who are mentally ill often can't work. They need care from the doctor. The NHS has to fund the care they get and the state has to support them if they can't work. This is very expensive.
>
> Politically it is a good thing if the government funds mental health care. People will feel that the government is looking after them and will vote for the government.
>
> Morally it is good if the government funds mental health care. The government has a duty to look after people. It is wrong if people can't get the health care they need.
>
> So the government should increase funding to improve mental health care.

Comment

This student has tried hard to put ideas into the categories of economic, political and moral reasons. However, there are two areas that could be improved. First of all, the student really needs to focus on the reasons on the conclusion, which is about increasing funding to improve mental health care. Their reasons are generally about whether the government should fund mental health care at all.

Second, each paragraph is a collection of ideas; it isn't really a mini argument that functions as a strand of reasoning. So, how can we edit and improve this argument?

First, we can get the framework reasoning clear and focused on the idea of increasing funding to improve mental health care.

Let's ask:

Why should the government increase funding for mental health care? Perhaps:

- There isn't enough money at the moment (economic).
- There is a problem with mental health care (what is the problem?) Are people not getting treated? Are the physical symptoms being treated but not the mental ill health that causes the symptoms? Are people being blamed for being fat or lazy or stupid when in fact they are clinically depressed or anxious or otherwise ill?

And:

- The consequences of this problem with mental healthcare need to be sorted out, because:

- people are missing work
- people are unhappy
- people are turning to crime
- people are harming others.

All of these cost the state money (economic).

And:

■ More money will have an effect on the problem (economic).

Why should the government increase funding?

■ Our UK healthcare system depends on NHS, government (practical, political).

■ Cheaper than curing symptoms (economic).

■ Duty (moral).

■ Right to health care (moral).

■ Why not private? – political outcry if only rich can get necessary treatment (moral principle about equal access).

■ If there is a problem, government needs to be seen to deal with it (political).

So, let's sort these ideas out into framework reasoning for an argument:

The government should increase funding for mental health care because:

■ there is an expensive problem with the current state of mental health care

■ morally, it is right for the government to take action on this issue by increasing funding

■ politically, it would be harmful to the government not to take action on this issue by increasing funding.

Now we have three key reasons, which we need to *support* with reasons (making them key intermediate conclusions). Let's try an edited version of the argument:

Answer B

The government should increase funding for mental health care.

The main reason for this is that there is an expensive problem with the current state of mental health care. People who are mentally ill for example with severe depression, some phobias or disorders like schizophrenia – often can't work. They therefore depend on support from the state, which is expensive. Many people with poor mental health do not get treatment, or they only get treatment for the symptoms of their ill health, for example they might be told to go on an AA programme instead of getting treatment for the reasons they need to drink so much, which can often be deep-rooted psychological problems. It would be much cheaper for the government to increase funding to improve mental health care for people like this. Relatively cheap treatment might enable people to stay in work, and not depend on benefits.

Secondly, it is morally right for the government to increase funding for mental health care, because people have a right to access to appropriate health care, and this includes care for illnesses like depression or schizophrenia. Furthermore, the government has a duty to look after people. Some people with mental illnesses harm themselves or others, so the government would be fulfilling its duty to ill people and those around them by increasing funding for mental health care.

Thirdly, the government should take action on this issue rather than leaving it to individuals, because we have a strong belief in the National Health System, resting on our moral belief that everyone should have equal access to health care. If the government is seen to be ignoring a problem, or undermining the NHS or treating people unfairly, it will get negative press attention, and may become unpopular. To be re-elected, the government needs to be seen to take action – so it should take effective action by increasing the funding for mental health care.

Comment

This argument is still not perfect, but it would now gain a high mark in the OCR Unit 4 exam. The student's original ideas have been included in a much stronger argument.

You may disagree with this argument, or want to support the claim differently. That's acceptable, but you can use some of these strategies of thinking about framework reasoning and writing mini-arguments. If you want to challenge the claim, think about *how*:

- The government should *not* increase funding for mental health care.

- The government should *decrease* funding for mental health care.

- The government should take no role at all in funding any type of health care.

REMEMBER !

A strand of reasoning has to have strong support between the evidence, reasons and intermediate conclusion. Writing down two or three ideas on the same topic is not enough to make a strand of reasoning.

ACTIVITY

Write a short argument to support or challenge one of the following conclusions. Plan your argument and consider strands of reasoning.

- Public art is a waste of public money.
- Young people should not be exposed to traumatic issues in the classroom.
- Couples should not be allowed to choose the sex of their baby.
- The government should make cars illegal.

WORKED EXAMPLE 17

'Public art is a waste of public money.' Write a short argument to support or challenge this conclusion.

Answer

Public art is not always a waste of money

Some ugly monuments

Some artists unrelated to people

Some public art unskilled

beautiful spaces — civic pride

improves recovery for ill people

Flower in BA — beauty, national pride, tourists, money

talking point — pedestal in TS
            — issues important in Soo

Reminds us that we're human, and being creative is human

History — connectedness
            identity

What is
public art — statues?
       architecture?
       sculpture?

CA
1. Can be a waste of money if ugly, bad, unskilled, irrelevant.
   But: not a waste of money ✗

IC
2. It has an important function for people/community
     IC re beauty
     IC re identity, connectedness, pride, history, symbol
     IC re talking point
     IC re human creativity

If is possible to see public art as a waste of money, especially if you think of ugly, monstrous statues plonked in public places with no thought for their purpose or the people around them. However, public art is (C) not always a waste of money. Indeed, with (IC) it has an important function for people and/or the community, it can be a very valuable way to spend money.

Public art can be stunningly beautiful. Many people respond to beautiful buildings, images, fountains or sculptures with a rush of joy or an increase in contentment. In our busy, pressured lives, anything which reminds us that there is beauty and makes us glad – however briefly – to be alive, is good. These positive feelings can also make us generally healthier. Even when we are not aware of it, beautiful surroundings can improve our well-being. So, beautiful public art can be worth spending money on.

Another reason why it can be good to spend money on public art is that art is a celebration of being human and being creative. We are required to be efficient and productive, so it can be a wonderful relief to respond to something creative. Furthermore, seeing other people's efforts can sometimes inspire us to use our creativity ourselves, making us generally more whole and happier, so giving valuable return on the money spent.

In addition to these reasons, public art can become a symbol of the place we live in, and help us to be connected to our history and our place. For example, a statue of Robin Hood could keep people connected to ideas about giving to the poor, and to feel pride in their home. Another example is the Angel of the North. People used to hate this sculpture, but now local people are very attached to it, and believe it has allowed them to feel pride in their home and to see art and creativity as part of their identity.

This sort of symbol can attract tourists and money to a region as well. This definitely means the money is not wasted. The Eiffel Tower started up as an odd piece of public art, and not only symbolises Paris now, but earns more than it ever cost. There is a huge metal flower in a park in Buenos Aires; the petals reflect the sky and the trees, and they open and close with the light like a real flower. Many people pass this flower on the way to work, and their hearts lift. Tourists come to see it, and it symbolises the creativity and beautiful soul of a city that is not always beautiful.

Public art like the flower in Buenos Aires is definitely worth spending money on. We shouldn't reject all public art as a waste of money just because some of it is.

Comment

This is a structured argument which remains generally focused on supporting intermediate and main conclusions. The student has qualified the conclusion effectively; to show that public art is not always a waste of money only requires the student to show that some public art is a valuable use of money.

The first strand of reasoning about beauty is well structured and does give us enough reason to accept that beautiful public art can be worth spending money on.

The second strand of reasoning to do with creativity expresses an important idea which does give some support to the claim that it can be good to spend money on public art. It has a reasonable structure, but is perhaps overstating the benefits of public art for rhetorical effect.

The idea of public art becoming a symbol is also an important way of supporting the claim that public art is not always a waste of money, because there are benefits. However, the structure of reasoning is looser here; although it is good that the student has brought in some real examples, they are relying too heavily on assertion and example. It feels as though the student has lost focus a little here.

The last strand is also an important idea but is again driven by the examples, and almost loses its way into an appreciation of one piece of public art. However, the student recovers, and relates the examples back to the main conclusion. The last sentence is an important and insightful point, but comes across more as a rhetorical flourish than as an integrated part of the reasoning.

Overall, the student has given us grounds to accept that public art is not always a waste of money, that is, they have supported their conclusion effectively. This argument would gain a high mark in the OCR Unit 4 exam.

■ Public art – a waste of public money?

ACTIVITY 35

a) Consider reasons for and against keeping murderers in prison until they die.

b) Consider what sort of evidence you might need to support these reasons.

c) Consider any principles that might help you.

d) Write two arguments to support or challenge the conclusion that murderers should remain in prison until they die. Make one argument as strong as you can. In the other argument, use as many appeals as possible, and target your audience's emotions.

e) Compare your two arguments with the mark scheme for writing your own arguments (Exam Café section of the CD-ROM).

WORKED EXAMPLE 18

Answer A

Murderers should always remain in prison until they die. We can't be allowing savage killers to roam free around our streets threatening innocent members of our society. Some people talk about comparison for killers – but what about justice? What about fit punishment? What if it was your child they'd killed? Would you want the person who ended your child's life to enjoy a life of freedom and leisure? No! They've taken a life, and that life can't be given back.

Answer B

Murderers should remain in prison until they die because their offence is so serious that it merits the most serious punishment that can be given out. Taking a life is wrong. Someone who murders takes a life even though they know it is wrong, so they must face strict consequences. If a murderer does not know that their action was wrong, we have all the more reason to keep them locked away from society for the rest of their lives. Society must be protected from those who do wrong. Furthermore, if we have strict penalties for serious crimes, we can hope that people will be prevented from committing such serious crimes.

Comment

Answer A is very emotive, ranting reasoning, which barely qualifies as reasoning. It would get a low mark in the OCR Unit 4 exam.

Answer B is much stronger. Although it is short, it is rational and focused. It has short strands of reasoning relating to seriousness of crime, protection of society and prevention of crime. This answer would gain quite a high mark.

Response to counter-argument

At AS Level Critical Thinking you probably included a counter reason or short counter-argument in your own arguments. You may have done this by stating the opposite of your own conclusion at the beginning of your argument. At A2 Level you will be expected to **respond to counter-arguments** and not just to state counter-claims.

So, how do you answer a counter-argument?

Ideally, you would refute a counter-argument. That is, you would show it not to work at all because it is flawed or inconsistent. However, in real-world reasoning you may find that an argument that opposes yours is quite strong, even if it isn't logically watertight. You can still counter, or respond to, this argument. You could:

- consider unacceptable consequences of the counter-argument or proposed cause of action and show why this undermines the counter-argument
- consider principles which conflict with the counter-argument and show why they mean that it cannot be accepted
- consider any logical weaknesses in the counter-argument and show why these mean that it does not undermine your argument
- consider any issues of language that affect whether the counter-argument holds up – for example use of key terms which is different from yours
- refer to any factual inaccuracies in the counter-argument – but beware of just saying 'The counter argument is wrong.'

Let's look at some examples:

Argument:
R murderers should be punished
R we would be protected
R future murderers should be deferred
C murderers should remain in prison until they die because:

Counter argument:
C Murderers should not always remain in prison until they die because:
R they are human and have rights too

STRETCH AND CHALLENGE

Once a murderer always a murderer? Does that one action of murder dominate your identity for the rest of your life? If we see people who have committed murder as people who have done a bad action, rather than as "murderers", does this change our attitude? Can people who have committed serious crimes make different choices and become good citizens? How can we help them?

The counter-argument here is opposing (countering) the argument on the basis of a principle. So, you need to show that the principle does not apply in this case, or that it does not oppose your argument, or that the consequences of applying this principle would be unacceptable. Let's look at how your might do this.

> Murderers should remain in prison until they die because they have committed a serious crime and should be seriously punished. Some people argue that murderers should not always remain in prison until they die because even murderers have human rights. However, this does not mean that they should be set free. By violating someone else's human right to life, murderers lose their own right to freedom. It is possible to deprive them of freedom but to maintain their human dignity and other rights.
>
> Furthermore…

Here, the counter argument has been answered by showing that not all human rights apply to murderers. This response is successful in showing that murderers should lose their freedom; it does not show that they should do so permanently, nor does it deal with the 'not always'. Nevertheless, it is quite a good response and would be well rewarded in the OCR Unit 4 exam.

Alternatively you could argue as follows:

> Murderers should remain in prison until they die because they have committed a serious crime and should be seriously punished. Some people argue that murderers should not always remain in prison until they die because even murderers have human rights. However, the consequences of setting murderers free so that they can reoffend are unacceptable. Not only might more people be murdered but people will be afraid of murder, and future murderers will not be deferred by a soft penalty. So murderers must be deprived of their right to freedom.
>
> Furthermore…

Here the response to counter argument is based on the unacceptable consequences of applying the principle. Again, it is quite strong but perhaps relies a little too strongly on rhetorical persuasion. Being let our before you die is not necessarily a 'soft' penalty.

Write down the counter-argument

Make sure that you write down the counter-argument. It will ensure that you are clear about what you are responding to.

Responding to counter-argument

A counter-argument might support a conclusion which is opposite to or subtly different from your own. On the other hand, it might consist of objections to your own argument. In either case you need to make sure that you answer the counter-argument. Have you thought of a reason for the conclusion that would help you answer the counter-argument?

Suppose that you want to support the claim:

> 'We have too much choice in modern life.'

There are strong reasons to support counter-claims which point out/highlight the many benefits of choice. You would need to consider these.

1 Think of lots of ideas to support the conclusion of your argument, and to counter your argument.

   a) Support the argument:

   - Having a wide choice of lots of baked beans is unnecessary.
   - Who needs to choose between hundreds of ring tones?
   - People can suffer from anxiety about making the wrong choices.
   - Sometimes one option is best: one directory enquiries with one number to remember; just one police force and one fire service.
   - It is uncertain whether choice in education is good or bad.

   b) Counter-argument:

   - Choices make us free and allow us to live our own lives as we wish to.
   - Life without choice would be boring and restrictive.
   - Choice helps us decide who we really are.
   - If we didn't have choices, we would be forced to do lots of things we don't want to do.

2 Select the key points for and against your argument, thinking about strands of argument; for example, some of the points in the list we have written about, such as baked beans, ring tones and TV are very much the same. There is no fixed rule about how many points you should make; in an exam with time pressure, you should probably have about two, three or four strands of reasoning. One of these might be dealing with counter-argument. Have you thought of a reason for the conclusion that would help you answer the counter-argument?

3 Begin to structure your argument:

   R1 Too many choices waste time in an unnecessary way (for example, baked beans, TV, ringtones).

   R2 In some cases it may be fatal to have a choice (for example, having one number for the fire services makes it easy to remember in an emergency, whereas the time taken to look up and choose between competing services could mean the difference between life or death).

   R3 In other cases, choice can cause problems (for example, health, education).

   CA Choices make us free and allow us to live our own lives as we wish to.

   R4 (Response to CA) Yes, but not choices about baked beans.

   C So, we have too much choice in modern life.

4 Expand each reason into a strand of reasoning with examples, evidence and further reasons, so that each reason becomes an intermediate conclusion.

5 Write it down.

6 Edit it.

ACTIVITY 36

Write a developed version of the argument outlined to support the claim that 'We have too much choice in modern life'.

Now write an argument to challenge the claim that 'We have too much choice in modern life'. Make sure you work through all six steps outlined above.

■ Would we be happier if there was less choice in life?

WORKED EXAMPLE 19

Answer

> Challenge
>   Don't have <u>too much</u> choice in modern life?
>   Don't have <u>enough</u> choice in modern life?
>
> CA: Confusing   Choose where we live
>   Fire services   Education – choose subjects ⎤ no choice bad
>   Waste time   Life – choose career   ⎦ waste life / potential
>   Choice makes us who we are – choices make us free
>   Boring, restrictive, forced
>   R3
>   R̶X̶ choice makes us individuals / free
>   R̶2̶ c̶h̶o̶i̶c̶e̶ s̶e̶t̶s̶ u̶s̶ f̶r̶e̶e̶
> R2   R̶X̶ lack of choice is wasteful
>   CA choice can be wasteful / fatal
> R1   R̶X̶ (RCA) – choices v choice
>   C   don't have too much choice

Some people argue that we have too much choice in modern life because choices (e.g. between tins of baked beans) can waste time or, in the case of emergency services, can prove fatal. This argument doesn't hold up. It may be the case that choosing between emergency services would prove fatal sometimes, but you can't argue that there is too much choice in modern life on the basis of something that doesn't actually happen. In modern life in the UK there is only one number to call. Moreover, this argument conflates choice with choices. We can choose not to spend time making choices, baked bean brands, by always buying our favourite brand. Moreover, we can be glad that there are choices.

Lack of choice is wasteful of life and human potential. In past societies people didn't always get a choice about their education or career. For a gifted musician to become a farmer is wasteful of that life and that potential. For a person who is in tune with nature and the seasons to study religion rather than farming is a waste of that person's talents. It is much better in our modern society in Britain, where everybody gets some opportunity to choose what to do with their life and career. However, there are still restrictions on this power of choice, if you want to be a successful musician or investment banker or large-scale farmer your choice will be limited if you don't have money for lessons, or contacts, or land. So in terms of life choice, we don't have too much choice because there are still some areas in which we don't have enough choice.

Furthermore, choice makes us the individuals we are. The ability to choose our path in life allows us to be free, happy people who can express ourselves. Restricting our choice and therefore our ability to be ourselves would be wrong because it would force us into patterns of living that are wrong for us. For example, knowing that you can choose to stop working tomorrow can give you the strength to keep going. It doesn't mean you will stop working, but it makes you feel free and happy and that is important. Having the choice between watching football or going to the ballet allows you to be who you are. We might even argue that social pressures and conventions about who should watch football or ballet is a restriction on our choice that limits who we can be. So, far from having too much choice, we don't have enough choice.

Overall we can see that there is not too much choice in modern life.

Comment
This is a very strong argument. It is well structured and focused. The response to counter-argument is astute and focused – it really provides an answer which relates to the reasoning (other than just disagreeing with it or saying it is wrong).

Claim and counter-claim

It is possible to write an argument which consists of a series of claims and counter-claims. This structure is encouraged in some subjects, and you can certainly apply your understanding of how to respond to counter-argument in those subjects. However, this is not the best structure to use when you are writing your argument in your A2 Level Critical Thinking exam.

You need to be able to show that you can respond to anticipated counter-argument, but most of the marks are given for the structure of your main argument, with strands of reasoning in which reasons give really strong support to intermediate and main conclusions.

Students who write arguments based on a series of claims and counter-claims tend to focus on the content rather than the structure, and forget to concentrate on the way their main argument fits together. The marks in the exam are awarded for strong structure not for knowledge or understanding.

ACTIVITY 37

a) **Expand the short argument below into a more complex argument by answering the objections.**

> **R1** Exams cause many young people a great deal of stress.
> **R2** Many young people do not perform well in exams.
> **IC** Both these groups may suffer for much of their lives because of the exam system.
> **C** So, young people should not have to take exams.
>
> **Objections:**
> Exams show what students can do and are a good indicator of what they should do next.
> The problems suffered by a few students should not be a barrier to the progress and success of the rest.

REMEMBER

Plan your response to the objections.

b) **Write a short argument to support a claim of your own choice.**

c) **Swap with a partner and think of objections to your partner's argument.**

d) **Consider answers to your partner's objections to your own argument.**

e) **Write a more complex argument including a response to the objections.**

WORKED EXAMPLE 20

Answer

Young people should not have to take exams. Some people argue that exams show what students can do and are a good indicator of what they should do next. However, teacher assessment, practical work, work experience and job interviews can also show what students can do and they are far less stressful than exams. Exams are stressful because your whole life depends on what you can write in a one, two or three hour period when you are timed. Also, many young people do not perform well in exams, perhaps because of the high stakes pressure, perhaps because they are better at being reliable, good workers. Both these groups of young people may suffer for much of their lives because of the exam system. Some people argue we should keep exams because the problems suffered by a few students should not be a barrier to the progress and success of the rest. However, if we used work experience and teacher assessment instead of exams, these students would not necessarily suffer. So this argument doesn't give us a strong reason to keep exams when there are so many disadvantages to them.

Comment

This is a strong argument with effective responses to counter-argument.

EXAM TIP

In the exam the single most important point to remember is that your reasons must give strong logical support to the intermediate and main conclusions. Organising your ideas into topics and calling these 'strands' will not help if there are no strong logical links of inference between reasons and conclusions. Discussions or humorous rambles on a theme in which there is not a single claim which supports another will not gain high marks in the exam.

Writing an argument using all these skills together

Now that we have considered a number of different skills you can use when writing your arguments, it is time to pull them together and see what an argument in the exam might look like. An argument in the exam needs:

- reasons which give strong support to intermediate and main conclusions

- a clear structure including strands of reasoning

- response to anticipated counter-argument

- clarification of key or ambiguous terms.

'Technological change should be welcomed.' Write your own argument to support or challenge this claim.

We should welcome some technological change because it has the potential to improve our lives in terms of our health, the environment and our standard of living.

Technological change could improve our health. Advances in medical technology, such as new cloning techniques, could lead to cures and treatments for illnesses such as Parkinson's, cancer and Alzheimer's. Past technological change in medicine has led to longer life expectancy, through transplants and improved drugs. Future changes, including improvement in diagnostic technology, could mean that we are healthier for more of that longer life.

Technological change could help to conserve the environment. New technologies should allow us to gain more electricity from renewable sources without having a damaging impact on the environment. Changes in technology might allow small communities to generate their own electricity with small-scale equipment which will not be ugly or noisy like large-scale windfarms, for example. Technological change ought to make it possible for us to travel in a more environmentally friendly way.

Technological changes could help improve our standard of living as well. Improvements in computer and communication technology could allow more people to work from home and avoid commuting. This would perhaps represent a significant improvement in many people's lives. GM and other developing crop technologies should mean that more food can be grown, which should allow more people in the world to eat a nutritious diet.

Of course, many people will argue that we should resist technological change, because much of it is focused on warfare and surveillance, both of which are unpleasant and negative. Technological change can also have frightening consequences, such as global warming. However, just because some technological change can be negative does not mean that all of it is. We should use our judgement and be prepared to welcome change that is positive. (300 words)

EXAM TIP

If you are defining terms, make sure you use those definitions to inform your argument, qualify your conclusion and focus the reasons on the conclusion.

Evaluating arguments you have written

So, what makes this a strong argument which would gain high marks? Before you read through the commentary below, read through the argument again using your analytic and evaluative skills.

■ Identify the structure.

■ Look for assumptions, flaws and other weakness.

■ Question whether the reasons are focused precisely on the intermediate and main conclusions.

■ Identify any ambiguity or vagueness.

You can use these skills to help you improve your own arguments too.

Commentary

This is a strong argument with a clearly stated, qualified conclusion. The writer has focused precisely on technological change with an emphasis on the future rather than talking about technology in general or referring to past changes. Clarification of some of the terms has happened through the use of examples. There are three strands of reasoning and an anticipated counter-argument with a strong response. Most importantly, the examples support the reasons and the reasons support the intermediate conclusions and the intermediate conclusions support the main conclusion.

Analysis

R1	Advances in medical technology could lead to cures and treatments for illnesses.
Ex	Parkinson's, cancer and Alzheimer's.
Ex	New cloning techniques.
R2	Past technological change in medicine has led to longer life expectancy, through transplants and improved drugs.
R3	Future changes, including improvement in diagnostic technology, could mean that we are healthier for more of that longer life.
IC1	Technological change could improve our health.
R4	Changes in technology might allow small communities to generate their own electricity with small-scale equipment which will not be ugly or noisy.
Ex	Large-scale windfarms, for example.
IC2	New technologies should allow us to gain more electricity from renewable sources without having damaging impact on the environment.
R5	Technological change ought to make it possible for us to travel in a more environmentally friendly way.
IC3	Technological change could help to conserve the environment.

R6 Improvements in computer and communication technology could allow more people to work from home and avoid commuting.

R7 This would represent a significant improvement in many people's lives.

R8 GM and other developing crop technologies should mean that more food can be grown,

IC4 (This) should allow more people in the world to eat a nutritious diet.

IC5 Technological changes could help improve our standard of living as well.

CA (C) Of course, many people will argue that we should resist technological change, because (R) much of it is focused on warfare and surveillance, both of which are unpleasant and negative. (R) Technological change can also have frightening consequences, such as global warming.

RCA (R) However, just because some technological change can be negative does not mean that all of it is. (IC) We should use our judgement and be prepared to welcome change that is positive.

IC It (some technological change) has the potential to improve our lives in terms of our health, the environment and our standard of living.

C We should welcome some technological change.

ACTIVITY 38

Write a short argument to support or challenge one of the following claims:

a) **Religion is a tool of oppression.**

b) **Heroism is not restricted to the battlefield.**

c) **Britain should return plundered artworks to their countries of origin.**

d) **Fathers should have the right to the same length of paternity leave as mothers.**

Summary

You should now be able to write your own arguments with:

■ a clear structure of reasoning with reasons that support intermediate and main conclusions and strands of reasoning

■ anticipation of and response to counter-argument

■ clarification of key terms.

ExamCafé
Relax, refresh, result!

Relax and prepare

Before the exam

In Critical Thinking there is very little content to learn. What you have done mostly during the course is to acquire skills. You can apply these skills to any subject matter. There are a few things you can learn, however. These include key terms, explanations and examples of flaws.

Prepare

Read the newspapers, especially papers such as *The Times*, *Guardian*, *The Telegraph* and *The Independent*. This will make you familiar with the level of language and debate required at A2 Level Critical Thinking. It will improve your general knowledge and make you familiar with the kind of topic which might come up in the exam. The Comment, Debate and Analysis sections are most likely to contain arguments of the sort that you will find in the exam,

but it is useful to read any section of these papers. Train yourself to read quickly and precisely. A good way to do this is to read as much as you can.

Practise

- Make sure you are familiar with the kinds of question you might come across and the answers required.

- Use past papers and mark schemes. Every time your work is marked, compare your answers to answers in the mark scheme or another student's work which gained high marks. Don't be downhearted by your mark – look for ways to improve it.

- Work with a friend. Mark each other's answers and then take it in turns to explain why you have given the marks you have. Listen carefully to the explanations given.

Refresh your memory

General exam strategies

Think of the exam as a game which has to be played by certain rules. Think how you can make those rules work to your advantage. By doing this you can maximise your chances of doing as well as you possibly can.

a) Read the questions carefully!

The most important thing you can do is read carefully in the exam. No matter how profound your thinking, or how wonderful your reasoning, you will gain 0 marks if you have answered a question that hasn't been asked. Candidates lose too many marks by not reading carefully; for example, by answering the wrong question, or analysing the reasoning in the wrong paragraph.

b) Answer the questions in the order that suits you

You do not have to start at question 1 and complete each question in order. When you are practising, work out which bits of the paper you find it easiest to gain marks in. Do those sections first. So long as you label each answer clearly, it does not matter which order you do them in. For example, many candidates find that they gain their best marks in class in the questions on developing their own arguments. These questions are usually at the end of a paper, so candidates sometimes do not reach them. If you are one of these people, why not try writing your own arguments as soon as you have read the passage, or after you have finished the analysis questions?

c) Time yourself carefully

Make sure that you leave yourself enough time to attempt every question on the paper. You cannot get marks for a question you have not answered at all. There comes a point for each question when you have gained as many marks as you can, and need to move on to the next question. You may spend an extra 5 minutes on one question, but only gain 1 extra mark. If you move on to the next question, you may gain 7 marks in those 5 minutes. Knowing how long you are likely to need for each question is particularly important if you answer questions in the order that suits you.

d) Think quality not quantity

Most questions in Unit 4 are marked using descriptions of levels of performance. So, for example, you may be rewarded for having a 'clear' understanding of strength and weakness in an argument. Writing more will not necessarily move you up a level. To reach a higher level you would need to demonstrate a 'sound, thorough and perceptive evaluation' of strength and weakness in an argument.

So THINK before you write!

Strategies for Unit 4

- You will have 1 hour and 30 minutes for this part of the paper. There are 60 marks allocated for the questions. This gives you roughly a minute and a half per mark, but you do have to spend time reading the passage.
- Read the questions.
- Read the passage carefully.
- Think about the framework structure and the quality of reasoning as you read.
- Make notes on the passage in the Resource Booklet. You will need to develop your own techniques but here are some suggestions:
  a) The questions will refer you to a number of quotations from the passage. Highlight them so you can find them again easily.
  b) Annotate the framework structure. Short notes in pencil such as IC beside key claims should help you to navigate the passage.
  c) Circle and label obvious weaknesses so that you can find them again. You might like to use a pencil circle in the relevant part of the text with a label. 'Slip SI' or 'Doesn't follow'.
- Read the questions again, very carefully.
- Check how many questions there are, and how many marks you get for each. It will not necessarily be the same every year.
- Plan your answers. Time spent thinking in your Critical Thinking exam will be time well spent.
- Divide your time carefully. If a question is worth 9 marks, it does not make sense to spend 30 minutes answering it.
- Accept that good enough is good enough. The examiners know that you have a lot to do, and are looking for good answers under exam conditions. It is impossible to write thoroughly about everything. It is possible to get top marks even if you haven't written everything that could be written. You need to select key points to make, make them well, and move on.
- Write concise answers focused on the precise questions you have been asked.
  a) Explain the function of an element in the structure of an argument – explain that this intermediate conclusion is supported by the reason 'quote' and gives support to the further IC 'quote'.
  b) If you are asked to evaluate the support given to a specific claim, focus on the reasoning supporting that claim and quote the claim in your evaluative comments. 'The author has not shown that our culture is not based on words; she has only shown that pictures have become more common so she has not supported the claim that "our culture has slipped from one based essentially on words to one based essentially on pictures"' is a much stronger answer than 'Text language is still language and this weakens the conclusion.'
  c) Write a short, well-structured argument focused on the conclusion you have been given.
- Leave yourself enough time to re-read your answers and check your work.

Questions worth 9 marks or more

Questions worth 9 marks or more are marked using levels of description. Details of these levels can be found in the mark schemes, but all of them share a common framework:

▷ Level 4   Sound, perceptive and thorough analysis/evaluation/reasoning
▷ Level 3   Clear understanding/clear, effective reasoning
▷ Level 2   Basic understanding/reasoning
▷ Level 1   Limited understanding/reasoning
▷ Level 0   Nothing worth crediting.

As a rough guide, it seems reasonable to assume that a student should have a 'basic' understanding in order to meet the requirements to gain a pass in an A Level.

What is in the exam?

The Unit 4 exam paper lasts for 1 hour and 30 minutes. It consists of:

▷ a Resource Booklet (this will probably contain one longer passage but may contain more than one passage)
▷ a question paper including questions on:
    a) analysis
    b) evaluation
    c) developing your own reasoning to support or challenge a claim related to the main passage.

Unit 4 questions

Analysis questions

There are two main question types you are likely to find in the analysis part of Unit 4.

1. Name and briefly explain the function of the following element in the structure of the author's argument (see page XX): (example).
2. Analyse in detail the structure of the reasoning in paragraph X by identifying elements of reasoning (e.g. reasons, conclusion, assumptions, etc.) and showing their relationship to each other.

Evaluation questions

There are three main question types you are likely to find in the evaluation part of Unit 4.

1. How effectively does the author respond to counter-argument?
2. 'Key claim from argument.' (Paragraph Y) Evaluate the support given to this claim by the reasoning in paragraphs X–Z.
3. How effectively does Document 2 respond to the reasoning in Document 1?

Developing your own reasoning questions

There is likely to be one question type you will find in the developing reasoning part of Unit 4.

1. 'Claim.' Write your own argument to support or challenge this claim.

Exam tips

▷ There are 5 marks available for the quality of your written communication. These will be given for clear, succinct and precise communication of good Critical Thinking points using accurate terminology (such as assumptions, names of flaws, etc.).
▷ The number of questions in each section of the paper, and the marks allocated to each question, are likely to vary from year to year. It is really important to read the questions and look at the number of marks available.
▷ You will access the highest marks by making sure you answer the questions precisely. It may be tempting to just list flaws, but you must ensure that you relate all your answers to the specific question posed.
▷ You MUST write your own argument, using your own reasoning. Repetitions of the argument from the passage cannot be credited. Remember quality is more important than quantity. Think about your answers before you write them down.
▷ Remember that the claim you are supporting is different from the main conclusion. It is a good idea to go beyond the ideas in the passage and introduce new and different ideas.

Read the documents below, then answer questions 1–4 that follow.

Resources

Document 1

Let's reclaim the f-word
Katherine Rake

1 Roll up, roll up, for a spot of that old favourite, feminist-bashing. Anyone can have a go, it's easy. Trot out that readymade mythological figure of the dungaree-clad, scary, hairy and humourless feminist. It's just as insulting as the slights of 'noisy virago' and 'shrieking sisterhood' hurled at the founder of the Fawcett Society, Millicent Fawcett, when she was campaigning for women's right to vote more than 100 years ago.

2 And yet history is on the side of Millicent, on the side of the 70s feminists who campaigned for equal pay, on the side of the women in the early 90s who campaigned to make rape within marriage illegal. The stereotype of the mythological feminist, while ridiculous, is dangerous in that it gives the impression that feminism is first and foremost about how women should dress or whether they should wear make-up.

3 It belittles feminists' true legitimate and serious concerns – that the pay gap still exists, that violence against women is at crisis levels, that women's caring roles are so undervalued, that women are still woefully underrepresented in positions of power. Add to this the fact that there is no one organisation or definition of feminism, and it makes it all the easier for people to indulge in a spot of feminist-bashing; they can pick and choose and exaggerate the elements they want and then knock them down.

4 So why has feminism always provoked such hostility? Unlike other radical movements, feminism is calling for something many women and men find difficult: a profound change in the power relations between sexes – not only in the public sphere, but also, much more trickily, in the private sphere.

5 Feminists aim to transform not just who gets the top jobs in business, but also who gets the job of cleaning the toilet at home. Feminists want to change not just who walks the corridors of power, but also who feels safe walking home at night. Feminism is not just about allowing women to lead the same lives that men have for many years; it's about changing the rules of the game, mapping out a possible future in which activities that do not directly contribute to further swelling the coffers of UK plc, such as caring for family and others, are valued much more highly. It's about more than tinkering at the edges – and that feels threatening to a lot of people.

6   Although there are different strands of feminist thought, there is a common agenda on which we can unite. Women still need to work together on the issues that preoccupied 1970s' feminists but still are not resolved. The pay gap short-changes women every day; quality childcare is out of the reach of most parents; rape conviction levels are at their lowest ever; and more than 80% of MPs are men. And we now also have to contend with the hypersexualisation of our culture, a phenomenon that has developed and snowballed with hardly a murmur of dissent. Against a backdrop of ubiquitous images of women's bodies as sex objects, rates of self-harm among young women are spiralling, eating disorders are on the rise, and plastic surgery is booming.

7   We need to harness the beginnings of a third wave of feminism. A unified movement must include those whom feminism has failed to reach in the past, such as men, many ethnic minority women, working-class women, and young women. It is only together that we can reclaim the f-word. We must challenge the stereotypes. We must hold government and policy-makers to account. We must stand up and use our electoral power to call for change.

8   We need to map out the profound changes that feminism could bring – making it clear that our arguments are so much bigger than what women wear. This vision could be centred around five key freedoms: power, rights, autonomy, respect and choice.

9   In a world of equal power, women politicians would no longer be seen as a rare breed, whose clothes attract more comment than what they say. In a world of equal rights, women could expect to be paid the same as a man for a job of equal worth. True autonomy would mean your teenage daughter could go out without you worrying about her safety. Respect would mean that we valued – and paid – those who look after our children more than those who look after our cars. Choice would make it unremarkable to see a woman managing a Premiership football team, or a male nursery nurse.

10 This world, that feminism could deliver, is one that many ordinary men and women want to see – just imagine how powerful we could be together. To make it happen, we have to reclaim the f-word, show what we are really about and unite for change. If we do, we can put a stop to feminist-bashing forever.

Source: *The Guardian*, 8 August 2006

Document 2

A blogger responded to Document 1 as follows:

Some women actually admire female pop stars who sell sex and men who are macho stereotypes. Not many men wish to belong to a movement of women who think they can tell everyone else who should clean their toilets. Rake is talking the usual sexist feminist rubbish along the lines of, 'women never generalise, all men are rapists and we need to trample men to get them back for all that oppression'.

Analyse

1. Name and briefly explain the function of the following elements in the structure of Rake's argument:

   a) 'It's just as insulting as the slights of "noisy virago" and "shrieking sisterhood" hurled at women campaigning for women's right to vote more than 100 years ago.' Paragraph 1   [2]

   b) 'It [feminism] is about much more than tinkering at the edges – and that feels threatening to a lot of people.' Paragraph 5   [2]

   c) 'More than 80% of MPs are men.' Paragraph 6   [2]

   d) 'To make it happen, we have to reclaim the f-word, show what we are really about and unite for change.' Paragraph 10   [2]

2. Analyse in detail the structure of the reasoning in paragraph 2 by identifying elements of reasoning (e.g. reasons, conclusion, assumptions, etc.) and show their relationship to each other.   [12]

Evaluate

3. How effectively does the blogger's response in Document 2 counter Rake's reasoning in Document 1?   [20]

Develop your own reasoning

4. 'Equality is an unattainable dream.' Write your own argument to support or challenge this claim.   [20]

Glossary

Adequate evidence
This is enough to support a claim and does not need additional evidence. It would not be weakened by an alternative explanation.

Appeal to authority
Referring to an expert witness or recognised authority to support a claim.

Appeal to emotion
Any attempt to make us agree with a proposition by arousing emotions rather than giving good reasons.

Appeal to history
A form of argument which supports a prediction about the future with a reference to the past.

Appeal to popularity
A form of argument which justifies a conclusion by its popularity.

Appeal to tradition
A form of argument which supports a conclusion by saying it is traditional.

Assumption (A)
An unstated step in the reasoning which is essential to be able to draw the conclusion.

Attacking the arguer (*ad hominem* flaw)
A form of reasoning that dismisses an opposing view by attacking the person putting forward that view rather than addressing their reasoning.

Autonomy
Being able to make decisions concerning one's own life.

Beneficence
Doing good to other people.

Categorical Imperative
A command which applies universally, not just under particular circumstances. It is commonly associated with the philosopher Kant.

Choices
The different options that might be available to us when we are responding to situations where decisions need to be made.

Collective
Refers to situations where groups of people are affected as a whole rather than just on an individual level.

Collective decisions
Are those made by, or on behalf of, society or institutions as a whole, as in the state or any organisation we might belong to, such as school, business, family and so on.

Conclusion (C)
A claim which is intended to persuade the reader and is drawn from a reason or reasons.

Conflation
Bringing different concepts together and treating them as if they were the same.

Consequentialist
Making moral choices and judgements on the basis of consequences only.

Counter-argument (CA)
An additional argument that is against, or counter to, what the conclusion seeks to establish. The writer normally presents the counter-argument in order to dismiss it. (See page 148 for fuller explanation.)

Counter-assertion
A claim or piece of evidence which would oppose the author's argument.

Credible/Credibility
Whether the evidence is believable.

Criteria
The plural of *criterion*, which is a standard by which something may be judged or decided.

Deontological
Making moral choices and judgements on the basis of rights, rules or duties, irrespective of consequences.

Dilemma
A situation where a difficult and important choice has to be made between two conflicting options, each of which will result in some undesirable consequences.

Divine Command ethics
Ethical principles which are obeyed because they are said to have been given by God.

Entail
To have as a necessary consequence.

Equity
Fairness and impartiality.

Equivocation
Changes in meaning from one use of a word to another within an argument.

Ethical principles
These are general rules or guides to action which can be applied in a range of contexts and are concerned with the notion of what is morally good or bad.

Ethics
Systematic thinking about morality.

Evidence (Ev)
Facts, figures, statistics and specific information that can be used to support a claim.

Example (Ex)
A specific instance which is used to illustrate a claim. An example does not support a reason in the same way as evidence, although a counter example can be used to demonstrate that a claim is false.

Flaw of causation
Reasoning which assumes a causal connection without good reason, oversimplifies causal relationships or confuses cause and effect. This flaw is also known as *post hoc*.

Framework reasoning
The main structural outline of reasoning in an article.

Generalisation
Drawing a general conclusion from specific evidence.

Human rights
Fundamental needs of every individual person which, it could be argued, should be protected by their fellow citizens and government.

Inconsistency
Parts of the argument which pull in different directions, or which would support different conclusions; often both cannot be true at the same time.

Independent reasoning
Two or more reasons which each give separate support to a conclusion on their own.

Inductive argument
An argument in which reasons give logical support to a conclusion and make the conclusion plausible, but do not mean that it must be true. Most everyday arguments are inductive.

Infer/Inference
An *inference* is a conclusion that can be reached on the basis of the evidence and reasoning given.

Intermediate conclusion (IC)
A claim which is supported by reasons and which gives support to a further conclusion.

Invalid
In an invalid argument, the truth of the conclusion cannot be derived from the truth of the reasons.

Joint reasoning
Two (or more) reasons which work together to support a conclusion. Both or all of them are needed to support the conclusion.

Morality
An idea, or set of ideas associated with how we should behave.

Natural Law ethics
Ethical principles which are based on nature, especially human nature.

Non-maleficence
Not harming other people.

Paternalism
The view that certain people are unfit to make decisions affecting their own lives, and that other people should therefore make those decisions on their behalf.

Principle
A general rule – a guide to action which can be applied beyond the immediate situation in a range of contexts. It may relate to a variety of areas, e.g. ethical, scientific, business.

Principle of liberty
The principle that the only justification for limiting the freedom of a sane adult is in order to protect other people.

Plausible
Could reasonably be the case, not far-fetched.

Reason (R)
Normally a general statement which supports a conclusion by giving us grounds or information which helps us to believe, accept or agree with the conclusion.

Reasoning
A thread of persuasive thought, connected in a logical manner.

Relevance
In Critical Thinking relevance relates to logical reasoning, and in that it refers to a precise link, focusing upon a reason or conclusion. Just being about the same topic does not make information relevant to the conclusion.

Reliable evidence
Evidence that comes from a source which is reputable, authorative and without a clear vested interest to mislead.

Representative evidence
Evidence based on a sample which is large enough for the results to be applied more generally and is typical of the group or set from which it is taken.

Responding to a counter-argument
This involves showing that the counter-argument is weak or irrelevant or can be answered.

Rhetorical persuasion
An attempt to persuade or to get us to agree with a claim or to adopt an attitude through use of words and emotive language rather than good reasons.

Significance
The weight of support or importance of evidence.

Slippery slope
Reasons from one possibility, through a series of events which are not properly, logically linked, to an extreme consequence.

Social Contract
A theory that the authority of governments is based on the consent of the governed and that citizens must therefore obey the laws which those governments impose.

Strands of reasoning
Developed lines of thought, possibly with evidence, examples, reasons and intermediate conclusion(s).

Straw person
This flaw misrepresents or distorts an opposing view in order to dismiss it.

Suppositional reasoning
Reasoning that presents a situation and draws out the consequences. Unlike hypotethical reasoning, the supposition does not intimate acceptance, it is simply posing a possibility and its consequences.

Sweeping generalisation
A generalisation that moves from some or many to all, creating a stereotype. It may sometimes move back to one individual again.

Syllogisms
A traditional deductive argument structure that began with Aristotle. It involves a format that relates two reasons and a conclusion.

Teleological ethical theories
Ethical theories which consider an end or consequence. These are not quite the same as consequentialist ethical theories, but the terms are often treated as if they were the same.

Utilitarianism
A family of ethical theories based on trying to achieve the greatest good of the greatest number.

Valid
In a valid argument, the conclusion must be true if the reasons are true.

Verify
To check, or use extra information to confirm a claim or conclusion.